THE COMPLETE MUSICIAN

THE COMPLETE MUSICIAN

STUDENT WORKBOOK, VOLUME I

An Integrated Approach to Tonal
Theory, Analysis, and Listening

Second Edition

Steven G. Laitz
Eastman School of Music

New York   Oxford
OXFORD UNIVERSITY PRESS
2008

Oxford University Press, Inc., publishes works that further Oxford University's objective of excellence in research, scholarship, and education.

Oxford   New York
Auckland   Cape Town   Dar es Salaam   Hong Kong   Karachi
Kuala Lumpur   Madrid   Melbourne   Mexico City   Nairobi
New Delhi   Shanghai   Taipei   Toronto

With offices in
Argentina   Austria   Brazil   Chile   Czech Republic   France   Greece
Guatemala   Hungary   Italy   Japan   Poland   Portugal   Singapore
South Korea   Switzerland   Thailand   Turkey   Ukraine   Vietnam

Copyright © 2003, 2008 by Oxford University Press, Inc.

Published by Oxford University Press, Inc.
198 Madison Avenue, New York, New York 10016
http://www.oup.com

Oxford is a registered trademark of Oxford University Press

ISBN 978-0-19-530109-0

Printing number: 9 8 7 6 5 4 3 2

Printed in the United States of America
on acid-free paper

CONTENTS

PREFACE

Workbook 1 contains 144 exercises that accompany Chapters 1–23 of *The Complete Musician*. Exercises are carefully gradated, ranging from basic, introductory tasks (such as identification and comparison), to more active writing exercises within a highly regulated yet musical context, to elaborate and creative compositions that present students with more creative choices. The varied activities include not only the usual writing and analytical exercises found in many textbooks (such as spelling, error detection, figured bass, melody harmonization, and roman-numeral and formal analysis), but also crucial skill-development exercises such as singing model progressions (through arpeggiation), extensive keyboard studies, improvisation, and many types of harmonic dictation (with an emphasis on the music literature, and all performed on the instruments designated by the composers).

The second edition features a new layout: exercises are structured to fit a consistent format of discrete assignments (from four to eight assignments per chapter) fitting on usually two sheets of paper (front and back) so that students can easily tear them out and hand them in. Each assignment builds on the previous assignment and contains diverse tasks, such as analysis, dictation, four-part writing (figured bass, melody harmonization, freer illustrations, etc.), and keyboard. Thus, the instructor need not deal with the perennially thorny issue of assigning a mix of exercises that are drawn from throughout a workbook chapter, or discover that the next assignments were on the back sides of previously submitted work sheets.

In addition to the integrated assignments, numerous supplementary exercises appear at the end of each workbook chapter. Workbook 1 includes two DVDs of musical examples. These recordings—from solo piano to full orchestra—present the vast majority of exercises contained in the workbook, and are played by students and faculty from the Eastman School of Music. Between the two workbooks, there are a total of nearly 2,000 recorded analytical and dictation examples.

Many people have contributed to this enterprise, and I have acknowledged them in the main text, but I would like to give special recognition and thanks to the following reviewers, each of whom worked through both workbooks and made countless suggestions: Mary I. Arlin, Ithaca College; Robert Peck, Louisiana State University; and Eliyahu Tamar, Duquesne University.

THE COMPLETE MUSICIAN

CHAPTER 1

The Pitch Realm:
Tonality, Notation, and Scales

ASSIGNMENT 1.1

PERFORMING

EXERCISE 1.1 Singing Scales

In a comfortable register, be able to sing a one-octave major scale beginning on any given pitch in both ascending and descending forms. Use scale degrees or solfège.

EXERCISE 1.2 Singing Scales

In a comfortable register, be able to sing any of the three forms of the minor scale beginning on any given pitch in both ascending and descending forms. Use scale degrees or solfège.

EXERCISE 1.3 Singing Scale Fragments

Be able to sing any three- to five-note stepwise fragment from any major or minor scale using pitch names. You will be given $\hat{1}$ each time. For example, given the instruction to sing $\hat{3}$–$\hat{2}$–$\hat{1}$ in the key of B♭ major, you would be given the pitch B♭, and then you would sing "D–C–B♭", each note being a whole step from the other. Below are sample patterns to sing:

A. In G minor, sing $\hat{5}$–$\hat{4}$–$\hat{3}$–$\hat{2}$–$\hat{1}$.

B. In A major, sing $\hat{7}$–$\hat{1}$–$\hat{2}$–$\hat{3}$.

C. In F major, sing $\hat{6}$–$\hat{5}$–$\hat{4}$–$\hat{3}$.

D. In C (melodic) minor, sing $\hat{6}$–$\hat{5}$–$\hat{4}$–$\hat{3}$.

E. In D major, sing $\hat{5}$–$\hat{6}$–$\hat{7}$–$\hat{1}$.

F. In E (melodic) minor, sing $\hat{8}$–$\hat{7}$–$\hat{6}$–$\hat{5}$.

LISTENING

EXERCISE 1.4 Melodic Dictation

Notate scale degree numbers for the major-mode melodic fragments.

A. ___ ___ ___ ___ ___   B. ___ ___ ___ ___ ___

C. ___ ___ ___ ___ ___ ___ ___   D. ___ ___ ___ ___ ___ ___ ___

E. ___ ___ ___ ___ ___ ___ ___   F. ___ ___ ___ ___ ___

WRITING

EXERCISE 1.5 Writing Scale Fragments

Study each scale fragment below and determine in which major scales the fragments could be members; write out the complete scales and include scale degrees. For example, given the fragment A and B♭ and the instruction to list the major scales to which the pitches belong, the answer would be F major and B♭ major. List as many major scales as would fit each fragment; there may only be a single solution or there may be multiple solutions.

i. D–E   ii. A–B   iii. C–D♭   iv. B♭–D

v. G–C   vi. E♭–G   vii. F♯–A♯

KEYBOARD

EXERCISE 1.6 Identification of Notes

Using alternating hands, find and play the Gs on the keyboard. Begin by locating middle C and identifying all the Gs, first by descending in octaves and then by ascending. Continue this exercise in the same manner with the following pitch classes: D, C♯, A, F♯, B, E, C, B♭, E♭, F, and A.

EXERCISE 1.7 Matching Pitches

Play the following pitches on the keyboard and then sing each pitch. Begin by playing the pitches in the middle of the piano, then branch out and play pitches in other registers (i.e., in different octaves above and below the original octave). When you sing these pitches, you will need to find a comfortable register.

A   F   B   E♭   G   C♯   A♭   D   F♯   B♭   E

ASSIGNMENT 1.2

PERFORMING

EXERCISE 1.8 Singing Major- and Minor-Mode Scale Fragments

Be able to sing any three- to five-note fragment from any major or minor scale using pitch names. You will be given $\hat{1}$ each time. For example, given the instruction to sing $\hat{1}$–$\hat{2}$–$\hat{4}$–$\hat{3}$ in the key of B♭ major, you would be given a B♭ and then you would sing "B♭–C–E♭–D". Arrow direction indicates whether you are to leap up or down from a given note. Below are sample patterns to sing:

A. In C major, sing $\hat{1}$–$\hat{4}$–$\hat{3}$

B. In D (harmonic) minor, sing $\hat{1}$–$\hat{7}$–$\hat{1}$–$\hat{3}$

C. In A major, sing $\hat{1}$–$\hat{3}$–$\hat{5}$–$\hat{6}$–$\hat{5}$

D. In B (melodic) minor, sing $\hat{1}$–$\hat{3}$–↓$\hat{1}$–$\hat{7}$–$\hat{6}$–$\hat{5}$

E. In E major, sing $\hat{1}$–↓$\hat{5}$–↑$\hat{1}$–$\hat{2}$–$\hat{3}$

F. In B♭ major, sing $\hat{3}$–$\hat{5}$–$\hat{1}$–$\hat{4}$–$\hat{3}$

LISTENING

DVD 1
CH 1
TRACK 2

EXERCISE 1.9 Melodic Dictation

Notate scale degree numbers for the minor-mode fragments.

A. ___ ___ ___ ___ ___ ___   B. ___ ___ ___ ___ ___ ___

C. ___ ___ ___ ___ ___ ___   D. ___ ___ ___ ___ ___

E. ___ ___ ___ ___ ___ ___   F. ___ ___ ___ ___ ___ ___

WRITING

EXERCISE 1.10 Scale Fragments

Study each scale fragment below and determine in which minor scales the fragments could be members; write out the complete scales and include scale degrees. For example, given the fragment A and B♭ and the instruction to list the minor scales to which the pitches belong, the answer would be B♭ melodic and harmonic minor, G minor, and D harmonic minor. Make sure that you specify the form of minor.

i. D–E   ii. A♭–C   iii. A♭–B   iv. F♯–G

v. B–F   vi. F–A   vii. C♯–F

EXERCISE 1.11 Scale Practice: Error Detection

Below are misspelled major scales; correct the errors by adding the appropriate accidentals and/or pitches. Extra credit: transpose scales that appear in the bass clef down a whole step and scales that appear in the treble clef up a fifth.

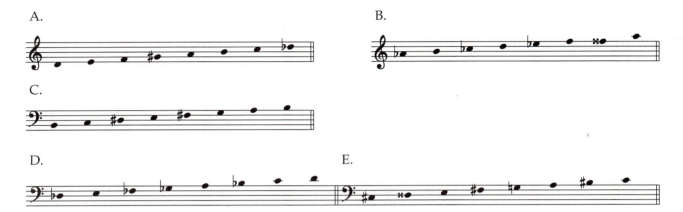

A.

B.

C.

D.

E.

KEYBOARD

EXERCISE 1.12 Bass and Treble Reading

Play the following pitches on the keyboard and then sing each pitch. Begin by playing the pitches in the middle of the piano, then branch out and play pitches in other registers (i.e., in different octaves above and below the original octave). When you sing these pitches, you will need to find a comfortable register. Ledger lines appear in this exercise.

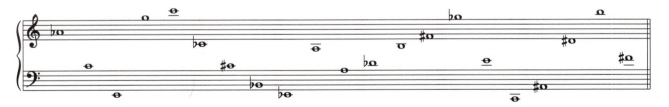

EXERCISE 1.13 Half and Whole Steps

Be able to play half and whole steps above and below the following pitches: D, G, F, B, A♭, E♭, B, C♯. Then, give yourself the starting pitch and sing half and whole steps above and below those pitches. To become fluent with this task and to sing in tune, view the given pitch as a scale degree within a key. For example, to sing a half step above D, consider D to be $\hat{7}$, and resolve this leading tone to $\hat{8}$, which is E♭. Similarly, to sing a whole step below D, consider D to be $\hat{2}$ in C major and then fall to $\hat{1}$, which is C.

ASSIGNMENT 1.3

PERFORMING

EXERCISE 1.14 Singing Scale Degrees

A. Play $\hat{1}$ in any major or minor key. Sing this pitch, and then be able to sing any other scale degree(s) in that key above or below it. In the beginning, you may find it easier to sing to the required scale degree if you sing the scalar pitches between it and $\hat{1}$. For example, given the scale of E (natural) minor and $\hat{1}$, and the instruction to sing $\hat{5}$, you would sing $\hat{1}$–$\hat{2}$–$\hat{3}$–$\hat{4}$ and then $\hat{5}$.

B. Given $\hat{3}$ or $\hat{5}$ of any major or minor key, be able to sing to any other scale degrees.

LISTENING

DVD 1
CH 1
TRACK 3

EXERCISE 1.15 Melodic Dictation

Notate scale degrees of the minor-mode melodies.

A. ___ ___ ___ ___ ___ ___   B. ___ ___ ___ ___ ___

C. ___ ___ ___ ___ ___   D. ___ ___ ___ ___ ___

E. ___ ___ ___ ___   F. ___ ___ ___ ___ ___ ___

WRITING

EXERCISE 1.16 Writing Scale Fragments

Study each scale fragment below and determine in which major *and* minor scales the fragments could be members; write out the complete scales and include scale degrees. For example, given the fragment A and C♯ the answer would be:

Major scales: A, D, E

Minor scales: B (melodic), C♯ (harmonic), D (melodic and harmonic), E (melodic and harmonic), F♯ (melodic and/or harmonic). Make sure that you specify the form of minor.

i. E♭–F–G   ii. F♯–G   iii. C–E   iv. G–D

v. A–B–C   vi. F–G–A♭   vii. E–B♭

EXERCISE 1.17 Scale Practice: Error Detection

Below are misspelled minor scales; correct the errors by adding the appropriate accidentals and/or pitches. Accidentals apply only to pitches they precede; they do not carry over.

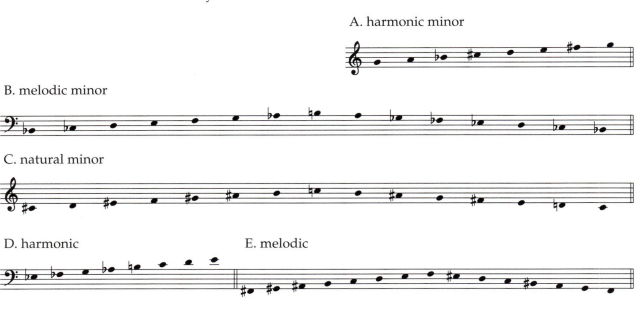

A. harmonic minor

B. melodic minor

C. natural minor

D. harmonic   E. melodic

KEYBOARD

EXERCISE 1.18 Scales

Since scales have eight notes (seven different pitches and an octave duplication of the first pitch) and we have four fingers and one thumb on each hand, there is an easy method of playing scales: use the four fingers of your left hand beginning with the smallest finger (finger numbers 5–4–3–2) to play the first four notes of a scale (referred to as the first tetrachord). Use the four fingers of your right hand to play the next four notes of the scale beginning with the index finger (finger numbers 2–3–4–5). Below is an illustration in D major:

	D	E	F#	G			A	B	C#	D
LH:	5	4	3	2	RH:		2	3	4	5

Play each scale in ascending and descending forms. Sing as you play. Play the major and three forms of minor scales (natural, harmonic, and melodic) in keys through two sharps and two flats. Play two notes, then sing the next two, playing the following two, and so on. Also, be able to jump immediately to any scale degree in a scale.

EXERCISE 1.19 Playing Major Scales Derived from Nontonic Pitches

Construct the major scale derived from the scale degree function of the given pitch. For example, given the pitch G and $\hat{5}$, you count down five scale degrees to C and then play a C major scale.

Given pitch:	C	F#	A	B♭	E	B	D	C#	B
Given scale degree:	$\hat{4}$	$\hat{3}$	$\hat{7}$	$\hat{4}$	$\hat{3}$	$\hat{3}$	$\hat{3}$	$\hat{7}$	$\hat{3}$

ASSIGNMENT 1.4

LISTENING

DVD 1
CH 1
TRACK 4

EXERCISE 1.20 Melodic Dictation

Notate scale degrees of the major- and minor-mode melodies that are played in different keys.

A. ___ ___ ___ ___ ___ ___ ___   B. ___ ___ ___ ___ ___

C. ___ ___ ___ ___ ___ ___ ___   D. ___ ___ ___ ___ ___ ___ ___

E. ___ ___ ___ ___ ___ ___ ___   F. ___ ___ ___ ___ ___ ___ ___

WRITING

EXERCISE 1.21 Key Signatures, Relative and Parallel Keys

A. Write the following key signatures from memory: A major, E♭ major, D minor, B major, G minor, F♯ minor, B♭ minor.

B. Name the relative minor keys of E♭ major, A♭ major, B major, and F major; then write their scales using accidentals, not key signatures.

C. Name the relative majors of C minor, F minor, G minor, and A♭ minor; then write their scales using accidentals, not key signatures.

D. Name the parallel minors of A, B, F♯, D, E♭, then write their scales using accidentals, not key signatures.

E. Transpose the tune below as follows: Brahms, "O Wüsst ich doch den Weg"

i.   to the relative minor (use accidentals)

ii. up a fifth (use key signature)

iii. down a whole step (use accidentals)

iv. to the parallel minor (use key signature)

O wüsst' ich doch den Weg zu - rück, den lie - ben Weg __ zum Kin - der-land!
O if I only know the road back to the dear _ way back __ to child __ land!

EXERCISE 1.22 Brain Twister

Below is a series of sharps and flats that will become key signatures. Notate these correctly on staff paper. Then, write the following required scales, which bear no relation, and often contradict the given key signatures. Notate the required scales using appropriate accidentals. For example, given the key signature of two sharps (i.e., F♯ and C♯), write a B♭ major scale. You would notate: B♭, C♮, D, E♭, F♮, G, A, B♭. Given the following key signatures:

A. One sharp, write an E♭ major scale.
B. Three flats, write a D major scale.
C. Three sharps, write a C natural minor scale.
D. Four flats, write a C♯ harmonic minor scale.

ANALYSIS

EXERCISE 1.23 Scale Analysis: Minor Keys

Determine the minor scale/key by considering the following: the key signature for minor scales is derived from the natural minor scale, composers must raise $\hat{7}$ to create a half step between it and $\hat{8}$, the tonic. Thus, you will encounter an added sharp when the key signature contains sharps or an added natural when the key signature contains flats. For example, in E minor, the relative minor of G major, F♯ appears in the key signature. You will also encounter the chromatic pitch D♯ rather than D♮ on $\hat{7}$, since composers usually use a leading tone. One of the examples ends on its tonic; which one is it?

A. Schumann, "Hör ich das Liedchen klingen" ("When I Hear the Little Song"), *Dichterliebe*, op. 48

B. Schumann, "Wilder Reiter," *Album für die Jugend*, op. 68, no. 8

C. Schumann, "Es leuchtet meine Liebe" ("My love gleams"), op. 127, no. 3

D. Mozart, Symphony no. 40 in G minor, K. 550 *Allegro molto*

KEYBOARD

EXERCISE 1.24 Playing Melodic Minor Scales from Nontonic Pitches

Construct the minor scale derived from the scale degree function of the given pitch. For example, given the pitch G and $\hat{5}$, you count down five scale degrees to C and then play a C minor scale.

Given pitch:	A	D	F	B♭	B♭	F♯	B	G	D
Given scale degree:	$\hat{4}$	$\hat{3}$	$\hat{3}$	$\hat{3}$	$\hat{6}$	$\hat{5}$	$\hat{2}$	$\hat{3}$	$\hat{5}$

(descending form)

EXERCISE 1.25 Keyboard Scale Fragments

A. Given the following 2- or 3-note scale fragments, play the major scale(s) of which they are members. Hint: Remember that half steps occur both between $\hat{3}$ and $\hat{4}$ and between $\hat{7}$ and $\hat{8}$.

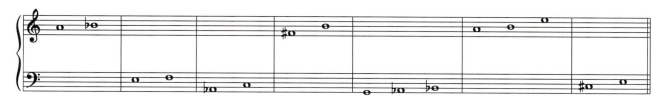

B. In the following example, you are given 2-note scale fragments. Play the minor scale(s) of which they are the members.

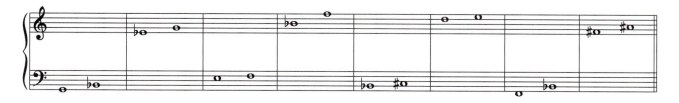

Additional Exercises

TRANSPOSITION

EXERCISE 1.26 Transposition and Performance

For each melodic fragment (A–I, below), label scale degree numbers and perform the fragment on your instrument. Then, perform the fragment again, transposing it to the key implied by the given pitch. Note: The given pitch will be the first pitch of the fragment, but, like the fragment, may not necessarily be the tonic.

For example, given the fragment D–G–A–B–F♯–G and the first pitch of the transposed version (B♭), you would:

1. Study the melody to determine the key. The sample solution is in G major.
2. Label the scale degrees of the melody ($\hat{5}$–$\hat{1}$–$\hat{2}$–$\hat{3}$–$\hat{7}$–$\hat{1}$).
3. Transfer the scale degree number of the first pitch of the original melody to the given new pitch, since this will be the first pitch of the transposed version. Given that the first pitch of the original melody is D, which functions as $\hat{5}$ in G, then the given B♭ will also function as $\hat{5}$, but now in the key of E♭ major.
4. Play the transposed version: B♭–E♭–F♯–G–D–E♭. (Notice that F♮ is necessary to cancel the retained F♯ from G major.)

Sample solution

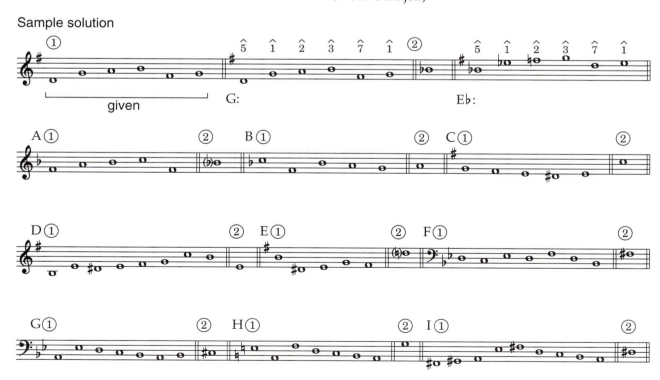

EXERCISE 1.27 Scale Fragments and Transposition

A. Transpose each given major scale opening three (3) fifths forward (clockwise) on the circle of fifths. For example, given D–E–F♯ (1̂–2̂–3̂ in D major) you would write B–C♯–D♯, because three fifths up from D is B major (D–A–E–B)

B. Transpose each natural minor scale opening three fifths backward (counter-clockwise) on the circle of fifths.

EXERCISE 1.28 Intervals

On a separate sheet of manuscript paper, notate pitches above or below the given pitch name at the required interval and in the appropriate register. Possibilities are diatonic half step, chromatic half step, whole step, fifth, and octave. You may be asked to notate pitches using enharmonic spellings.

Sample solutions

1. What pitch lies a fifth above A♭4? Answer: E♭5

2. What pitch lies a chromatic half step below C^3? Answer: C♭^{2}

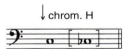

What pitch lies:

A. A whole step above Db^3? ____

B. A diatonic half step below G^2? ____

C. An octave above A♭4 (use an enharmonic equivalent)? ____

D. A fifth above B♭^{2}? ____

E. A whole step below B5 (use an enharmonic equivalent)? ____

F. A chromatic half step above F♯^{4}? ____

G. A fifth below E^3? ____

H. A diatonic half step above E^6? ____

I. An octave below A^4 (use an enharmonic equivalent)? ____

J. A whole step above B^5? ____

EXERCISE 1.29 Correction

Renotate Examples A–H to reflect what is played. Use a separate sheet of manuscript paper.

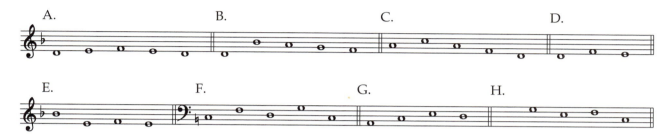

CORRECTION

EXERCISE 1.30 Error Detection and Correction

The minor scales in Examples A–D contain pitch errors. On a separate sheet of manuscript paper, renotate each scale correctly and then transpose the scale up a whole step.

A. melodic minor
C. natural minor

B. harmonic minor
D. harmonic minor

CHAPTER 2

Pulse, Rhythm, and Meter

Exercises for Rhythmic Notation and Duration

ASSIGNMENT 2.1

ANALYSIS

EXERCISE 2.1 Matching

Each rhythm in column X can be matched one-to-one with the same total duration, in column Y. The first example in column Y is completed for you.

WRITING

EXERCISE 2.2 Rhythmic Values

Subdivide each of the rhythmic series (A–D) into various rhythmic groupings, each of which sums to the original value. Follow the instructions provided for parts A–D. You have at your disposal the following devices: shorter note values, ties, dots, and rests.

Sample solution

Given is a dotted quarter note, followed by various divisions:

A. Given a half note and dotted quarter note: write six different rhythmic solutions for the given half note and the dotted quarter note, each of which contains ever-shorter note values.

B. Given a half note: write four different solutions for the half note, each of which includes the use of at least one dotted note value.

C. Given a quarter note: write six different solutions, each of which includes the use of ties.

D. Given a dotted quarter note: write four different solutions, each of which displays the use of rests.

KEYBOARD

EXERCISE 2.3 Keyboard: Scale Fragments in Both Hands

Using both hands, which are placed one octave apart, play the following scale degree patterns. Then, play the pattern in one hand while singing it. Finally, try playing and/or singing the exercises by beginning one hand before the second hand. Start the second hand as the first plays the third note of each pattern. Try singing and playing this way as well. Such **canons** are common in tonal music.

scale degrees in A minor:	$\hat{1}$	$\hat{2}$	$\hat{3}$	$\hat{2}$	$\hat{1}$;			in B♭ major
scale degrees in D minor:	$\hat{3}$	$\hat{2}$	$\hat{1}$	$\hat{2}$	$\hat{3}$;			in E♭ major
scale degrees in G minor:	$\hat{5}$	$\hat{4}$	$\hat{3}$	$\hat{2}$	$\hat{1}$	$\hat{2}$	$\hat{3}$;	in D major

EXERCISE 2.4 Two Notes in Each Hand

Simultaneously play the following pairs of scale degrees in the hand requested. As you play, sing first the lower and then the higher pitch. Choose a comfortable singing range.

A. Play $\hat{1}$ and $\hat{5}$ (using fingers 1 and 5) in the following keys:
   Using the right hand: G major, B♭ major, E major
   Using the left hand: D minor, B minor, F minor

B. Play $\hat{1}$ and $\hat{3}$ (using fingers 1 and 3) for the following keys:
   Using the right hand: C major, B♭ major, D major
   Using the left hand: A minor, E minor, G minor

C. Play $\hat{2}$ and $\hat{5}$ (using fingers 2 and 5) for the following keys:
   Using the right hand: A major, B major, G major
   Using the left hand: C minor, D minor, B minor

D. Play $\hat{1}$ and $\hat{4}$ (using fingers 1 and 4) for the following keys:
   Using the right hand: A major, B major, G major
   Using the left hand: C minor, D minor, B minor

E. Play $\hat{2}$ and $\hat{4}$ (using fingers 2 and 4) for the following keys:
   Using the right hand: B♭ major, F major, A major
   Using the left hand: B minor, C♯ minor, A minor

EXERCISE 2.5

Return to Exercise 2.4, and fill in each of the given scale degree distances with the remaining scale steps.

LISTENING

DVD 1
CH 2
TRACK 1

EXERCISE 2.6 Rhythmic Completion

Below are incomplete rhythmic patterns. Listen to each example, notating the missing rhythms.

A. ♩ ♩ _____   B. ♩ ♩ _____

C. ♫ _____   D. ♪.♪ _____

E. ♩ ♩ _____   F. ♩ _____

ASSIGNMENT 2.2

ANALYSIS

EXERCISE 2.7 Matching

Match a rhythm from column X with one in column Y that has the same total duration. Ties and rests are included. There may be more than one correct answer. The first example in column Y is completed for you.

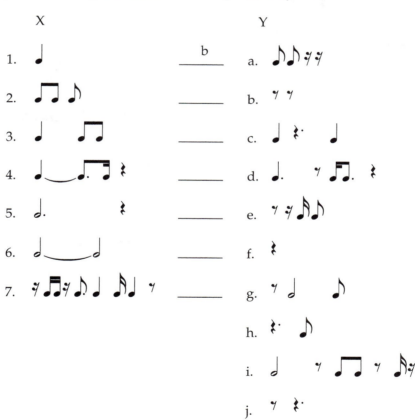

X

1.

2.

3.

4.

5.

6.

7.

Y

a.

b.

c.

d.

e.

f.

g.

h.

i.

j.

EXERCISE 2.8 Scale Analysis from the Literature: Major Keys

Determine the initial key of the excerpt, then bracket new major-key areas as they occur. Begin by looking for accidentals, since they imply a new tonal area. This method will reduce the 12 possible keys to only one, or at the most two. For example, if you encounter two sharps, F♯ and C♯, then you know that the major scale/key is D, since D major contains two sharps (review the circle of fifths, if necessary). Then, on a separate sheet, notate the scales in ascending form and in the order that they appear.

A. Schumann, "Ihre Stimme" ("Your voice"), Op. 96, no. 3

B. After Haydn, *Scherzando*, Piano Sonata in C♯ minor, Hob. XVI: 36

C. After Mozart, *Andante*, Violin Sonata in A major, K. 402

D. After Haydn, Symphony no. 38 in C major, Hob. I: 38

KEYBOARD

EXERCISE 2.9

Using the fingerings given, play the following pitch and rhythmic patterns. Determine the key(s) implied in each exercise. Then, be able to sing (and sustain) the bass by playing the first right-hand pitch.

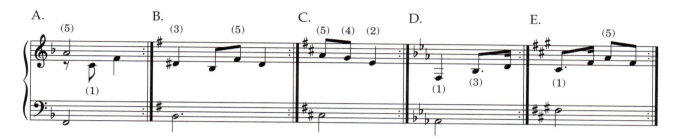

LISTENING

DVD 1
CH 2
TRACK 2

EXERCISE 2.10

Notate both pitch and rhythm for the following short melodic fragments.

Exercises for Meter (Simple and Compound), Beat Division, and Meter Signature

ASSIGNMENT 2.3

LISTENING

EXERCISE 2.11 Meter and Mode Identification: Simple and Compound Meters

Identify the meter and the mode (major or minor) in the following examples. Your choices are $\frac{2}{4}$, $\frac{3}{4}$, $\frac{4}{4}$, and $\frac{6}{8}$.

A. Brahms, "Wie Melodien zieht es mir" ("As If Melodies Were Moving"), *Five Songs for High Voice and Piano*, op. 105, no. 1:　　　　　　　　　　　meter: _____ mode: _____

B. Chopin, Nocturne in F minor, op. 55, no. 1 BI 152:　　　　　　　meter: _____ mode: _____

C. Schumann, "Reiterstück," *Album für die Jugend*, op. 85　　　　　meter: _____ mode: _____

D. Bach, Prelude in B♭ major, BWV 866, *Well-Tempered Clavier*, Book 1:　　meter: _____ mode: _____

E. Mozart, Trio in E♭ for Piano, Clarinet, and Viola, K. 498, *Allegretto*　　meter: _____ mode: _____

ANALYSIS

EXERCISE 2.12

Determine the most logical meter signature for each of the following examples. Support your answer in a sentence or two.

A. Beethoven, Piano Sonata in E♭ major, op. 7 *Adagio*

B. Brahms, Sonata in F minor for Clarinet and Piano, op. 120, no. 1

C. Haydn, *Allegro*, String Quartet in G minor, op. 74, no. 3

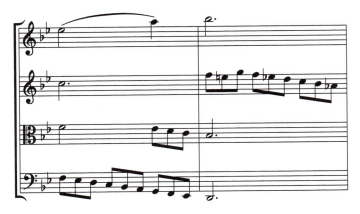

D. Josquin, Credo, from *Missa Pange Lingua*

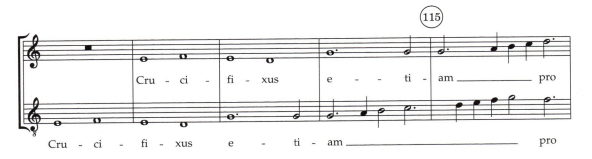

PERFORMING

EXERCISE 2.13 Conducting and Singing Fragments in Rhythm and Meter

This exercise presents melodic fragments in a meter, with a rhythmic pattern given below. First, practice the conducting patterns for $\frac{2}{4}$, $\frac{3}{4}$, $\frac{4}{4}$, and $\frac{6}{8}$. Then, using "ta" or other rhythmic syllables, conduct the meter and say the rhythm. Finally, conduct the meter and sing the scale degrees in rhythm. Continue each pattern until you return to the tonic.

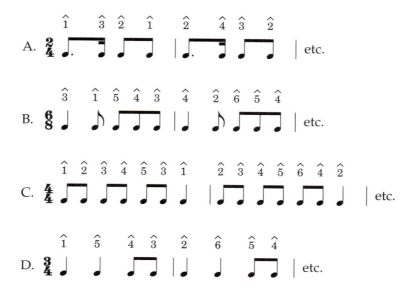

ANALYSIS AND WRITING

EXERCISE 2.14 Adding Bar Lines

Each of the following sets of rhythms has a meter signature but no bar lines. Supply bar lines based on the meter signature. The notation must reflect the meter. Thus, you may need to tie rhythms in order to insert a bar line. (For example, given the rhythm quarter, quarter, half, in $\frac{3}{4}$, you would need to tie the half note, which begins on beat 3 to the downbeat of the next measure.) Use beams when possible. All exercises begin on the downbeat, and the final measure is complete. After adding the bar lines, conduct the meter, and either clap or speak the rhythms.

ASSIGNMENT 2.4

KEYBOARD

EXERCISE 2.15 Scales in Rhythm

Play the major and three forms of minor scales (natural, harmonic, and melodic) in keys with three sharps and three flats. Determine a probable meter for each exercise. Use the tetrachordal fingering.

EXERCISE 2.16 Scale Fragments in Rhythm

Sing each fragment in rhythm. As you sing, tap the beat (for simple meters, it will be the quarter note; for compound, the dotted quarter note). Next, play the melodic fragments in rhythm on the piano with either hand) while you sing. Next, play the melodic fragments in rhythm on the piano with either hand while tapping the beat with the free hand. Finally, determine a possible meter for each example and conduct that meter while playing the melodic fragments.

ANALYSIS AND WRITING

EXERCISE 2.17 Determining Meter and Adding Bar Lines

The following examples are unmetered and lack bar lines. However, given the metrical groupings and other various musical hints (melodic parallelism, etc.), you should be able to determine the meter and add bar lines.

A. William F. Sherwin, Day Is Dying in the West (version 1)

B. Bach, Prelude in E minor, from *Six Little Preludes*, BWV 938

C. Bach, Prelude in A minor, BWV 865, *Well-Tempered Clavier*, Book I

D. Bach, "Erbarme dich," mein Gott ("Have Mercy, Lord, on Me"), *St. Matthew Passion*, no. 39, BWV 244

E. William F. Sherwin, Day Is Dying in the West (version 2)

1. Day   is   dy - ing   in   the   west;   Heaven   is   touch - ing   earth   with   rest:

WRITING

EXERCISE 2.18 Single-Measure Completion

Using either single rest ("R") or single note ("N") complete each measure.

Sample solution

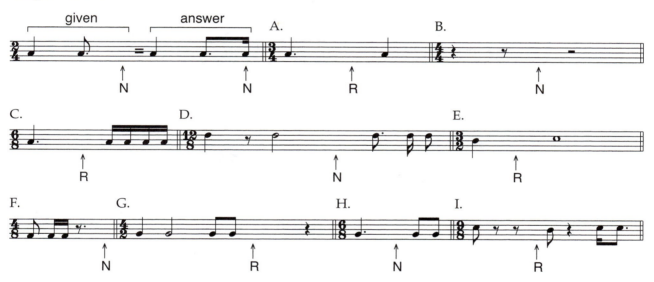

EXERCISE 2.19 Incomplete Measures

Some measures in the examples below do not contain enough beats. Add a single note value that completes any measure with too few beats. Add beams and/or ties when necessary.

ANALYSIS

EXERCISE 2.20 Scale Analysis: Minor and Major Keys

Determine the initial key of the excerpt, then bracket new major- and minor-key areas as they occur. Recall the added dimension of the leading tone in minor: $\hat{7}$ will need to be raised to create a leading tone, so you will encounter one more accidental in each key than is found in the key signature. For example, the key of B minor contains two sharps, F♯ and C♯, but you will also find A♯ which, of course, is not in the key signature, but is necessary to raise $\hat{7}$ to become a leading tone.

A. Mozart, Symphony no. 40 in G minor, K. 550

B.

C. Haydn, Piano Sonata in E minor

Exercises for Clarifying Meter and Borrowed Divisions

ASSIGNMENT 2.5

ANALYSIS AND WRITING

EXERCISE 2.21 Determining Meter and Adding Bar Lines

The following examples are unmetered (some are familiar tunes). Sing through the tunes, trying to determine the best meter according to the following criteria:

- Long notes usually fall on an accented part of the measure. Shorter notes usually follow longer notes and fall on an unaccented part of the measure.
- Changes in melodic contour often coincide with a downbeat or accented beat.
- All examples are in major. Note that $\hat{1}$, $\hat{3}$, and $\hat{5}$ often occur on accented beats.

After you have determined the meter and added bar lines, sing the tune again while conducting. Be aware, as shown in the sample solution, that you may need to omit ties (m. 2) or add ties (m. 6).

Sample solution

A.

B.

C.

D.

E.

F.

EXERCISE 2.22 Matching

Match a rhythm from column X with one in column Y that has the same total duration. Note: There may be more than a single correct answer, and not every letter is matched with a number. The first example in column X is completed for you.

EXERCISE 2.23 Rhythmic Correction

Below are several metered examples, each of which contains numerous rhythmic errors: there are too few or too many beats within most measures. Circle, then change when necessary, one or more given rhythmic values in each measure to make the measure agree with the time signature. Do not change rests or eliminate or add any notes. There may be many ways to correct a measure.

EXERCISE 2.24 Beaming

Below are examples whose rhythmic notation does not reflect the given meter clearly. Clap each rhythm. Then, clarify the meter by renotating each example using the following devices: adding or redistributing beams, adding or deleting ties, combining two or more note values into a single note value or breaking down a single longer note value into two note values. When you have corrected the notation, conduct the meter and either clap or say the rhythms.

ASSIGNMENT 2.6

ANALYSIS AND WRITING

EXERCISE 2.25 Adding Bar Lines

Renotate the following rhythms (on your own sheet of manuscript paper), replacing any note that does not fit in a measure with two smaller notes tied together. Then add beams. Note: Examples begin on downbeats but might not end on downbeats. If they do not, add any necessary rests (to complete the final measure). Do not change the given rhythms and maintain the prevailing "feel" of the meter; that is, do not contradict the given meter. For example, given that $\frac{6}{8}$ is generally felt in two large beats, group values around those metrical accents. When you have added the bar lines, conduct the meter and either clap or say the rhythms.

EXERCISE 2.26 Determining Meter and Adding Bar Lines

Determine the best meter for each of the melodies below. Then, add a meter signature and bar lines. Tunes may start with an anacrusis.

A.

B.

C.

D.

WRITING

EXERCISE 2.27 Metric Conversion

Rewrite the following simple meter examples in the equivalent compound meter and the compound meter examples in simple meter.

Sample solution

simple triple

compound duple

A.

Assignment for Metrical Disruptions

ASSIGNMENT 2.7

DVD 1
CH 2
TRACK 6

EXERCISE 2.28 Determining Meter and Adding Bar Lines

Determine the meter and add bar lines for each of the following examples drawn from the literature; there may be more than one possible answer. Begin by "scanning" the rhythms, noting repetitions that create larger patterns. Recall that accent, and therefore metrical emphasis, is often enhanced by durational accents and by changes of harmony, musical patterning, texture, register, and so on. List at least three criteria that you used to determine each example's meter.

A. Bach, Prelude no. 2 in D minor, *Clavier-büchlein für W. Fr. Bach*, BWV 926

B. Bach, Prelude no. 4 in A minor, from *Sechs kleine Préludien*, BWV 942

C. Grieg, *Lyriske stykker* (*Lyric Pieces*)

1. *Lyriske stykker I* (*Lyric Pieces I*), op. 12, no. 1
   This is the first of Grieg's sixty-six *Lyric Pieces*. The second excerpt, "Remembrances," was written almost a half-century later and is the last *Lyric Piece*. They are obviously contrasting works, but do you notice any similarities?

2. "Efterklang" ("Remembrances"), *Lyriske stykker X* (*Lyric Pieces X*), op. 71, no. 7

PERFORMING

EXERCISE 2.29 Singing Rhythmic-Metric Disruptions

Below are melodic fragments that illustrate syncopation and hemiola. Label and bracket examples of these disruptions. Then sing each pattern, continuing it until you return to the tonic. Finally, be able to conduct yourself while singing. Exercise A has been labeled for you.

ANALYSIS

EXERCISE 2.30 Analysis of Rhythmic-Metric Disruptions

DVD 1
CH 2
TRACK 7

Label and bracket examples of syncopation and hemiola in the examples below.

C. Brahms, Violin Concerto, op. 77, *Allegro non troppo*

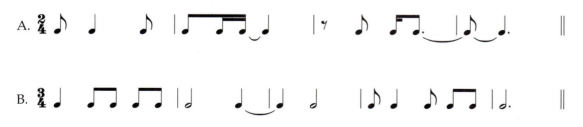

D. Corelli, Chamber Sonata in E minor, op. 2, no. 3

E. Brahms, Variation 7, *Variations on a Theme by Haydn*, op. 56b

PERFORMING

EXERCISE 2.31 Transforming Melodic Fragments

Sing each fragment as written and in any other major or minor key. Continue the pattern until you return to the tonic. Then, transform the tunes by adding syncopations or hemiolas. The easiest way to disrupt the rhythms is to move strong-beat accents to a weak beat by making the strong-beat duration shorter than that of the weak beat.

EXERCISE 2.32 Combining Rhythm, Meter, Singing, and Keyboard

Complete the following tasks while sitting at the keyboard.
A. Tap quarter notes on any pitch. Sing ascending and descending scales in quarter notes, then in eighth notes, and again in dotted quarter-plus-eighth rhythms.
B. Tap quarter notes with one foot and eighth notes with one hand on any pitch on the keyboard. Sing ascending and descending scales in quarter notes, then in eighth notes, then in dotted quarter-plus-eighth rhythms.
C. Tap the following rhythms on any pitch on the keyboard while singing scales in even quarter notes and eighth notes:

CHAPTER 3

Intervals and Melody

Exercises for Naming Generic, Melodic/Harmonic, Simple/Compound, and Specific Intervals

ASSIGNMENT 3.1

ANALYSIS

EXERCISE 3.1 Generic Intervals: Melodic and Harmonic, Simple and Compound

Fill in all three blanks for A–I.

1. The generic (numerical) size of each interval.
2. Whether the interval occurs melodically (mel) or harmonically (har).
3. Whether the interval is simple (s) or compound (c).

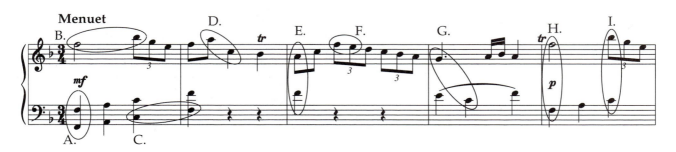

A. 1. __8__ 2. _har_ 3. __s__   F. 1. ____ 2. ____ 3. ____

B. 1. ____ 2. ____ 3. ____   G. 1. ____ 2. ____ 3. ____

C. 1. ____ 2. ____ 3. ____   H. 1. ____ 2. ____ 3. ____

D. 1. ____ 2. ____ 3. ____   I. 1. ____ 2. ____ 3. ____

E. 1. ____ 2. ____ 3. ____

EXERCISE 3.2

Identify *only* the perfect, major, and minor intervals; do not label the remaining intervals. Use the analytical technique that views the lower note as the tonic of a scale.

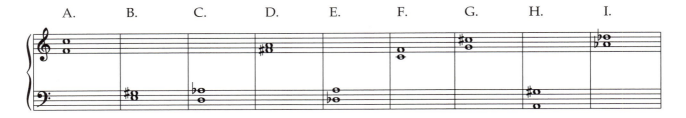

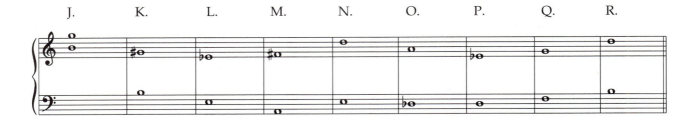

WRITING

EXERCISE 3.3

Notate the following intervals above the given pitches.

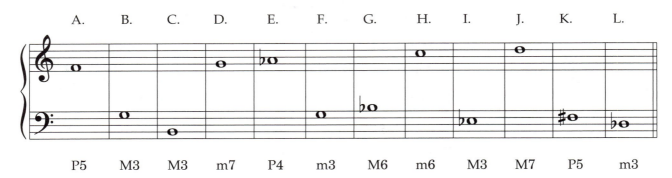

P5   M3   M3   m7   P4   m3   M6   m6   M3   M7   P5   m3

DVD 1
CH 3
TRACK 1

LISTENING

EXERCISE 3.4

The first note of a melodic interval is given. Label the interval you hear and notate the second note that forms that interval. Your choices are m2, M2, P5, and P8.

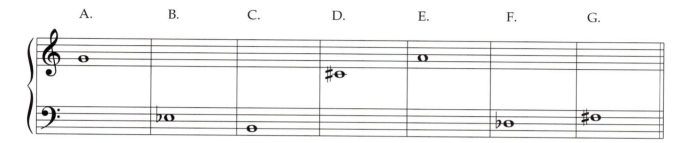

DVD 1
CH 3
TRACK 2

EXERCISE 3.5

The second note of a melodic interval is given. Label the interval you hear and notate the second note that forms that interval. Your choices are m2, M2, P5, P8, and compounds.

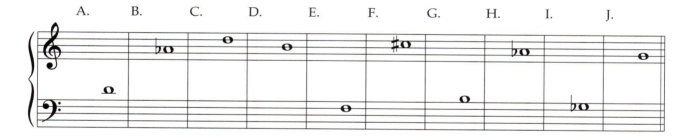

KEYBOARD

EXERCISE 3.6 Scales

Play major and minor scales with key signatures up to and including four sharps and four flats. Use the tetrachord fingering introduced in Chapter 1.

EXERCISE 3.7 Scales and Intervals

Using one finger in each hand, play the scale degree pairs below in the following keys: A♭, A, E♭, and E major and F, F♯, C, and C♯ minor. Be able to identify the melodic interval. Scale degrees:

$\hat{1} + \hat{4}$

$\hat{1} + \hat{6}$ (use harmonic/natural minor)

$\hat{2} + \hat{4}$

$\hat{2} + \hat{6}$ (major only)

$\hat{1} + \hat{7}$ (above; use all forms of minor)

$\hat{5} + \hat{3}$

ASSIGNMENT 3.2

LISTENING

DVD 1
CH 3
TRACK 3

EXERCISE 3.8

You now hear descending seconds, fifths, and octaves. Label all intervals; compound intervals are included in this exercise.

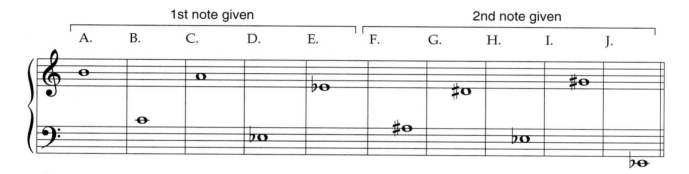

DVD 1
CH 3
TRACK 4

EXERCISE 3.9 Identifying and Notating Seconds and Perfect Fifths

You will hear intervals played harmonically. Notate and label intervals. For Exercises A–E, the lower note is given, and for F–J, the upper.

DVD 1
CH 3
TRACK 5

EXERCISE 3.10 Identifying and Notating Seconds and All Perfect Intervals

A mix of ascending and descending seconds, fifths, and octaves occur. To these intervals we add the perfect fourth. Notate and label intervals. For exercises A–E, the first note is given and for F–J, the second.

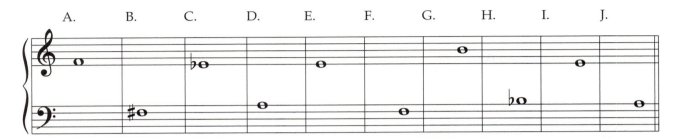

ANALYSIS

EXERCISE 3.11

Identify the interval notated.

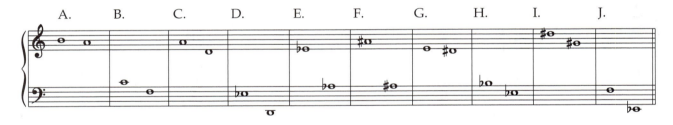

WRITING

EXERCISE 3.12

Notate the following intervals below the given pitches.

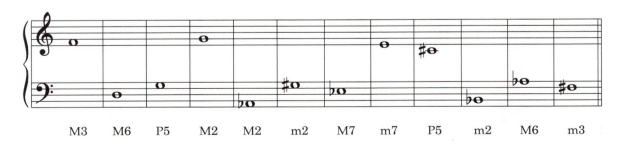

M3   M6   P5   M2   M2   m2   M7   m7   P5   m2   M6   m3

EXERCISE 3.13

Notate the intervals in the required clefs:

A. Treble clef: major seconds above and below:
   F, A, B♭, and F♯

B. Treble clef: minor thirds above and below:
   G, B, and E♭

C. Bass clef: perfect fourths above and below:
   F, A♭, and D

D. Bass clef: minor sevenths above and below:
   D, A, and C♯

PLAYING

EXERCISE 3.14

Be able to sing or play on your instrument any major, minor, or perfect interval above a given pitch.

EXERCISE 3.15 Two-Voice Step Motions in Parallel Motion on the Keyboard

Play in a steady tempo the two-voice exercises that focus on scalar seconds in major and minor keys up to and including four sharps and four flats. The lowest note in each exercise, 1̂, should be played using the thumb in the right hand and the fifth finger in the left hand. Play adjacent notes with adjacent fingers. Be able to sing one part while playing the other.

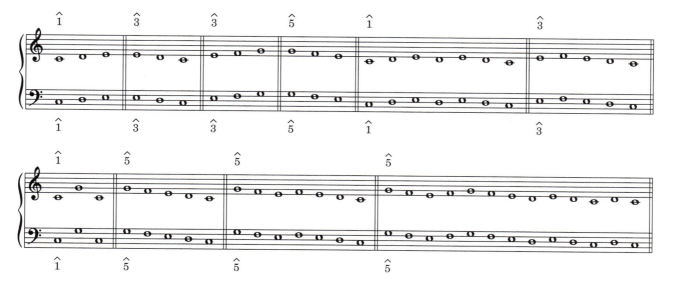

EXERCISE 3.16 Keyboard: Seconds, Fifths and Fourths

Using the instructions from Exercise 3.15, play the exercises below.

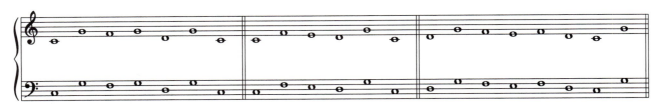

EXERCISE 3.17 Keyboard: More Interval Play

Below is a series of notated pitches. Play, then sing the given pitch on its letter name and play major and minor thirds, tritones, and perfect fifths and fourths above and below the given pitches.

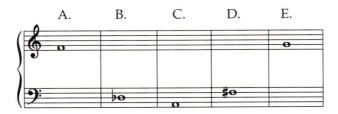

Assignments for Transforming Intervals (Including Augmented and Diminished), and Inversions

ASSIGNMENT 3.3

LISTENING

EXERCISE 3.18 Identifying and Notating Major and Minor Thirds and the Tritone

DVD 1
CH 3
TRACK 6

The lower note for melodic ascending intervals is given. Notate the second pitch and label the interval. Since the diminished fifth and augmented fourth are impossible to distinguish aurally, notate them both. Refer to compound thirds as major or minor tenths.

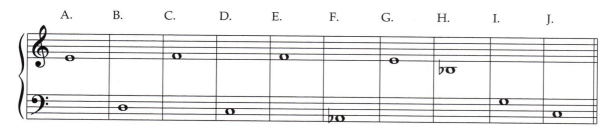

EXERCISE 3.19 More Thirds and Tritones

DVD 1
CH 3
TRACK 7

This exercise is identical to Exercise 3.18 except that the second, rather than the first, note is given.

DVD 1
CH 3
TRACK 8

EXERCISE 3.20 Yet More Thirds and Tritones

This exercise is similar to Exercise 3.19, but now descending thirds and tritones occur. For exercises A–E, the first note is given and for F–J, the second.

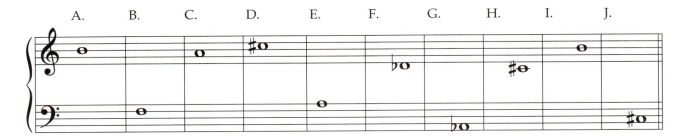

PERFORMING

EXERCISE 3.21 Keyboard

Given the series of pitches below, find a comfortable register in which you can sing the required intervals above and below the given pitch. Then complete the following tasks:

A. given E: Play and sing major and minor thirds and perfect fifths.

B. given A♭: Play and sing major and minor thirds, tritones, and perfect fifths.

C. given B: Play and sing all major and minor seconds and thirds and perfect intervals.

D. given E♭: Play and sing all perfect intervals and major and minor seconds and thirds.

EXERCISE 3.22 Keyboard: Two-Voice Exercises in Parallel Motion:
         Seconds and Thirds

Play the short melodies below; duplicate the pitches at the octave in the left hand. Play each exercise in a steady tempo as written and in G and E major and minor. The lowest note in each exercise, 1̂, should be played by using the thumb in the right hand and the fifth finger in the left hand. Play adjacent notes with adjacent fingers. Be able to sing one part while playing the other. Finally, play the left hand a sixth or tenth below what is written in the right hand, using the diatonic pitches from the key you are in. The result will be parallel sixth and parallel tenth motion. Reverse this process so that the right hand plays tenths and sixths above the left hand's given pitches.

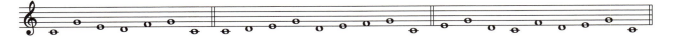

WRITING

EXERCISE 3.23 Writing Intervals

Complete the following tasks, making sure that you maintain the generic (numerical) size. For example, increasing the size of a P4 by a half step creates an A4, not a d5.

A. What would the following intervals become if you increased their size by a semitone?

i. P5 _____   ii. m3 _____   iii. M2 _____   iv. M7 _____   v. d3_____
vi. d8_____

B. What would the following intervals become if you decreased their size by a semitone?

i. m6 _____   ii. M3 _____   iii. P4 _____   iv. A6 _____   v. A8 _____
vi. M2 _____   vii. P5_____   viii. m3_____

EXERCISE 3.24

Name the pitches that occur above A, C, and E♭ at the intervals shown.

	A	C	E♭
P4			
m3			
M7			
d8			
m2			
A5			

Name the pitches that occur below D, B♭, and F at the intervals shown.

	D	B♭	F
M2			
P5			
m3			
D5			
M7			

ASSIGNMENT 3.4

LISTENING

DVD 1
CH 3
TRACK 9

EXERCISE 3.25

Notate the ascending and descending thirds and tritones that occur. For Exercises A–E, the first note is given and for F–J, the second.

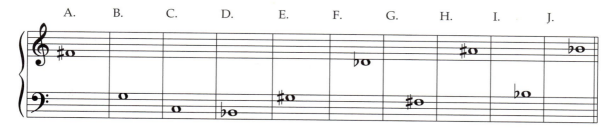

DVD 1
CH 3
TRACK 10

EXERCISE 3.26

Notate the thirds and tritones that are played harmonically. For exercises A–E, the lower note is given, and for F–J, the upper.

DVD 1
CH 3
TRACK 11

EXERCISE 3.27 Intervals: Seconds, Thirds, Fourths, Fifths, Octaves, and Tritones

Notate and label the ascending or descending intervals that you hear. The first note is given in A-E, the second in F-J.

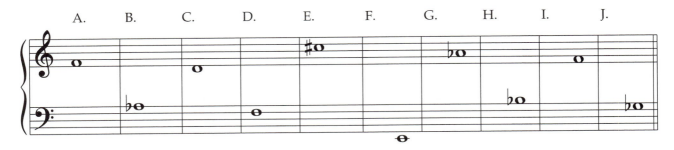

ANALYSIS

EXERCISE 3.28 Scale Analysis: Major and Minor Keys (Review)

Two or more major and/or minor keys occur in each of the following examples. Use accidentals as clues: Changes in type and number of accidentals signal a change in key. For example, a shift from flats to sharps or vice versa is a clear indication that the key has changed. Similarly, an addition or reduction in the number of accidentals indicates a new key. Bracket and label each key area. Then, notate the scales that appear in each example.

A.

B.

C. Modeled on Haydn, String Quartet in E♭ major, "Fantasias" op. 76, no. 6, Hob. III: 80

KEYBOARD

EXERCISE 3.29 Interval Play

Sing the pitches below, and say the letter name. Then play major and minor thirds, sixths, and sevenths above and below the given pitches. Finally, be able to sing the pitch and the interval above and below before you play it.

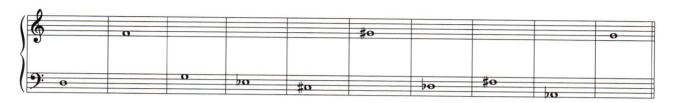

EXERCISE 3.30 More Interval Play

Play each pitch below in any register, then play the required intervals above and below that pitch. Finally, find a comfortable register in which you can sing the required intervals above and below the given pitch.

1. given F: Play major and minor sixths and thirds.
2. given D: Play major and minor sevenths and sixths.
3. given F♯: Play major and minor sevenths and thirds and perfect fifths.
4. given B: Play major and minor thirds, sixths, and sevenths.
5. given A: Play any of the intervals.
6. given E♭: Play and sing all perfect intervals and major and minor seconds and sixths.

Exercises for Generating All Intervals (Above and Below) Including Enharmonic Intervals; Consonance and Dissonance

ASSIGNMENT 3.5

LISTENING AND WRITING

EXERCISE 3.31 Intervals: Seconds, Thirds, Fourths, Fifths, Octaves, and Tritones

Label the harmonic intervals that you hear. The lower note is given in A–E, the upper in F–J. On a separate sheet of manuscript paper, renotate each interval enharmonically by changing the *upper pitch*.

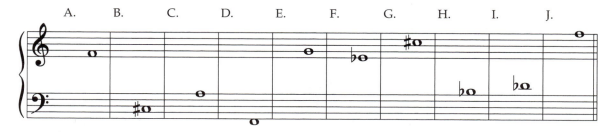

EXERCISE 3.32 Intervals: M6 and m6 and Sevenths; Review of Seconds, Thirds, Fourths, Fifths, and Tritones

You will hear ascending melodic forms of the m2, M2, m3, M3, m6, M6, and m7, M7, P4, P5, and tritone. The first note is given; notate the second note and label the interval. On a separate sheet of manuscript paper, renotate each interval enharmonically by changing the *lower pitch*.

KEYBOARD

EXERCISE 3.33

Play the various interval combinations below, transposing each by the required interval until you return to the starting pitch pattern (unless specified differently). You will need to employ enharmonic notation to return to the tonic (e.g., if you were to transpose the pitch D by major thirds, you could write either D–F♯–A♯–D or D–F♯–B♭–D; notice that a diminished fourth (shown in bold) occurs in both versions). Be able to identify each interval in the given pattern. Extra credit: Play the first pitch, and sing each subsequent pitch.

A. Transpose by ascending major seconds.

B. Transpose by ascending major thirds.

C. Transpose by descending major seconds.

D. Transpose by ascending perfect fourths (only four repetitions).

E. Transpose by ascending major seconds.

F. Transpose by descending major thirds.

G. Transpose by descending perfect fifth (only four repetitions).

Assignment for Interval Review and Melody (Characteristics, Writing, and Melodic Dictation)

ASSIGNMENT 3.6

LISTENING

EXERCISE 3.34 Notation of Diatonic Melodies

You will hear short melodic fragments (*c.* eight notes). Once you are given the tonality, quietly sing Î–3̂–5̂–3̂–Î to give yourself a tonal footing. Then memorize each fragment. Finally, use scale degree numbers to notate the fragment.

A.   B.
C.   D.
E.   F.

EXERCISE 3.35 Notation of Melodic Fragments

This time you are to notate the pitches on staff paper (noteheads without stems are adequate, since rhythm is not involved at this point) in the following keys.

A. E minor   B. F major   C. F♯ minor
D. C major   E. G minor   F. D major

Include an analysis of scale degrees and the intervals between each pair of pitches.

EXERCISE 3.36 Identifying All Intervals

You will hear a mix of melodic, harmonic, and ascending and descending intervals. Identify each on a separate sheet of paper.

WRITING

EXERCISE 3.37

Complete the following melodic intervals. Choose note durations that form a complete measure for the given meter. Ascending and descending intervals are indicated by arrow direction.

Sample solution

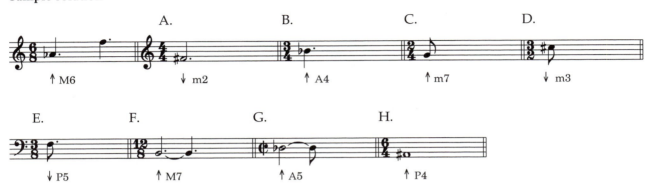

ASSIGNMENT 3.7

LISTENING

EXERCISE 3.38 Melodies: Temporal Elements Added

You will hear five short melodies. Determine:

1. Meter
2. Number of measures
3. Prevailing rhythmic motive (notate rhythm)

Be able to sing back the entire melody. Optional: Notate in a key of your choice.

EXERCISE 3.39 Melodies from the Literature

On a separate sheet of paper, determine the meter and number of measures for the five melodies heard now. Also, using scale degrees, label first and last note and lowest and highest.

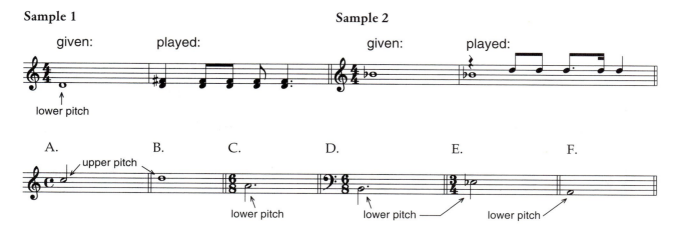

EXERCISE 3.40 Rhythm and Intervals

You will hear a single interval played in a one-measure rhythmic pattern. Notate the rhythmic pattern that will fill one measure of the given meter and identify the interval.

Sample 1   **Sample 2**

WRITING

EXERCISE 3.41 Writing Melodies

Write two or three short (12–16 pitches), unmetered melodies in major and minor keys. Strive for the characteristics of a good melody given in the text.

Additional Exercises

LISTENING

EXERCISE 3.42 M6, m6, M7, m7; Review of Seconds, Thirds, Fourths, Fifths and Tritones

This exercise is identical to Exercise 3.32 except that the second pitch descends.

EXERCISE 3.43 Major and Minor Sixths and Sevenths, and Review of Seconds, Thirds, Fourths, Fifths, and Tritones

This exercise is similar to Exercise 3.42, but now intervals are presented harmonically. Identify each interval you hear on a separate sheet of paper.

ANALYSIS

EXERCISE 3.44

Identify each boxed interval above its corresponding letter.

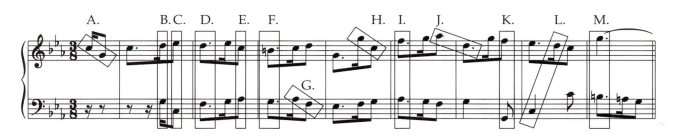

DVD 1
CH 3
TRACK 22

EXERCISE 3.45

In the following excerpt from Dello Joio's "Night Song," written in the late twentieth century, identify the boxed intervals and answer the questions. Examples E and F contain three pitches, and therefore two intervals.

1. How are the following intervals related?
   a. B and D
   b. B and C
   c. E and F (both contain two intervals)
   d. G, H, I, and J

2. Discuss any intervallic relationships that you found interesting.

EXERCISE 3.46 Melodic Analysis

Play each melody and briefly address the following questions:

1. Is there an overall shape? Is there a climax?
2. Is there an emphasis on the tonic triad, and is there a cadence?
3. What is the overall range and general tessitura?
4. Describe the primary type of melodic motion (conjunct or disjunct). Are any dissonant intervals involved in the leaps? Does the composer invoke the law of recovery?

A. Mozart, *Die Zauberflöte* (The Magic Flute), K. 620

1. Song, "Der Vogelfänger bin ich ja," act 1

2. Aria, "Zum leiden bin ich auserkoren," act 1

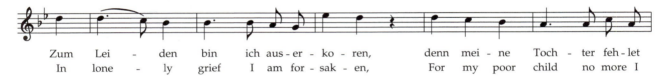

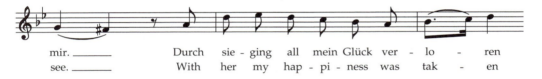

3. Aria, "Ach, ich fühl's, es ist verschwunden," act 2

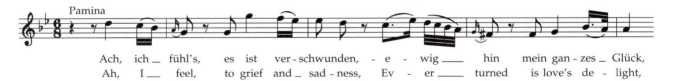

B. Beethoven, Piano Sonata in A♭ major, op. 31, 3 no. 3

C. Donizetti, "Regnava nel silenzio" cavatina from *Lucia di Lammermoor*, act I

Re - gna - va nel ___ si - len - zi - o   al - ta la not - te e   bru - na

D. Schumann, "Träumerei," *Kinderszenen* (Scenes from Childhood), op. no. 7

E. Chopin, Prelude in D♭ major, ("Raindrop,") op. 28

WRITING

EXERCISE 3.47

- Notate the pitch to form the requested melodic intervals.
- Choose note durations that form a complete measure for the given meter.
- Label the inversion beneath each given interval.

Sample solution

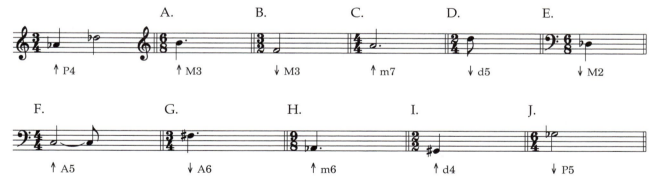

EXERCISE 3.48

Notate missing pitches based on the requested interval in this excerpt from the *Andante cantabile* of a Mozart string quartet (K. 465). Use a duration that will fill the measure. Consider the musical context to determine the appropriate octave.

A. a P4 above violin 2

B. a M10 above the cello

C. a diminished twelfth above the viola

D. a M6 below violin 1

E. a M3 above violin 2

F. a d7 above the cello

G. a m7 below violin 2

H. a M10 above the cello

I. a M6 below violin 1

CHAPTER 4

Controlling Consonance and Dissonance: Introduction to Two-Voice Counterpoint

Exercises for First-Species Counterpoint

ASSIGNMENT 4.1

WRITING

EXERCISE 4.1 Two-Part Writing: Error Detection

Below are two first-species, two-voice counterpoints that contain two types of errors: dissonant intervals (2, 4, and 7) and parallel perfect intervals (1, 5, and 8).

1. Label each interval.
2. Circle the errors and specify the type of error ("D" for dissonance and "PPI" for parallel perfect intervals).
3. Rewrite each of the counterpoint lines using only consonant intervals (do not change the cantus). Remember: (a) Aim for contrary motion, and (b) when writing in parallel motion, use only imperfect intervals. Try to make each line as stepwise (singable) as possible, and restrict nonstepwise motions mostly to skips of a third, with only one leap of a fourth or fifth. Avoid larger leaps altogether.

A. counterpoint

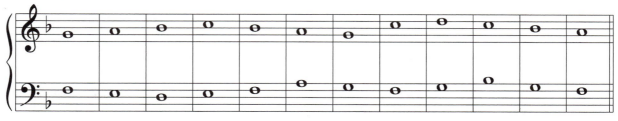

cantus

Key:

counterpoint

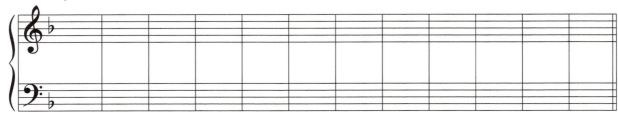

cantus

Key:

B.   counterpoint

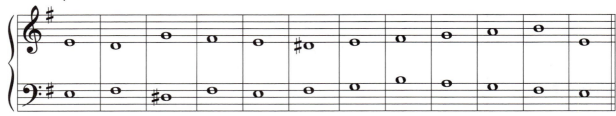

cantus

Key:

counterpoint

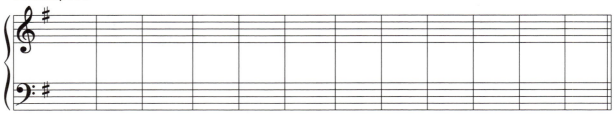

cantus

Key:

EXERCISE 4.2 Two-Part Writing: First Species

Below are two examples of cantus firmus. Write first-species counterpoint such that the added voice exhibits a pleasing melodic arch, mostly stepwise motion, and is easy to sing. There may be a few leaps, but remember that thirds are most common, and leaps by a fourth or fifth may occur no more than once in each exercise. Label each vertical interval (between your counterpoint and the cantus firmus), making sure that there are no dissonances and that any parallel intervals are restricted to thirds and sixths. Do not change any of the pitches of the cantus firmus.

Once you have completed writing your counterpoint, try inverting the parts; that is, if you wrote counterpoint above a cantus, place it an octave (or two) below, and vice versa. Does your solution still work (i.e., how are the melodic shapes and vertical intervals between the cantus and the counterpoint)? If it doesn't work, why not?

A.

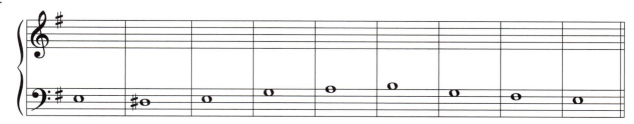

B.

LISTENING

EXERCISE 4.3 Dictation: Notation of One Voice in Two-Voice Counterpoint

DVD 1
CH 4
TRACK 1

You will hear examples of two-voice counterpoint. The cantus firmus is given. Using your ear and knowledge of permissible pitches, notate the counterpoint voice. Check your work by labeling the interval making sure that each is consonant.

ASSIGNMENT 4.2

DVD 1
CH 4
TRACK 2

LISTENING

EXERCISE 4.4 Dictation: Notation of One Voice in Two-Voice Counterpoint

You will hear examples of two-voice counterpoint. The cantus firmus is given. Using your ear and knowledge of permissible pitches, notate the counterpoint voice. Check your work by labeling the interval making sure that each is consonant.

WRITING

EXERCISE 4.5 First Species

Write first-species counterpoint against the examples of cantus firmus given below. Your added voice must be a good melody that is mostly stepwise in contour and easy to sing. There may be a few leaps in the counterpoint voice, but remember that thirds are most common, and leaps by a fourth or fifth may occur no more than once in each exercise. Label each vertical interval (between your counterpoint and the cantus firmus), making sure that there are no dissonances and that any parallel intervals are restricted to thirds and sixths. Do not change any of the pitches of the cantus firmus.

Once you have completed writing your counterpoint, try inverting the parts; that is, if you wrote counterpoint above a cantus, place it an octave (or two) below, and vice versa. Does your solution still work (i.e., how are the melodic shapes and vertical intervals between the cantus and the counterpoint)? If it doesn't work, why not?

A.

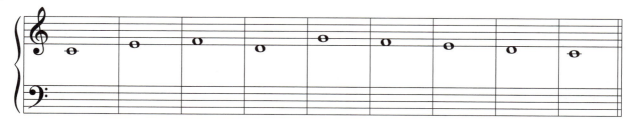

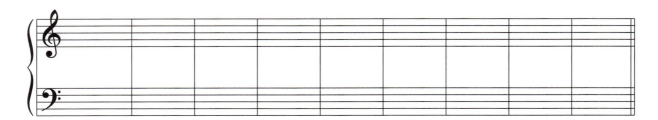

B.

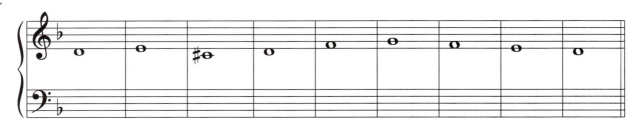

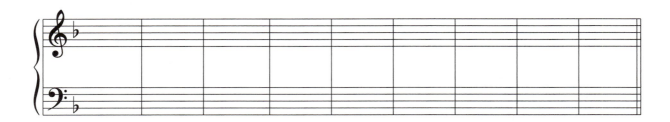

KEYBOARD

EXERCISE 4.6 First Species

Play the following exercises in the major mode, as written, and in the minor mode with a steady tempo. Begin by playing each hand separately; add the second hand only when you are comfortable with each hand alone. Play the lowest notes with the thumb of your right hand and the fifth finger of the left hand. Transpose each to the keys of G, E, and B♭ major and minor. Be able to sing one part while playing the other. Finally, analyze each exercise, marking the intervals and the types of contrapuntal motions.

A.   B.   C.   D.

E.   F.   G.

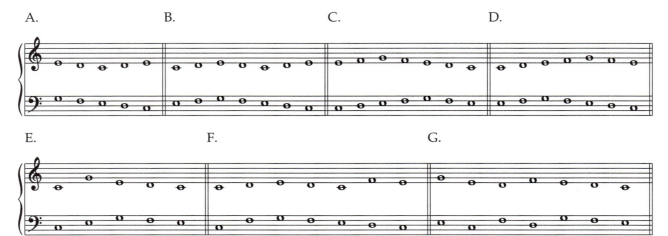

Exercises for Second-Species Counterpoint

ASSIGNMENT 4.3

ANALYSIS

DVD 1
CH 4
TRACK 3

EXERCISE 4.7 Analysis of Contrapuntal Motions

Determine the prevailing contrapuntal motion in each of the two-voice examples below. Then, using brackets, label two or more instances of other types of contrapuntal motions. Your choices are parallel (p), similar (s), oblique (o), and contrary (c).

A. Bach, Duette No. 1 in E minor, BWV 802

B. Grieg, "Gone," *Lyric Pieces*, op. 71

C.   Bach, Duette no. 4 in A minor, BWV 805

D. Haydn, String Quartet in G major, op. 20, no. 4, *Allegretto alla zingarese*

WRITING

EXERCISE 4.8 Two-Part Writing, Second Species: Error Detection

We now analyze and write second-species counterpoint. Label each interval and circle and label each error according to the model analysis in Textbook Exercise 4.4A. Then, rewrite each example, correcting the errors.

A.

B.

EXERCISE 4.9 Two-Part Writing, Second Species and Consonance

We now write second-species counterpoint. For this exercise, employ only consonance; thus, you may use steps (but only those involving the interval of a fifth to a sixth or vice versa), consonant skips, or consonant leaps. Label all intervals.

A.

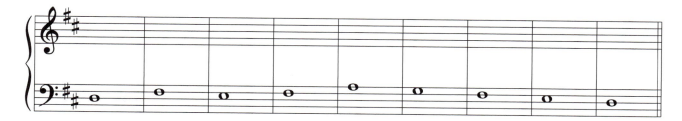

B.

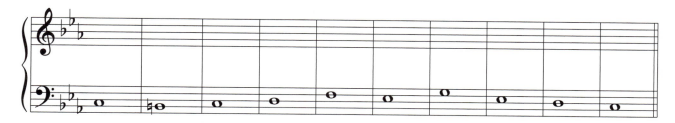

EXERCISE 4.10 Two-Part Writing, Second Species: Dissonance and Consonance

In this exercise you may use passing dissonance as well as consonant steps and leaps. Remember, however, that all dissonance must:

1. occur only on a weak beat
2. pass by filling the interval of a third

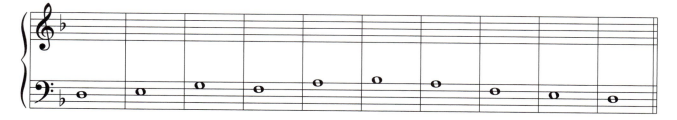

LISTENING

DVD 1
CH 4
TRACK 4

EXERCISE 4.11 Dictation: Notation of One Voice in Second-Species Counterpoint

Notate the second-species counterpoint above the cantus and label each interval.

ASSIGNMENT 4.4

DVD 1
CH 4
TRACK 5

LISTENING

EXERCISE 4.12 Dictation: Notation of One Voice in Second-Species Counterpoint

Notate the second-species counterpoint below the cantus and label each interval.

WRITING

EXERCISE 4.13 Second-Species Writing-Dissonance and Consonance

In this exercise you may use leaps (to consonances) and passing dissonances. Remember, however, that all dissonances must:

1. occur only on a weak beat
2. pass by filling the interval of a third that occurs on successive downbeats

A.

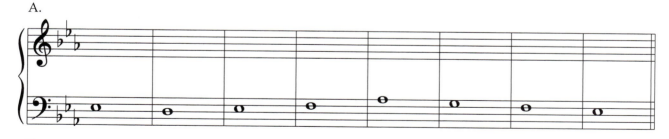

B.

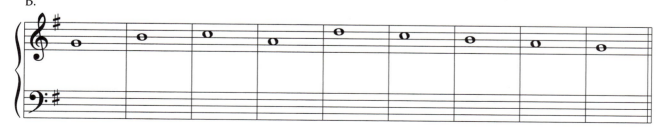

KEYBOARD

EXERCISE 4.14 Two-Voice Exercises

Below are exercises that contain various contrapuntal motions. Play as written and in the minor mode with a steady tempo. Begin by playing each hand separately; add the second hand only when you are comfortable with each hand alone. Play the lowest notes with the thumb of your right hand and the fifth finger of the left hand. Transpose each to the keys of D, F, and B♭ major and minor. Be able to sing one part while playing the other. Finally, analyze each exercise, marking the intervals and the types of contrapuntal motions.

ASSIGNMENT 4.5

LISTENING

DVD 1
CH 4
TRACK 6

EXERCISE 4.15 Analysis/Error Detection

Listen to the examples below that mix 1:1 and 2:1 counterpoint. Determine whether what you hear is what is notated. If it is, write yes, but if not, cross out the incorrect pitch(es) and write in the correct letter name. There may be up to four errors in an exercise. Label each example's key beneath the bass clef.

ANALYSIS

EXERCISE 4.16

The examples below are, like all tonal examples, held together by outer-voice counterpoint. Circle the structural outer-voice pitches that work together to create 1:1 counterpoint. Analyze each interval between these outer voices.

A. Schumann, Grosse Sonata, #1 in G minor, op. 11

B. Bach, Chorale from Cantata no. 5, BWV 5

C. Beethoven, *Adagio*, Violin Sonata no. 10 in G major, op. 96

D. Schumann, "Humming Song," Album für die Jugend op. 68, no. 3

E. Beethoven, Violin Sonata no. 9, in A minor, ("Kreutzer"), op. 4 Andante con Variazioni

Additional Exercises

LISTENING

DVD 1
CH 4
TRACK 8

EXERCISE 4.17 Notation of Two-Voice Counterpoint

Notate both the upper and lower voice of the short examples of two-voice counterpoint. Each example moves primarily in note-against-note style. Use the rhythms provided, and a few pitches are given. Check your work by analyzing each interval: all verticalities must be consonant (6, 3, 5, or 8) and weak-beat moving lines (oblique motion) may be dissonant (2, 4, and 7) but must pass between two pitches lying a third apart.

EXERCISE 4.18 More Notation of Two-Voice Counterpoint

Notate the following two-voice exercises. In this exercise a few pitches are provided. Analyze your work by labeling each interval. Exercises A and B are in B♭ major and C–E are in G minor.

A.   B.

C.   D.

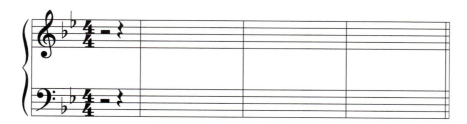

E.

WRITING

EXERCISE 4.19 Two-Part Writing: Error Detection

Below is a first-species, two-voice counterpoint that contain two types of errors: dissonant intervals (2, 4, and 7) and parallel perfect intervals (1, 5, and 8). Label each interval, circle the errors, and specify the type of error ("D" for dissonance and "PPI" for parallel perfect intervals). Then, rewrite each of the counterpoint lines using only consonant intervals (do not change the cantus).

1. Aim for contrary motion.
2. When writing in parallel motion, use only imperfect intervals.
3. Make each line as stepwise (singable) as possible, and restrict nonstepwise motions mostly to skips of a third, with only one leap of a fourth or fifth. Avoid larger leaps altogether.

cantus

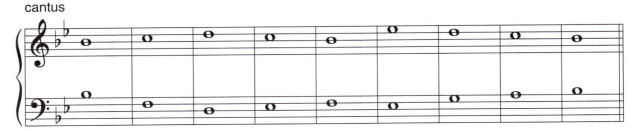

counterpoint

Key:

cantus

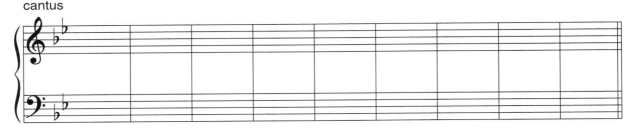

counterpoint

Key:

EXERCISE 4.20 Writing Fragments in First- and Second-Species Counterpoint

Below are two cantus firmus fragments. Consider these fragments to be taken from the interior portion of longer cantus firmi. On a separate sheet of paper, write as many different possible solutions for each of the cantus firmus fragments, first in first species, and then in second species, above and below the given fragments.

A.   B.

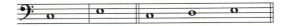

CHAPTER 5

Triads, Inversions, Figured Bass, and Harmonic Analysis

Exercises for Triads: Types, Spelling,
Voicing (Spacing and Doubling), Inversion

ASSIGNMENT 5.1

ANALYSIS AND WRITING

EXERCISE 5.1

A. Below each requested triad, notate the pitches in the required clef.

1. D major: bass   2. B minor: treble   3. F♯ minor: treble   4. A major: bass

5. E♭ minor: bass   6. C♯ major: treble   7. D♯ major: treble   8. E♯ major: bass

B. Error Detection

Below are incorrectly spelled root-position major, minor, and diminished triads. On the given staff, notate the corrected triad and label the triad type. The errors include enharmonic spelling (e.g., a C major triad must be spelled in thirds: C–E–G, not C–F♭–G) and wrong-note spelling (e.g., a G minor triad is spelled G–B♭–D, not G–B♭–E♭). There may be two possible answers in some cases.

Assume that the root is correct.

Sample solution

F – G♯ – C

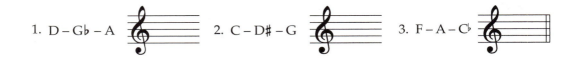

1. D – G♭ – A   2. C – D♯ – G   3. F – A – C♭

4. A – C – D♯   5. D – F – G♯   6. E – G – B

DVD 1
CH 5
TRACK 1

EXERCISE 5.2 Writing Root Position Triads in Close and Open Positions

Below are notated the roots of various major, minor, and diminished triads.

1. Notate in close position the missing pitches of the required triad type.
2. Renotate each triad in open position (three voices; there are several arrangements possible).
3. On a separate sheet of manuscript paper, renotate each triad in four voices (two voices in the treble and two in the bass staves): double the root (there are several arrangements possible).

Sample solution

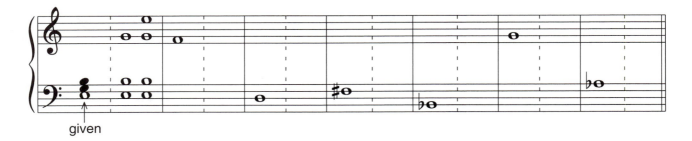

	A.	B.	C.	D.	E.	F.
e minor	F major	d minor	f♯ minor	B♭ major	g diminished	A♭ major
close open	close open	close open	close open	close open	close open	close open

given

LISTENING AND WRITING

DVD 1
CH 5
TRACK 2

EXERCISE 5.3 Hearing and Writing Root Position Triads

Each of the following pitches is the root of a triad. Listen to the recording and notate in close position the type of triad you hear. Next to each triad, write a four-voice version in open position.

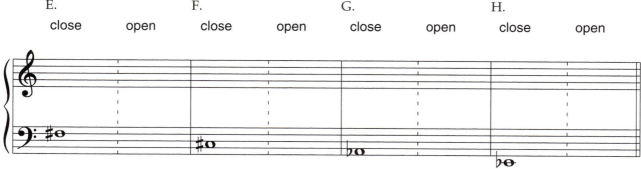

PLAYING

EXERCISE 5.4 Keyboard: Triads in Various Spacings: Three Voices

Below are seven sets of two notes of a root-position triad. Determine the missing chordal member and play it below the soprano voice to create a three-part texture. If a fifth is given, the triad could be major or minor, since the third of the chord is not specified; be able to play both triad types. Finally, be able to sing the missing note before playing it.

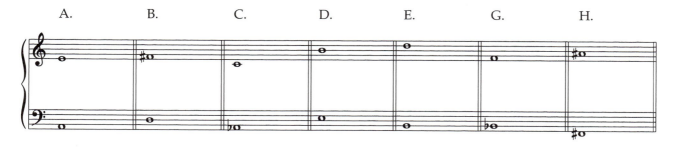

ASSIGNMENT 5.2

EXERCISE 5.5 Constructing Triads

Below is a series of pitches, each of which is either the root, third, or fifth of a major, minor, or diminished triad.

1. Listen to the given pitch, and then the triad that includes the pitch. Determine the type of triad and whether the given pitch is the triad's root, third, or fifth.
2. Notate the triad in close position.

Sample solution

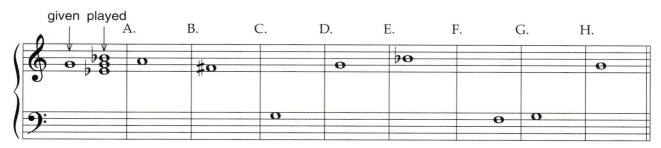

Eb major
third is given

EXERCISE 5.6 Writing Triads in Inversion and Other Triadic Manipulations

The given pitch is the bass note. Build triads above the given pitch according to the instructions. Label each triad by letter name. Refer to the sample solution.

Sample solution

1st inversion
major triads

Bb

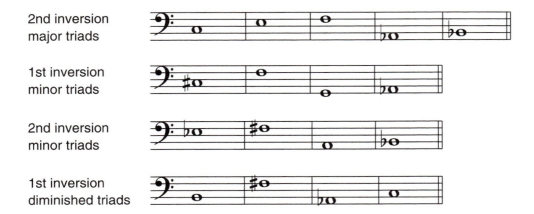

2nd inversion major triads

1st inversion minor triads

2nd inversion minor triads

1st inversion diminished triads

EXERCISE 5.7

Fill in the blanks from the information given.

Sample solution

Fifth	A	____	____	____	D♯	____	____	____	____	G♯	B
Third	(F♯)	A	G♭	____	____	____	F♯	C♯	____	____	____
Root	(D)	____	____	B	____	C♭	____	____	F	____	____
Type	M	M	m	d	m	M	d	M	d	m	M

EXERCISE 5.8

Each pitch below is a potential member of nine triads (we will consider major, minor and diminished triads only). For example, given the pitch D, it could be the

1. root of a D major, D minor, or D diminished triad
2. third of a B♭ major, B minor, or B diminished triad
3. fifth of a G major triad or G minor triad, or G♯ diminished triad

Determine the nine possible major, minor, and diminished triads of which each of the following pitches could be members:

	Root:	Third:	Fifth:
A. C:			
B. F:			
C. B♭:			
D. C♯:			
E. F♯:			

ASSIGNMENT 5.3

WRITING

EXERCISE 5.9

From each of the following pairs, make as many different types of triads as possible. (Use a separate sheet of manuscript paper.) We will consider all four triad types (major, minor, diminished, and augmented). For example, given the pair of pitches G and B, you can make four different triads: G–B–D (major), G–B–D♯ (augmented), E–G–B (minor), and E♭–G–B (augmented).

A. A and C
B. D and F♯
C. B♭ and D♭

D. F and C
E. C and A♯
F. C♯ and E

EXERCISE 5.10

Add a third pitch to each pair of pitches below to form the specified triad as shown for the first case. Label the root name of each triad in the space provided. Do *not* alter any of the given pitches.

DVD 1
CH 5
TRACK 3

EXERCISE 5.11 Triad Identification and Bass Voice

Label bass member (B) as 1, 3, 5 (root, third, and fifth, respectively), and chord quality (Q) as M, m, d.

A. ____ | ____
    B   Q

B. ____ | ____
    B   Q

C. ____ | ____
    B   Q

D. ____ | ____
    B   Q

E. ____ | ____
    B   Q

F. ____ | ____
    B   Q

G. ____ | ____
    B   Q

H. ____ | ____
    B   Q

I. ____ | ____
    B   Q

J. ____ | ____
    B   Q

DVD 1
CH 5
TRACK 4

EXERCISE 5.12 Triad Identification: Aural Recognition

This exercise is identical to Exercise 5.11, but now you must also identify the member of the chord that is in the soprano (S) in addition to bass (B) and quality (Q)

A. ____ | ____ | ____
    B   S   Q

B. ____ | ____ | ____
    B   S   Q

C. ____ | ____ | ____
    B   S   Q

D. ____ | ____ | ____
    B   S   Q

E. ____ | ____ | ____
    B   S   Q

F. ____ | ____ | ____
    B   S   Q

G. ____ | ____ | ____
    B   S   Q

H. ____ | ____ | ____
    B   S   Q

I. ____ | ____ | ____
    B   S   Q

J. ____ | ____ | ____
    B   S   Q

Exercises for Figured Bass

ASSIGNMENT 5.4

KEYBOARD

EXERCISE 5.13 Building Triads

The following intervals require a third pitch to make a triad. The lowest note is the bass, from which you will construct major, minor, and diminished triads. For example, given a perfect fifth, only a root-position triad is possible since the interval of a fifth is not formed with the bass in inverted triads. Similarly, the fourth would belong only to a second inversion triad ($\frac{6}{4}$). However, if a third or sixth is given, there is more than one type of triad to which they may belong. For example, the third occurs in both a root-position triad ($\frac{5}{3}$) and a first-inversion triad ($\frac{6}{3}$). Further, depending on the specific type of third, fifth, or sixth given, several triads are possible. For example, given C and E♭, you could construct C minor, C diminished, A♭ major (in $\frac{6}{3}$ position), and A diminished (in $\frac{6}{3}$ position) triads.

Determine the missing pitch, say the triad and its position, and then play it. Where there are two or more possibilities, play them all (see Examples). Finally, spread out each triad, playing the bass in the left hand and the upper voices with the right.

Exercises

examples:

exercises:

EXERCISE 5.14 Triads in Various Spacings: Three Voices

Two voices are given; add one pitch to create triads. Depending on the given interval, create $\frac{5}{3}$, $\frac{6}{3}$, and $\frac{6}{4}$ major, minor, and diminished triads. Each example presents the opportunity to make triads of at least two different qualities. Add the third pitch either above or below the given right-hand pitch.

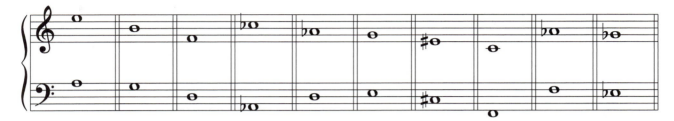

EXERCISE 5.15 Figured Bass in Three Voices

Realize the figured bass by adding the two missing notes in the right hand. Play each harmony in two different voicings.

LISTENING

DVD 1
CH 5
TRACK 5

EXERCISE 5.16 Triad Completion

Two of the three voices are provided for each of the following examples. You will hear each example twice: the first time you will hear only the two voices; the second time you will hear the complete three-voice triad. Notate the missing member of the triad in the required register (bass = B, alto = A, soprano = S). The three types of triads (major, minor, and diminished) may be inverted. Analyze each of the triads by identifying triad type (M, m, d) and figured bass (show any chromaticism). Example A is worked for you.

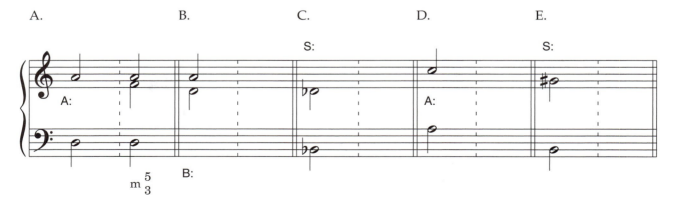

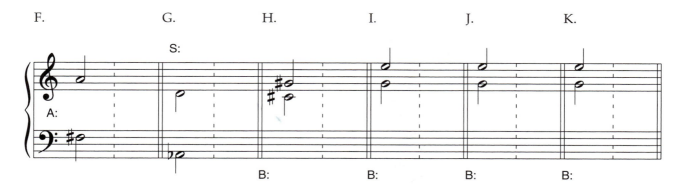

WRITING

EXERCISE 5.17 Figured Bass Practice: Construction, Playing, and Singing

Construct chords above each bass note following the figured bass. There is no underlying key in this exercise, thus no key signature, so add any necessary accidentals. Provide root and quality for each. There is more than one possible solution for each exercise. After playing the series of chords, return to the beginning of the exercise and play only the given bass pitch, singing the intervals above as required.

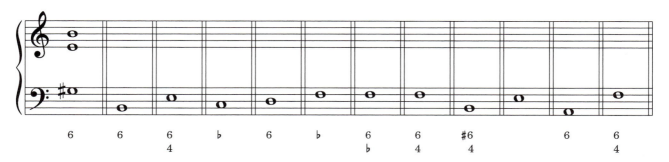

ANALYSIS

EXERCISE 5.18 Triads in Four Voices and in Various Spacings

1. Determine the root and quality of the triad.
2. Determine which member of the chord is in the bass: root (1), third (3), or fifth (5).
3. Determine which member of the triad is doubled: root (1), third (3), or fifth (5).
4. Provide a full (i.e., no shorthand) figured bass analysis that shows accidentals (i.e., consider the exercise to be in C major).

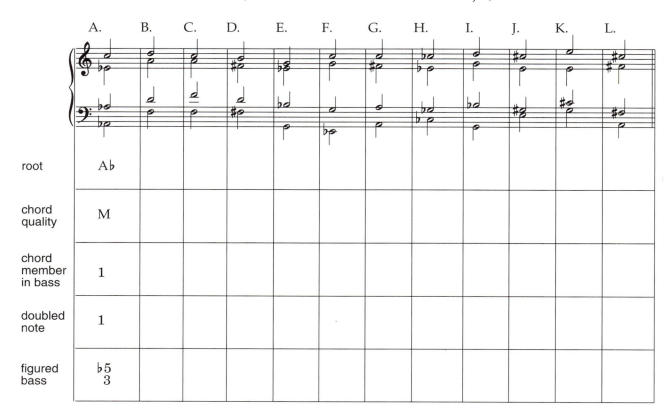

	A.	B.	C.	D.	E.	F.	G.	H.	I.	J.	K.	L.
root	A♭											
chord quality	M											
chord member in bass	1											
doubled note	1											
figured bass	♭5 3											

Exercises for Figured Bass and Harmonic Analysis

ASSIGNMENT 5.5

ANALYSIS

EXERCISE 5.19 Triads in Four Voices and in Various Spacings

1. Determine the root and quality of the triad.
2. Determine which member of the chord is in the bass: root (1), third (3), or fifth (5).
3. Determine which member of the triad is doubled root (1), third (3), or fifth (5).
4. Provide a full (i.e., no shorthand) figured bass analysis that shows accidentals (i.e., consider the exercise to be in C major).

	A.	B.	C.	D.	E.	F.	G.	H.	I.	J.
root	D									
chord quality	m									
soprano chord member	5									
chord member in bass	3									
doubled note	1									
figured bass	6 3									

EXERCISE 5.20 Figured Bass Realization

Given the following bass notes and figures, identify the key, and add the missing two voices above each bass note in close position. Write the root of each chord beneath the figures and identify the triad quality.

Sample solution

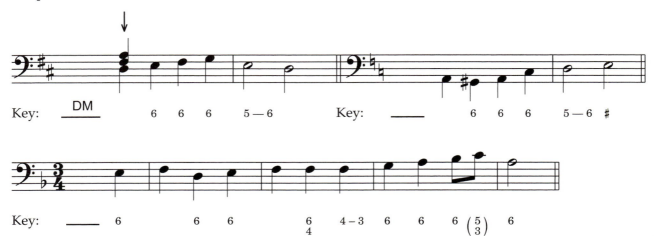

Key: _____ DM _____   6   6   6   5 — 6   Key: _____   6   6   6   5 — 6   ♯

Key: _____   6   6   6   6   4 – 3   6   6   6 (⁵₃)   6
                                                  4

KEYBOARD

EXERCISE 5.21 Outer Voices and Keyboard Style (I)

You are given a right-hand note and its chordal function, the root of the triad appears in the bass. Complete each triad by adding the missing note. Then, add a doubled root in your right hand as close to the other two notes as possible to create a four-voice texture, as shown is the sample solution. Finally, arpeggiate the right hand through the three various voicings while sustaining the left-hand note.

Sample solution

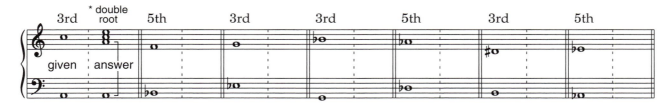

EXERCISE 5.22 Outer Voices and Keyboard Style (II)

In the following examples, the bass is always the root of the triad. Determine the chordal function of the soprano, then add the missing triad note(s); double the root. Play three voices in the right hand and the root in the left. Analyze with roman numerals.

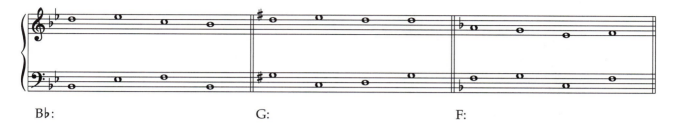

Bb: G: F:

EXERCISE 5.23 Soprano Voice and Building Chords

You are given a soprano line, the chordal function of each note (1 = root, 3 = third, 5 = fifth), and the key. Play the resulting triads below the soprano, using keyboard style to create a four-voice texture. The root will be in the bass. Name the quality of each triad. Note: Triads built on $\hat{5}$ will be major in both major and minor keys; that is, raise $\hat{7}$.

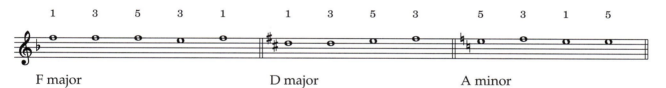

F major   D major   A minor

ASSIGNMENT 5.6

WRITING

EXERCISE 5.24 Writing Triads Generated from Various Scale Degrees

The given pitches represent the chordal roots of triads within a given key. However, no key signature is provided, nor required accidentals for any of the given pitches. Complete each triad in close position by adding two pitches and any necessary accidentals (based on the given key) and roman numerals.

For example, given the key of A major and the pitch C, you must first sharp the C, since C♯, not C natural, occurs in A major. Then, add two pitches a third and a fifth above the C♯. Given that the key of A major contains three sharps, you will also need to sharp the G. Add the roman numeral "iii," since a triad built on C♯ in A major is built on 3̂. You can check your work: iii in major should be a minor triad; sure enough, C♯–E–G♯ is a minor triad.

A. Given the key of D major and the following scale degrees:

B. Given the key of B♭ major and the following scale degrees:

C. Given the key of G minor and the following scale degrees:

EXERCISE 5.25 Notating Triads in Root Position and Inversion Within a Key

Notate triads in close position as requested; use accidentals rather than key signatures. Then, revoice each triad in four voices, chorale style, open position. Double the root.

sample solution   A.   B.   C.   D.   E.   F.   G.   H.

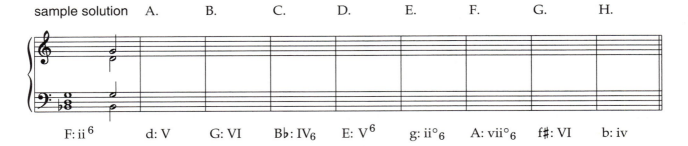

F: ii^6 d: V   G: VI   B♭: IV$_6$ E: V^6 g: ii°$_6$ A: vii°$_6$ f♯: VI   b: iv

EXERCISE 5.26 Brain Twister

Complete the following. Name three major and three minor keys in which each of the following triads appear. Use roman numerals for your answers. For example, A major: I in A major, IV in E major; V in D major, III in F♯ minor, V in D minor, and IV in E minor.

	Major keys	**Minor keys**
1. D major:		
2. A minor:		
3. F major:		
4. B♭ major:		

KEYBOARD

EXERCISE 5.27 Soprano Voice and Building Chords

You are given the soprano and the letter name of the triad. Add necessary notes to create complete right-hand triads; then double the root in the bass to create a four-voice, keyboard-style texture. Notice how little each voice moves to the next chordal pitch; often, in fact, there is no motion, given the common tones between the chords.

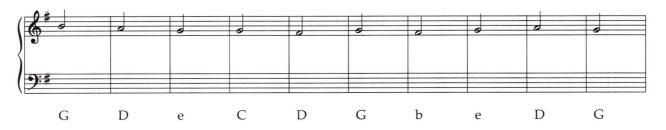

G   D   e   C   D   G   b   e   D   G

EXERCISE 5.28 More Triads and Doublings

Inversions are included in this exercise. Add missing pitches in the right hand below the soprano to create full triads, and play the bass note as required by the figured bass and given root. Double the root of the chord.

F   g$^6_3$ g   C   d   B♭$^6_3$ g$^6_3$ C$^6_3$ F$^6_3$ F$^6_4$ C   F

ASSIGNMENT 5.7

KEYBOARD

EXERCISE 5.29 Figured Bass and Doublings

In keyboard style, realize the figured basses below. Double the root in each example. When shifting to the next chord, move the right hand the shortest possible distance—by step preferably, or, not at all if there is a common tone.

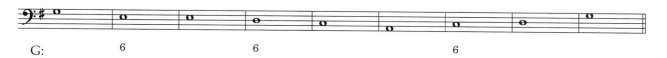

ANALYSIS

EXERCISE 5.30

The following triads appear in four voices and in various inversions.

1. Label the key.
2. Identify triad roots with roman numerals.
3. Include a figured bass for inverted triads.

KEY:

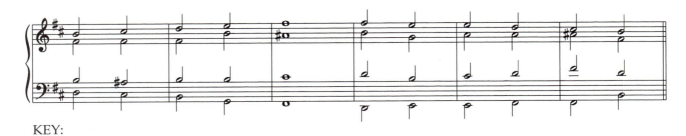

KEY:

EXERCISE 5.31 Analysis

Label the key for each example below. Provide roman numerals and figured bass for each harmony. In the spaces above each chord, write both the scale degree number and chordal member of the doubled pitches within the chord.

scale degree of doubled pitch:

chordal member of doubled pitch:

scale degree of doubled pitch:

chordal member of doubled pitch:

CHAPTER 6

Seventh Chords, Musical Texture, and Harmonic Analysis

Assignments for Root-Position Seventh Chords

ASSIGNMENT 6.1

ANALYSIS

DVD 1
CH 6
TRACK 1

EXERCISE 6.1 Identification of Root-Position Seventh Chords

Listen to the following series of root-position seventh chords that are written in close position.

1. Identify the type of seventh chord by choosing among Mm (major-minor), MM (major), mm (minor), dm (half diminished, °7), and dd (diminished, °7).
2. Transform each seventh chord as follows: Mm ↔ dd, MM ↔ dm, transpose mm up a minor third.

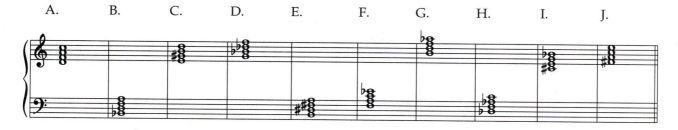

WRITING

EXERCISE 6.2. Error Detection

The pitches of the following seventh chords do not conform to the label beneath them. Renotate the pitches in each given seventh chord so that they conform to the respective labels.

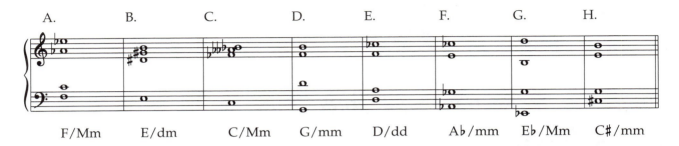

EXERCISE 6.3 Errors in Mm Seventh Chords

Below are incorrectly spelled root-position Mm seventh chords. The errors include enharmonic spelling (e.g., a Mm seventh built on C must be spelled in thirds: C–E–G–Bb, not C–E–G–A#) and wrong-note spelling (e.g., a Mm seventh built on G is spelled G–B–D–F, not G–B–D#–F#). Renotate each chord correctly, then after the dashed vertical line, transpose and notate each chord a major third higher.

LISTENING

DVD 1
CH 6
TRACK 2

EXERCISE 6.4 Seventh Chord Completion (I)

Listen to the examples below and add the two missing pitches to complete the root-position seventh chord you hear. The lowest pitch is the root. Identify each seventh chord (see the two worked examples). Your choices are MM, Mm, mm, dm, and dd. Finally, provide a plausible roman numeral and key in which each seventh chord would function (there will be multiple possibilities for some of the chords).

Sample solutions

DVD 1
CH 6
TRACK 3

EXERCISE 6.5 Seventh Chord Completion (II)

You will hear seventh chords of the following qualities: Mm, mm, MM, dm, and dd. Based on what you hear, construct root-position seventh chords above the notated roots, first in close position, then in an open position.

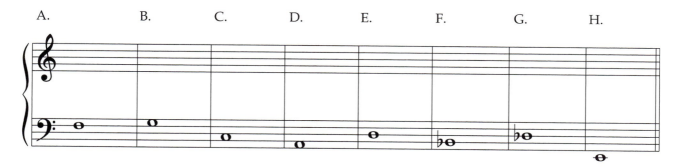

EXERCISE 6.6 Seventh Chord Completion (III)

Each of the given pitches is either the root, third, fifth, or seventh of Mm, MM, mm, dm7, or dd7 seventh chords. Listen to the given pitch, then to the root-position seventh chord in close position. Identify both the type of seventh chord and the pitch's placement as the root, third, fifth, or seventh of the chord.

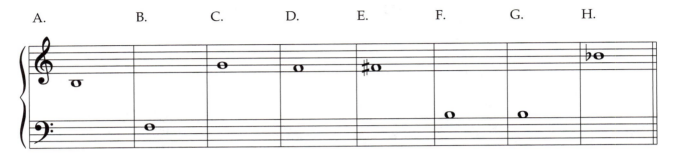

KEYBOARD

EXERCISE 6.7 Major-Minor Seventh Chords

Below are three notes of dominant seventh chords. The root is in the bass. Play the missing member in the right hand with the other two given notes. Return to the beginning of the exercise, play the given voices, then sing the missing voice.

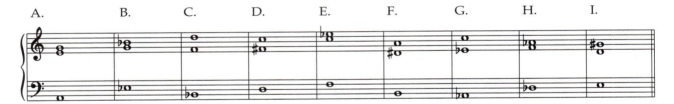

Assignments for Root-Position and Inverted Seventh Chords

ASSIGNMENT 6.2

WRITING

EXERCISE 6.8 Writing More Seventh Chords

A. Spell the seventh chords given the following:

1. C is the third of a Mm Seventh chord: _____
2. A♭ is the third of a MM Seventh chord: _____
3. B♭ is the fifth of a mm Seventh chord: _____
4. D is the seventh of a dm Seventh chord: _____
5. E is the fifth of a dd Seventh chord: _____

B. Write the seventh chord in which both given pitches are the specified members:

Sample solution:

    Given: F and D of Mm sevenths

    answer: B♭: B♭–D–F–A♭   and   G: G–B–D–F

    This answer is deduced as follows: F and D form the interval of a minor third, and in a Mm Seventh chord, there is a minor third between the third and the fifth of the chord (i.e., B♭–D–F–A♭) and between the fifth and the seventh of the chord (i.e., G–B–D–F). One of the exercises has only one solution, rather than two. Which one is it, and why?

1. A♭ and C of MM seventh chords _____ _____
2. C♯ and F♯ of MM seventh chords _____ _____
3. B and A of mm seventh chords _____ _____
4. B and D of dd sevenths (consider enharmonic equivalents) _____ _____

LISTENING

EXERCISE 6.9 Constructing Seventh Chords

You will hear the given pitch followed by an open position seventh chord played in root position or one of the inversions.

1. Determine the type of seventh chord and whether the given pitch is the chord's root, third, fifth, or seventh.
2. Notate the missing pitches in close position and label the chord.
3. Renotate each chord a minor sixth higher than its original position.

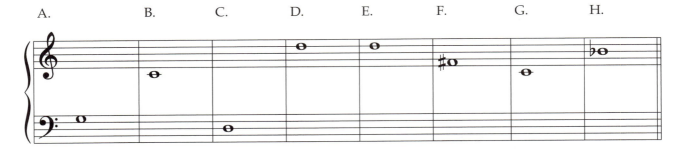

ANALYSIS

EXERCISE 6.10 Figured Bass Analysis

Determine the quality of the following seventh chords occurring in root position and inversion and then supply the appropriate full figured bass (don't forget to include accidentals).

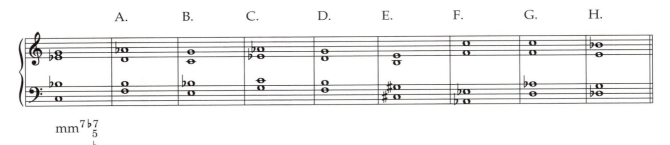

PERFORMING

EXERCISE 6.11 Singing Major-Minor Sevenths in Inversion

Given that Mm seventh chords occur more often than other seventh chords do, you must be familiar not only with their root-position sound but also with the sound of their inverted forms. Be able to arpeggiate from root position through each inversion until you return to root position. For example, given a B♭ Mm chord, you would sing B♭–D–F–A♭, D–F–A♭–B♭, F–A♭–B♭–D, A♭–B♭–D–F, B♭–D–F–A♭.

KEYBOARD

EXERCISE 6.12 More Mm Seventh Chords

Given are three notes of Mm Seventh chords, but the bass may or may not be the chord's root. From the three given notes, determine the missing member of a dominant seventh chord and play it in the right hand. Play the right-hand notes in two different spacings as shown in the example below. Return to the beginning of the exercise, play the given voices, then sing the missing voice.

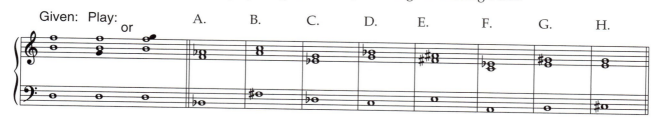

ASSIGNMENT 6.3

WRITING

EXERCISE 6.13 Figured Bass: Construction

Realize each of the following figured basses by writing in four voices. Remember that there are no doublings for seventh chords because they contain four different pitches. Label each type of seventh chord according to its quality (Mm, mm, MM, dm, or dd). Assume that there are no sharps or flats in the key signature.

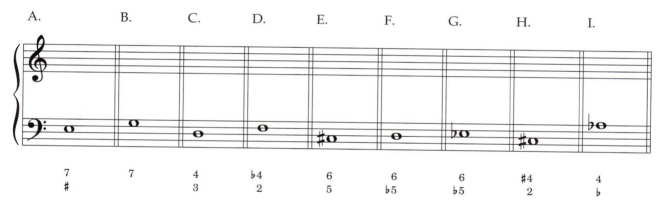

ANALYSIS

EXERCISE 6.14 Analysis: Identification of Seventh Chords in Root Position and Inversion

Below are notated root-position and inverted seventh chords. Identify:

1. The root of the chord.
2. The type of seventh (Mm, MM, mm, dm, dd).
3. The member of the chord (1, 3, 5, 7) that appears in the bass. Provide full figured bass that includes any chromaticism.

member of chord in bass:	1							
root:	A							
type of seventh:	dm							
figured bass:	7 b5 3							

PERFORMING

EXERCISE 6.15 Singing and Playing Major-Minor and Minor-Minor Seventh Chords from Given Pitches

Given any pitch, treat it as the root, third, fifth, or seventh of a Mm or mm seventh chord. For example, given the pitch C, consider it to be the root of each of the specific seventh chords. Then, consider C to be the third of a Mm 7 chord (which would be built on A♭) then as the third of a mm 7 chord (which would be built on A), and so on. You may either sing or play the resulting chords.

LISTENING

EXERCISE 6.16 Aural Identification of Root Position and Inverted Major-Minor Seventh Chords

DVD 1
CH 6
TRACK 6

Listen to and focus on the given bass pitch of the following Mm seventh chords that may appear in root position or in any inversion. Then, singing softly, arpeggiate up or down until you find the root and can identify which chord member is in the bass. Use figured bass notation to indicate the inversion of the chord you hear, and then spell the four-note chord in ascending thirds from the root.

A. C_____   B. G♯_____   C. E♭_____   D. D_____

E. E_____   F. A♭_____   G. C♯_____   H. B♭_____

KEYBOARD

EXERCISE 6.17 Figured Bass and Seventh Chords

Construct seventh chords in keyboard style according to the figured bass. Watch accidentals. Identify the quality of each seventh chord. Since there is no underlying key in this example, thus no key signature, you must add necessary accidentals.

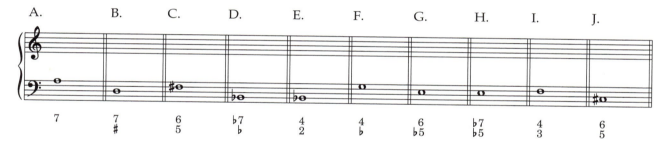

ASSIGNMENT 6.4

WRITING

EXERCISE 6.18 Seventh Chords Through the Octave

On a separate sheet of manuscript paper, write the specified root-position seventh chord. Then, renotate the chord at the interval specified. When you begin to encounter double flats and sharps, use enharmonic equivalents for easier notation.

A. Major-major seventh chord that begins on F and ascends through major thirds until the return to F.

B. Major-minor seventh chord that begins on G and ascends through major seconds until the return to G.

C. Minor-minor seventh chord that begins on A and descends through minor thirds until the return to A.

EXERCISE 6.19 Figured Bass: Construction

Below is a figured bass that incorporates triads and seventh chords in root position and inversion. Realize each chord according to the figured bass by writing in four voices (thus, for triads you will double the root; there are no doublings for seventh chords, since they contain four different pitches). Then label triad and seventh chord types. Since there is no underlying key in this exercise, thus no key signature, you must add any necessary accidentals.

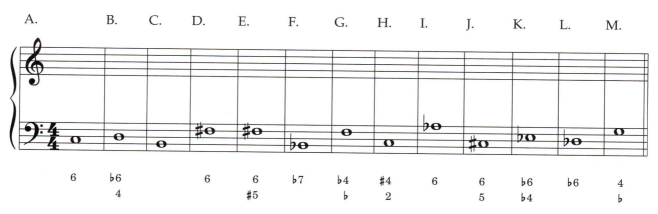

LISTENING

DVD 1
CH 6
TRACK 7

EXERCISE 6.20 Seventh-Chord Completion

Notated below are incomplete seventh chords: only three voices of their four voices are provided. Listen to each example, which will be played twice: the first time you will hear only the incomplete chords as written; the second time you will hear the complete seventh chord. Notate the missing member(s) of the triad as shown (bass = B, tenor = T, alto = A, soprano = S). The five types of seventh are Mm, MM, mm, dm, and dd; only the Mm will appear in inversion. Analyze each of the seventh chords, identifying the root and the type of seventh, and giving the full figured bass symbols (show all chromaticism). The first exercise, in which the tenor voice is missing, is completed for you.

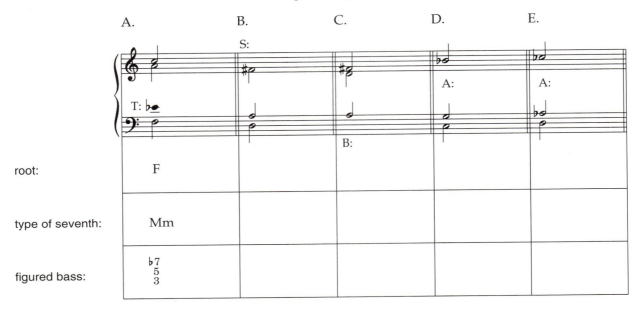

	A.	B.	C.	D.	E.
root:	F				
type of seventh:	Mm				
figured bass:	♭7 5 3				

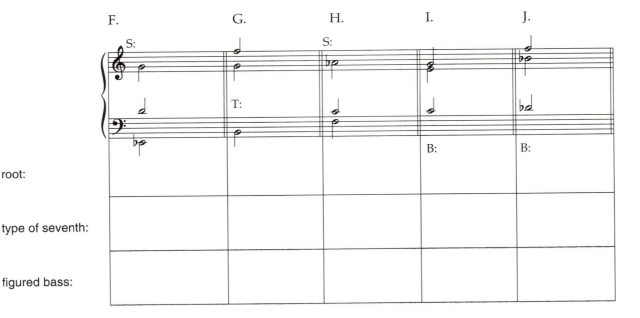

	F.	G.	H.	I.	J.
root:					
type of seventh:					
figured bass:					

Assignments for Musical Texture and Harmonic Analysis

ASSIGNMENT 6.5

ANALYSIS AND LISTENING

DVD 1
CH 6
TRACK 8

EXERCISE 6.21 Error Detection

Notated below are three- and four-note chords in various textures. Listen to each chord, noting whether what you hear is what is notated. If it is, write "Yes," and if it is not, write "No" and supply the correct answer. For example, if a major triad in root position is notated but you hear a minor triad in first inversion, you would write "No, minor triad, $^6_3$" There is a maximum of one wrong note per chord.

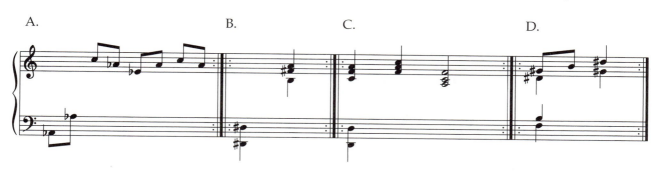

A. _____   B. _____   C. _____   D. _____

E. _____   F. _____   G. _____

EXERCISE 6.22

This exercise develops immediate comprehension of triads and seventh chords in various textures. Notes in parentheses are nonchord tones. Listen to each example and determine:

1. Size (triad, seventh chord).
2. Root name and quality (for triads: major, minor and diminished; beware, there is one instance of an augmented triad; for seventh chords: Mm, MM, mm, dm, mm). *Do not use roman numerals in your analysis.*
3. Member of chord in the bass (1, 3, 5, 7).

A. Tchaikovsky, "Morning Prayer," *Children's Album*, op. 39, no. 1

B. Corelli, Concerto Grosso no. 9 in F major, op. 6, *Adagio*

C. Brahms, "Ich stund an einem Morgen" ("One morning I stood"), *Deutsche Volkslieder*, WoO 32, no. 9.

ANALYSIS

DVD 1
CH 6
TRACK 10

EXERCISE 6.23 Functional Analysis

Determine the key and provide a roman numeral analysis.

A. Tchaikovsky, "Morning Prayer," *Children's Album*, op. 39, no. 1

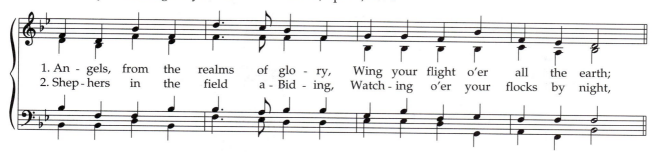

1. An - gels, from the realms of glo - ry, Wing your flight o'er all the earth;
2. Shep - herds in the field a - Bid - ing, Watch - ing o'er your flocks by night,

B. Corelli, Concerto Grosso no. 9 in F major, op. 6, *Adagio*

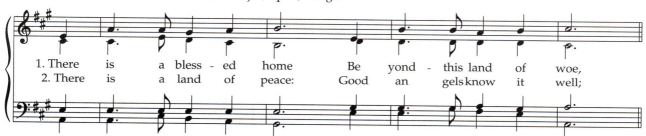

1. There is a bless - ed home Be yond - this land of woe,
2. There is a land of peace: Good an gels know it well;

C. Brahms, "Ich stund an einem Morgen" ("One morning I stood"), *Deutsche Volkslieder*, WoO 32, no. 9.

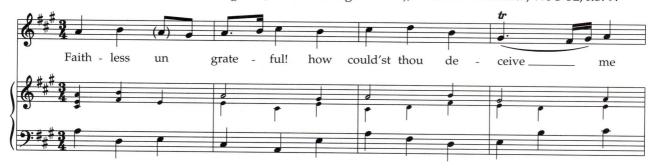

Faith - less un grate - ful! how could'st thou de - ceive _____ me

WRITING

EXERCISE 6.24 Writing Seventh Chords Generated from Scale Degrees

Complete the required tasks (including roman numeral analysis, construction of chords, and adding key signatures) from the information provided.

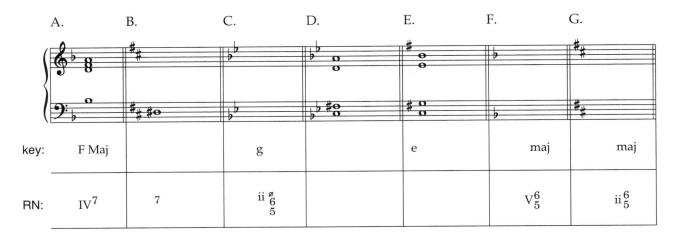

	A.	B.	C.	D.	E.	F.	G.
key:	F Maj		g		e	maj	maj
RN:	IV^7	7	ii$^{\o6}_{5}$			V$^6_5$	ii$^6_5$

ASSIGNMENT 6.6

ANALYSIS

EXERCISE 6.25

DVD 1
CH 6
TRACK 11

This exercise develops immediate comprehension of triads and seventh chords in various textures. Listen to each example and determine:

1. Size (triad, seventh chord).
2. Root name and quality (for triads: major, minor and diminished; for seventh chords: Mm, MM, mm, dm, and mm). *Do not use roman numerals in your analysis.*
3. Member of chord in the bass (1, 3, 5, 7).

A. Bach, Christ ist erstanden," Cantata no. 66, *Erfreut euch, ihr Herzen*, BWV 66

B. Schumann, "Anfangs wollt ich fast verzagen" ("At First I Almost Despaired"), *Liederkreis*, op. 24, no. 8

C. Debussy: *Canope, Preludes*, Book 2, no. 10. Identify only the sonorities enclosed in boxes.

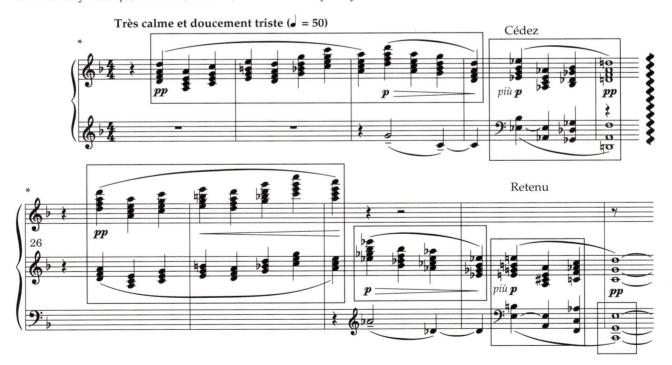

EXERCISE 6.26 Functional Analysis

Determine the key and provide a roman numeral analysis.

A. Bellini, "Sola, furtiva, al tempio" ("Alone, Furtive, to the Temple") from *Norma*, act I, scene vii

Consider the left-hand bass notes to occupy two beats of each measure because they continue to "ring."

B. Mozart, Sonata for piano and Violin in F major, *Tema* K. 377

WRITING

EXERCISE 6.27 Writing Seventh Chords Generated from Scale Degrees

Construct seventh chords based on the following information, which varies from providing the key signature to roman numeral ("RN") to the key.

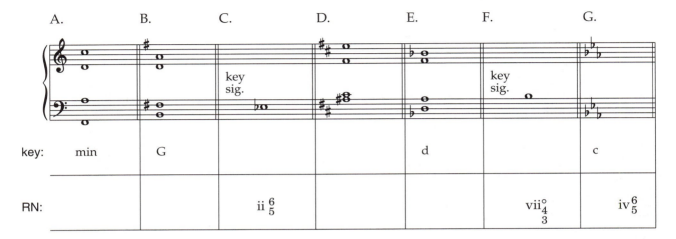

PERFORMING

EXERCISE 6.28 Singing Seventh Chords from Given Scale Degrees

Choose a major key, play its tonic pitch, and arpeggiate an ascending and descending MM seventh chord constructed above $\hat{1}$. Continue singing seventh chords built on the other diatonic scale degrees in the following manner: $\hat{1}–\hat{3}–\hat{5}–\hat{7}$ $–\hat{5}–\hat{3}–\hat{1}$, $\hat{2}–\hat{4}–\hat{6}–\hat{1}–\hat{6}–\hat{4}–\hat{2}$, $\hat{3}–\hat{5}–\hat{7}–\hat{2}–\hat{7}–\hat{5}–\hat{3}$, and so on. Do the same for a minor-mode key.

Additional Exercises

ANALYSIS

DVD 1
CH 6
TRACK 13

EXERCISE 6.29 Harmonic Analysis in Various Textures

Below are short excerpts in various textures. Complete the following tasks:

1. Circle each harmony and label root, type of harmony (for triads: Maj, min, dim; for seventh chords: Mm, MM, mm, dm, dd) and inversion, if any (for triads: $\frac{6}{3}$, $\frac{6}{4}$; for seventh chords $\frac{6}{5}$, $\frac{4}{3}$, $\frac{4}{2}$).
2. Describe the harmonic rhythm in terms of its rate of change (fast or slow), and whether or not it is regular.
3. Make a reduction on manuscript paper that includes the following:
   a. a bass note (which may or may not be the root, depending on whether the chord is inverted)
   b. two upper voices, added to complete triads, and three upper voices, added to complete seventh chords. Use close position, with highest note of the texture functioning as the soprano.

A. Corelli, Concerto Grosso no. 2 in F major, *Allegro*

B. Beethoven, Finale, Piano Trio in E♭, op. 1/1, *presto*

C. Haydn, String Quartet op. 20, no. 5, III, *Adagio*
    Include a roman numeral analysis.

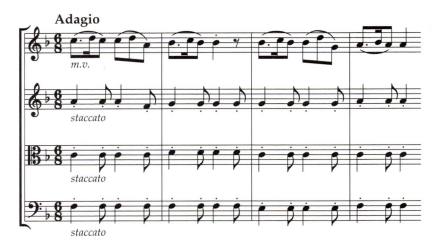

D. Bach, Prelude in C major, BWV 846, from *Well-Tempered Clavier*, Book 1
   Include a roman numeral analysis. Compare this example with the preceding example by Haydn.

E. Boismortier, *Allegro*, Sonata no. 1 for Two Bassoons in D minor

WRITING

EXERCISE 6.30

Write seventh chords in the key requested, first in close position (c) then open position (o). Use correct stem directions for soprano, alto, tenor, and bass. Exercises A and B are solved.

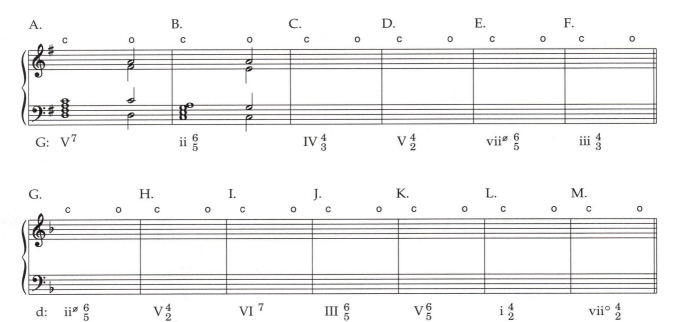

CHAPTER 7

Hierarchy in Music: Consonance, Dissonance, Unaccented Dissonance, and Melodic Fluency

Assignments for Tones of Figuration (PT, N, CL, and ARP)

ASSIGNMENT 7.1

ANALYSIS

DVD 1
CH 7
TRACK 1

EXERCISE 7.1 Harmonic and Melodic Analysis

Analyze, marking the following on the scores. Do *not* analyze with roman numerals.

1. Size of chord (triad or seventh chord)
2. Root name and quality (triad: M, m, d; 7th: Mm, MM, mm, dm, dd)
3. Member of the chord that is in the bass and soprano (e.g., root, third, etc.)
4. Label the following tones of figuration in the upper-voice melodies according to these types:

   a. passing tones and whether they are consonant or dissonant: "CPT," "DPT"

   b. neighboring tones and whether they are upper or lower types: "UN," "LN"

   c. chordal leaps: "CL"

A. Haydn, Piano Sonata no. 53 in E minor, Hob. XVI:34, *Adagio*

B. Mozart, Variation 6, *Variations on "Ah vous dirais-je, Maman,"* K. 265

Both the "Twinkle tune" and the harmony appear in the right hand, while the faster figuration notes appear in the left hand. Thus, you will need to consider the right-hand chords as you distinguish between chord tones and nonchord tones in the left hand (ignore the G^5 and F^5 in the right hand of mm. 3 and 4, enclosed in parentheses). Circle and label all nonchord tones in the bass.

C. Chopin, Waltz in B minor, op. posth. 69, no. 2, BI 35

D. Beethoven, Violin Sonata no. 3 in E♭ major, op. 12, no. 3, Rondo

E. Bach, Cello Suite no. 5 in C minor, BWV 1011, *Allemande*

DVD 1
CH 7
TRACK 2

EXERCISE 7.2 Verticalization

The examples below are written in a florid style. However, each depends on the flow of harmonies. Rewrite each example in chorale (vertical) style (four voices: soprano, alto, tenor, and bass) and provide an analysis that includes chord type and inversion. Do *not* use roman numerals unless specified in the example.

A. Schumann, "Wiegendlichen" no. 43, *Kinderszenen*, op. 68
Analyze mm. 1–6 using roman numerals.

B. Beethoven, Piano Sonata in C major, op. 2, no. 3, Trio

C. Strauss, "Heimkehr" "Homecoming", op. 15, no. 4
Identify the five tones of figuration (marked by arrows).

ASSIGNMENT 7.2

ANALYSIS

DVD 1
CH 7
TRACK 3

EXERCISE 7.3 Harmonic and Melodic Analysis

Analyze, marking the following items on the scores. Do *not* analyze with roman numerals. Ignore all pitches in parentheses.

1. Size of chord (triad or seventh chord)
2. Root name and quality (triad: M, m, d; seventh: Mm, MM, mm, dm, dd)
3. Member of the chord that is in the bass and soprano (e.g., root, third, etc.)
4. Label the following tones of figuration in the upper-voice melodies according to these types:

   a. passing tones and whether they are consonant or dissonant ("CPT" or "DPT")
   b. neighboring tones and whether they are upper or lower types ("UN" or "LN")
   c. chordal leaps ("CL")

A. Schubert, Waltz in A♭ major, *36 Originaltänze*, op. 9a, D. 365
Like many waltzes, the left-hand downbeat note controls the harmony throughout the measure; consider it sounding even though Schubert has not specified that it be sustained.

B. Bach, "O Ewigkeit, du Donnerwort" ("O Eternity, You Thunderous Word"), Cantata no. 20, BWV 20
Try playing the outer voices together on the piano, then play one of the outer voices while singing the other voice.

DVD 1
CH 7
TRACK 4

EXERCISE 7.4 Verticalization

Each of these examples is written in a florid style. However, each depends on the flow of harmonies. Rewrite the examples in chorale (vertical) style and provide an analysis of each chord type and inversion. Do *not* use roman numerals unless specified in the example.

A. Tito Mattei, "Non è ver?" (Romanza)

B. Schubert, "Ständchen" from *Schwanengesang*

C. Schumann, "Ich will meine Seele tauchen" from *Dichterliebe*

There are two chords in the first half beat of m. 7: A and C are members of both chords, while G (second 32nd note) and F♯ (fourth 32nd note) each belong to two different chords. Arrows indicate tones of figuration; label each.

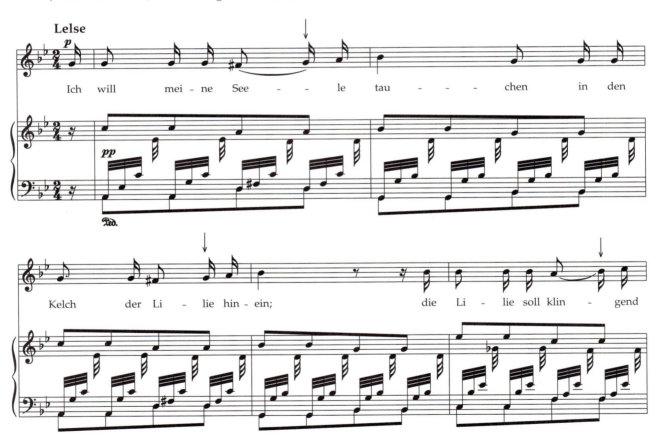

D. Beethoven, Rondo, op. 51, no. 1

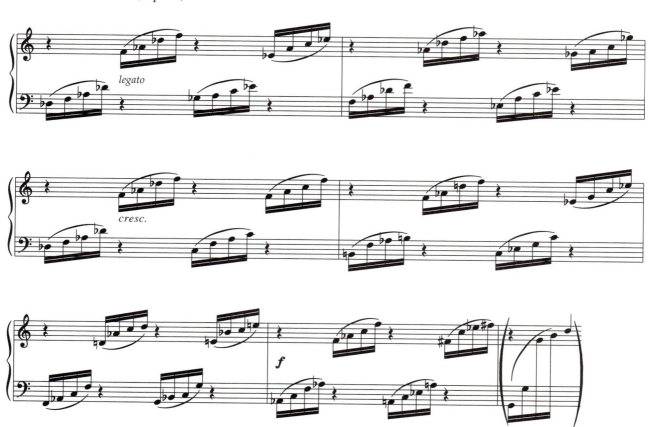

Assignments for Melodic Fluency

ASSIGNMENT 7.3

ANALYSIS

EXERCISE 7.5 Verticalization

DVD 1
CH 7
TRACK 5

These two excerpts from a Haydn string quartet are in a florid style. However, each depends on the flow of harmonies. Rewrite both in chorale (vertical) style and provide an analysis of each chord type and inversion. Do *not* use roman numerals.

A. Haydn, String Quartet in C major, op. 20, no. 2 *Adagio*

B. Haydn, String Quartet in C major, op. 20, no. 2 *Moderato*

EXERCISE 7.6 Melodic Fluency

Circle the pitches that participate in the structural melodic line. The pitches that you choose must be consonant with the bass (or chord tones, which include the chordal seventh) and must be accented in some way (e.g., metrically, rhythmically). Look for parallel musical relationships to support your connections. Notice in the sample solution that an overall stepwise descent of a fifth occurs, from C6 to F5. Beethoven clearly marks the stepwise descent in the following ways:

1. The descent from C to B♭ mm 1-64 occurs in parallel melodic/rhythmic contexts (see mm. 1–2 and 5–6)
2. Measures 5–8 and 9–12 are near repetitions of each another. However, note that the abrupt leap of B♭ down an octave (m. 5), the sudden shift to *piano* and *dolce*, and the incomplete descent only to A ($\hat{3}$) reveals that mm. 5–8 are subordinate to 9–12, where the original register is recaptured as is the dynamic level, and the structural melodic line completes its descent from B♭5 to F5.

Beethoven, Symphony no. 8 in F major, op. 93, *Allegro vivace con brio*

A. Mozart, "Notte e giorno faticar" from *Don Giovanni*, K. 527, act 1, scene 1

B. Schumann, "Winterszeit" *Album Für die Jugend*, op. 68, no. 12

C. Haydn, String Quartet in F minor, op. 20, no. 5, *Allegro moderato*

D. Mozart, Rondo in F major, K. 494

EXERCISE 7.7 Melodic Fluency, Harmony, and Tones of Figuration

The florid soprano melody of each example below depends upon more slowly moving stepwise lines that emerge when we listen to and study the examples. Complete the following tasks.

1. Listen to each example and circle and stem each note of the structural step-wise line, then beam them together.
2. For example C, identify harmonies; use roman numerals for the bass notes with horizontal dashes beneath them.
3. Label the type of tone of figuration for each soprano pitch beneath an arrow.

A. Beethoven, German dance

B. Verdi, "La donna è mobile" from *Rigoletto*, act 3

C. Albinoni, Sonata in C for Oboe and Basso Continuo, *Menuet*

PERFORMING

EXERCISE 7.8 Two-Voice Counterpoint and Figured Bass

Add the required pitches in the treble clef by studying the given figured bass and playing the bass notes with the left hand. Transpose the two-voice counterpoint to one other key of your choice.

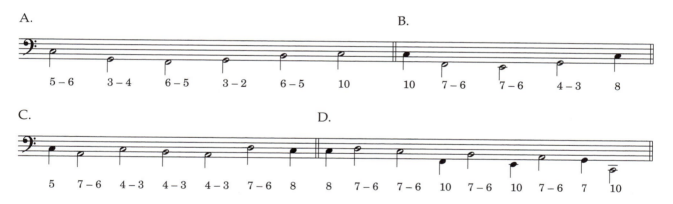

ASSIGNMENT 7.4

ANALYSIS

DVD 1
CH 7
TRACK 7

EXERCISE 7.9 Melodic Fluency

Circle the pitches that participate in the structural melodic line. The pitches that you choose must be consonant with the bass and must be accented in some way (e.g., metrically, rhythmically). Look for parallel musical relationships to support your connections.

A. Mozart, "Porgi, amor, qualche ristoro" from *Le Nozze di Figaro (The Marriage of Figaro)*, K. 492, act 2, scene 1

B. Mozart, String Quartet in E♭ major, *Adagio* K. 171
Compare this excerpt with the one from *Figaro*.

C. Bach, Prelude in C minor, BMV 871, *Well-Tempered Clavier*, Book 2

WRITING

EXERCISE 7.10 Melodic Fluency

Using any of the sample figurations below (each of which ornament the pitch "E"), or creating your own, embellish each note of the given melodic line to create an 8- to 12-measure melody.

ornamenting E

ASSIGNMENT 7.5

ANALYSIS

DVD 1
CH 7
TRACK 8

EXERCISE 7.11   Melodic Fluency

Circle the pitches that participate in the structural melodic line. The pitches that you choose must be consonant with the bass and must be accented in some way (e.g., metrically, rhythmically, etc.). Look for parallel musical relationships to support your connections.

A. Mozart, "Non più andrai" from *Le Nozze di Figaro (The Marriage of Figaro)*, K. 492, act 1, no. 9

(continues on next page)

po - so,　Nar - ci - set - to, A - don - ci - no　d'a - mor,　　del - le
o - ver,　Che - ru - bi - no,　my young　ca - va - lier,　　such di -

bel - le　tur-ban-do il ri - po - so,　Nar - ci - set - to, A - don - ci - no　d'a-mor.
ver - sions　are done with and o - ver,　Che - ru - bi - no,　my young ca - va - lier.

B.　Beethoven, Symphony no. 3 in E♭ major, "Eroica," op. 55, fourth Movement

CHAPTER 8

Tonic and Dominant as Tonal Pillars and Introduction to Voice Leading

Assignments for Hearing I and V, Cadences

ASSIGNMENT 8.1

LISTENING

EXERCISE 8.1 Warm-Up for Metrical Hearing

We now review metrical patterns, since the upcoming harmonic dictations will nearly always be cast in a meter. We focus on three meters for our dictations: $\frac{3}{4}$, $\frac{4}{4}$, and $\frac{6}{8}$. (We will also encounter $\frac{2}{4}$, $\frac{2}{2}$, $\frac{9}{8}$, and $\frac{12}{8}$ in analysis and writing.) $\frac{3}{4}$ and $\frac{4}{4}$ are easily distinguished. $\frac{6}{8}$ is a compound meter: it subdivides the beat into threes, rather than into the twos of $\frac{3}{4}$ and $\frac{4}{4}$. Listen to the following excerpts from the literature and identify a probable meter and an appropriate tempo indication that would correspond to that meter. If you hear the following patterns, for example,

two possible meters arise, one a fast $\frac{4}{4}$ (or $\frac{2}{4}$) (as notated above), and the other a slow $\frac{4}{4}$, notated as follows:

Your tempo indications are *andante* (slowish, walking), *allegro* (fast), and *molto allegro* (very fast).

	Meter	Tempo		Meter	Tempo		Meter	Tempo
A.	_____	_____	B.	_____	_____	C.	_____	_____
D.	_____	_____	E.	_____	_____	F.	_____	_____
G.	_____	_____						

DVD 1
CH 8
TRACK 2

EXERCISE 8.2 Identification of Tonic

Below are chord progressions that employ numerous diatonic chords. Label only tonic (I or i) harmonies in the appropriate box; leave remaining boxes blank. Each exercise is in a different key; you will hear I–V–I in the appropriate key to orient you. It is best to sing the tonic triad softly before listening to the exercise. The durations of harmonies are shown by the proportional length of dashes. Identify cadences in each example, except for example C.

A. $\frac{4}{4}$: ____ ____ ____ ____ | ____ ____ _____ | cadence type:

B. $\frac{4}{4}$: ____ | ____ ____ ____ ____ | ____ ____ _____ | cadence type:

C. $\frac{4}{4}$: ____ ____ ____ ____ | ____ ____ ____ ____ |

D. $\frac{4}{4}$: ____ ____ ____ ____ | _____ _____ | cadence type:

E. $\frac{3}{4}$: _____ ____ | _____ ____ | _____ ___ | _____ | _____ ___
       | _____ | _____ | cadence type:

DVD 1
CH 8
TRACK 3

EXERCISE 8.3 Identification of Tonic and Dominant

Once again, you will hear progressions that use numerous diatonic chords. Label only the I (or i) and V chords, using roman numerals. Identify cadence types.

A. $\frac{4}{4}$: __ __ __ __ | ____ ____ | __ __ __ __ | _____ | cadence type:

B. $\frac{3}{4}$: __ | __ __ __ __ __ | _____ __ | _____ __ | _____ cadence type:

C. $\frac{4}{4}$: ____ ____ | ____ ____ | ____ ____ | _____ | cadence type:

D. $\frac{4}{4}$: ____ ____ | __ __ ____ | ____ ____ | _____ | cadence type:

E. $\frac{6}{8}$: ____ __ _____ | ____ __ _____ | _____ ___ __ | _____ |
       cadence type:

ANALYSIS

DVD 1
CH 8
TRACK 4

EXERCISE 8.4

Each literature example below contains not only tonic and dominant harmonies, but also other harmonies. In each exercise, label the following:

1. Key.
2. Only root-position tonic and dominant harmonies (use roman numerals). (An occasional seventh may be added to the dominant; you may ignore it for now.) Many harmonies are to be left unlabeled at this point.
3. The type of cadence that closes each excerpt.

A. Foster, "Jeanie with the Light Brown Hair"
Label tones of figuration in the vocal line.

Key: ____

B. Couperin, L'Amphibie, *Pièces de Clavecin*, Book IV, 24e ordre.

C. Corelli, Concerto Grosso in G minor, "Christmas Concerto," op. 6, no. 8, *Vivace*

ASSIGNMENT 8.2

LISTENING

DVD 1
CH 8
TRACK 5

EXERCISE 8.5 Differentiating Between I and V

Listen to the following progressions that employ only tonic and dominant chords in root position. Vertical slashes represent bar lines, and note values represent durations of harmonies, below which you will write either I or V to indicate the sounding harmony. Be aware that the same harmony may be repeated in different spacings. The first four are in D major, the second four are in B minor. The first one has been done for you.

Sample Solution

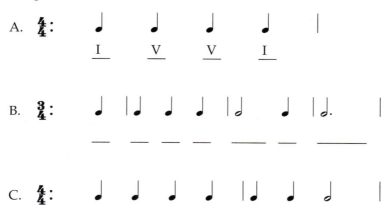

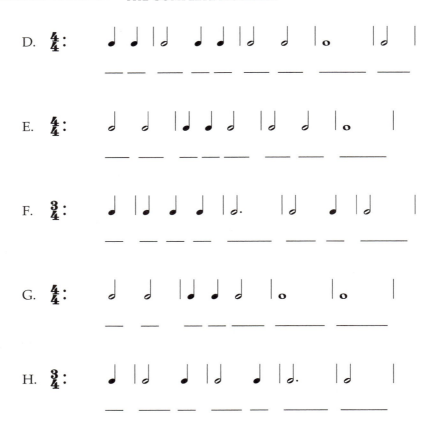

ANALYSIS

EXERCISE 8.6

Determine the following for the chord progressions given:

1. Whether the harmony is tonic or dominant (use roman numerals)
2. Whether close (c) or open position (o) is used
3. Which note is doubled (circle the doubled pitch class and indicate whether it is the root, third, or fifth (r, 3, 5)

Assignments for Voice Leading

ASSIGNMENT 8.3

LISTENING

EXERCISE 8.7 Identification of Tonic and Dominant
from the Literature

Label only tonic and dominant harmonies in the appropriate spaces below, ignoring any other diatonic harmonies. Identify the final cadence in each excerpt.

A. Schubert, "Frühlingstraum" ("A Dream of Springtime"), *Winterreise*, D.911, no. 11

m.:   1   2   3   4   5   6   7   8

$\frac{6}{8}$: ____ | ____ | __ __ | ____ | ____ | ____ | __ __ | ____ | cadence type:

B. Handel, "Air" Concerto Grosso no. 10 in D minor, Op. 6, HWV 328

m.:   1   2   3   4

$\frac{3}{4}$: _____ __ | _____ | ___ ___ | _____ | cadence type:

C. Schubert, Impromptu in A♭ (major), *Six Moments musicaux*, op. 94, D. 780

m.:   1   2   3   4   5   6   7   8

$\frac{3}{4}$: _____ | _____ | _____ | _____ | _____ | _____ | _____ | _____ |
cadence type:

D. Chopin, Mazurka in G minor, op. 67, no. 2

m.:   1   2   3   4   5   6

$\frac{3}{4}$: ____ | ____ | ____ | ____ | ____ | ____ | cadence type:

E. Schubert, Waltz in A major, *17 Ländler*, D. 366

m.:   1   2   3   4   5   6   7   8

$\frac{3}{4}$: _____ | _____ | _____ | _____ | _____ | _____ | _____ | _____ |
cadence type:

ANALYSIS

EXERCISE 8.8 Error Detection Involving I and V

Each example contains one or two errors, including errors in construction (e.g., missing chordal member, poor spacing, incorrect doubling, etc.) and voice leading (e.g., parallels, direct intervals, nonresolution of tendency tones, etc.). Identify and label the key; label and circle each error.

EXERCISE 8.9 Extended Error Detection

Analyze key and roman numerals. Then label chord construction and voice leading errors. Only tonic and dominant occur. The sample solution includes a shorthand labeling system you may wish to use (or, just describe the error in prose).

Sample solution

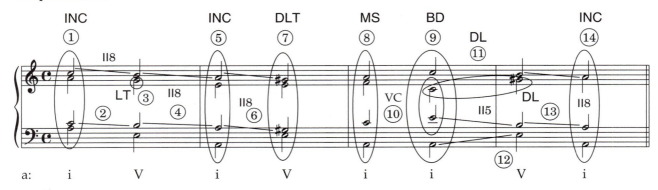

1. An incomplete chord (INC) is a poor way to begin. (Although the fifth is the only chordal member that can be omitted, its absence is justified only if it makes the voice leading smoother. At the beginning of an exercise, where many options are possible, there is no reason to omit it.)
2. Tenor-soprano parallel octaves (P8, with parallel lines showing which voices are involved and the pitches that create the parallels).
3. The $\hat{7}$ must be raised to create a leading tone (LT). In minor, you must add this chromaticism to the pitch.
4. Tenor-soprano parallel octaves.

5. No third in the tonic chord (INC). Remember, only the fifth may be absent in a chord.
6. The parallel octaves continue in tenor and soprano.
7. Double leading tone (DLT).
8. Misspelled tonic harmony: F is not a member of the chord (MS).
9. Doubled third for no reason; in fact, it creates problems (see item 10). Remember, you may double anything (except for dissonant notes or the leading tone), since smooth voice leading is the goal, but keep in mind that doubled roots are most common. Note: "BD" means bad doubling.
10. Voice crossing (VC).
11. Difficult, dissonant leap in alto (DL).
12. Contrary ("antiparallel") fifths (C^5, with contrary-motion lines showing voices involved).
13. Parallels between soprano and tenor.
14. Four roots and no third or fifth.

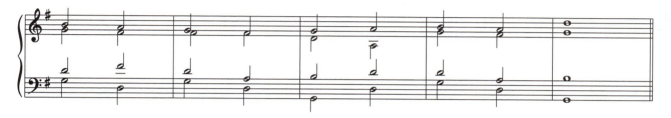

WRITING

EXERCISE 8.10 Completion of Missing Voices

Determine the key and add roman numerals to the incomplete root-position tonic and dominant triads. Then, decide which voice(s) is/are missing and the appropriate chordal member needed to create an SATB texture.

ASSIGNMENT 8.4

ANALYSIS

EXERCISE 8.11 Error Detection Involving I and V

Each example contains two or more errors, including errors in construction (e.g., missing chordal member, poor spacing, incorrect doubling) and voice leading (e.g., parallels, direct intervals, nonresolution of tendency tones). Identify and label the key; label and circle each error.

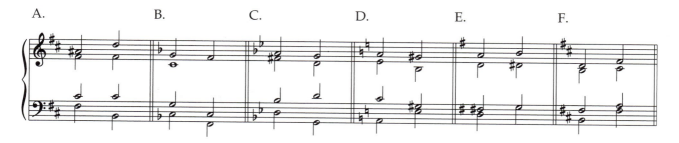

EXERCISE 8.12 Extended Error Detection

Analyze key and roman numerals. Then label chord construction and voice leading errors. Only tonic and dominant occur.

WRITING

EXERCISE 8.13   Completion of Missing Voices

Determine the key and add roman numerals to the incomplete tonic and dominant triads. Add the appropriate pitches to create a four-voice (SATB) texture. Double the chord's root and use only root-position tonic and dominant triads.

EXERCISE 8.14   Part Writing Tonic and Dominant in Major

1. In D major, notate in a meter of your choice the following soprano scale degrees: $\hat{1}$—$\hat{7}$—$\hat{1}$, $\hat{1}$—$\hat{2}$—$\hat{3}$, $\hat{3}$—$\hat{2}$—$\hat{1}$.
2. Add a bass line that implies only tonic and dominant harmonies in root position.
3. Fill in the alto and tenor voices to create a four-voice chorale texture. Remember that stems go up for soprano and tenor and down for alto and bass.
4. Analyze and then transpose to the keys of F and A major.

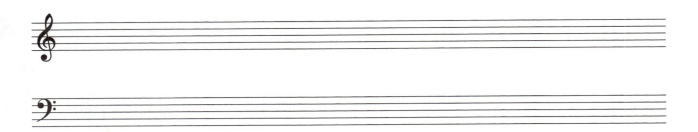

EXERCISE 8.15 Dictation

Notate the bass and soprano voices. Next, provide roman numerals for each chord and identify the type of cadence for the following homophonic progressions. Observe the following steps:

1. Listen to the entire exercise, notating the first harmony and final cadence.
2. Listen for individual chords, focusing on soprano steps and leaps.
3. Check your final product.
   a. Are there any missing notes?
   b. Are there any contradictions between harmony and melody? For example, remember that a dominant harmony cannot support $\hat{3}$ in the melody and that it is important to use the leading tone (i.e., raised $\hat{7}$, whether it is sharped or naturaled) in minor.

KEYBOARD

EXERCISE 8.16 Soprano Harmonization

In keyboard style, harmonize each pitch of the following soprano fragments. Use only root-position I and V chords. Except for $\hat{5}$, no other soprano scale degrees provide you with multiple chord choices. Play as written in both major and parallel minor and transpose to F and D major and minor.

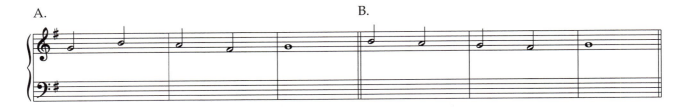

ASSIGNMENT 8.5

WRITING

EXERCISE 8.17 Part Writing Tonic and Dominant in Minor

Using the soprano scale degrees $\hat{1}$–$\hat{7}$–$\hat{1}$, $\hat{1}$–$\hat{2}$–$\hat{3}$, $\hat{3}$–$\hat{2}$–$\hat{1}$, harmonize using only i–V–i in the key of B minor. Remember that in minor the dominant triad is major, so $\hat{7}$ must be chromatically raised to create a leading tone Add alto and tenor voices and analyze. Transpose to G minor and E minor.

EXERCISE 8.18 Figured Bass

Realize the following figured basses in four voices (SATB), including roman numerals. Change the upper-voice spacings for any repeated bass notes (or octaves).

LISTENING

DVD 1
CH 8
TRACK 8

EXERCISE 8.19 Dictation from the Literature

Listen to the following literature excerpts that employ only I and V. Notate the single controlling bass pitch for each measure. Provide roman numerals (when you encounter an accompanimental figure, focus on the lowest sounding pitch, since it determines the harmony).

A.   B.

C.

KEYBOARD

EXERCISE 8.20 Bass Line Harmonization

Play a soprano in note-against-note style that works with the given bass and harmonize, using only I and V chords in root position. Then add inner voices (played along with the soprano in the right hand). Transpose the bass to D major and add a different soprano melody and inner voices.

ASSIGNMENT 8.6

WRITING

EXERCISE 8.21 Potpourri of Activities

Complete the tasks below in four voices as required. Use only root-position tonic and dominants. Chromatically raise $\hat{7}$ in minor. Label key, add key signatures, and roman numerals.

A. Write a passing soprano line

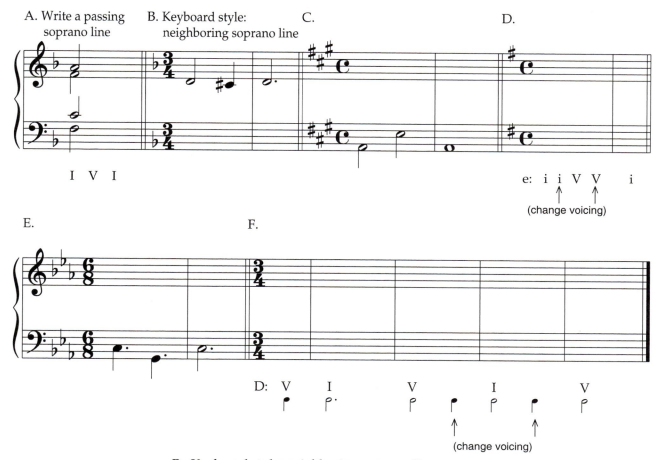

B. Keyboard style: neighboring soprano line

LISTENING

DVD 1
CH 8
TRACK 9

EXERCISE 8.22 Dictation from the Literature

Listen to the following literature excerpts that employ only I and V. Notate the single controlling bass pitch for each measure. Provide roman numerals (when you encounter an accompanimental figure, focus on the lowest sounding pitch, since it determines the harmony).

A. Mozart, Symphony in F major, *Andante*, K. 112
B. Mozart, Symphony in G minor, *Allegro*, third movement, K. 113

A.   B.

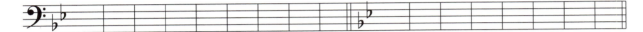

KEYBOARD

EXERCISE 8.23 Soprano Harmonization

Add a bass line to the soprano melody using only I and V harmonies in root position. Then, add tenor and alto. Transpose to F major. Be able to sing either outer voice while playing the remaining three voices.

Additional Exercises

WRITING

EXERCISE 8.24 Part Writing Progressions

Below are two chord progressions: I–V–V–I and i–i–V–i. Above the progressions are various soprano melodic fragments that can be harmonized by the progression that is given beneath. Choose a meter and a rhythmic setting for the soprano fragments. The final scale degree, harmonized by the tonic, must appear on a downbeat. Notate the outer-voice counterpoint. Then add inner voices, and analyze and label cadences.

Major mode

A. $\hat{1}$	$\hat{7}$	$\hat{2}$	$\hat{3}$	(in F and D)
I	V	V	I	
B. $\hat{3}$	$\hat{2}$	$\hat{7}$	$\hat{1}$	(in G and E♭)
I	V	V	I	
C. $\hat{1}$	$\hat{7}$	$\hat{2}$	$\hat{1}$	(in B♭ and A)
I	V	V	I	
$\hat{1}$	$\hat{2}$	$\hat{7}$	$\hat{1}$	(in E and B)
I	V	V	I	

Minor mode

D. $\hat{1}$	$\hat{3}$	$\hat{2}$	$\hat{3}$	(in D and B)
i	i	V	i	
E. $\hat{3}$	$\hat{1}$	$\hat{2}$	$\hat{3}$	(in C and F♯)
i	i	V	i	

EXERCISE 8.25 Harmonizing Cadential Soprano Progressions

Choose a meter, then write four-voice cadential progressions using only root-position tonic and dominant harmonies based on these soprano fragments. Your order of composition should be bass line, then alto and tenor lines. Analyze with roman numerals and label the cadence.

A. $\hat{3}$	$\hat{2}$	$\hat{1}$	$\hat{7}$	$\hat{1}$	(D minor, B minor)
B. $\hat{1}$	$\hat{7}$	$\hat{1}$	$\hat{2}$	$\hat{3}$	(A♭ major, E major, C minor)
C. $\hat{1}$	$\hat{2}$	$\hat{3}$	$\hat{5}$	$\hat{5}$	(F major, B♭ major, C minor)

EXERCISE 8.26 Unfigured Bass and Soprano

Figured basses are the first steps in understanding harmony because they prescribe harmonic content precisely, leaving you no choice in what chords to use. Unfigured basses are much more challenging, since a given bass note can be harmonized by more than one harmony (e.g., any bass note could be the root, third, or fifth of a triad). Thus, unfigured basses require mastery of the most typical and logical harmonic progressions, and they will regularly occur in the following chapters. An intermediate step between figured bass and unfigured bass is the unfigured bass with a given soprano, since the addition of the soprano voice restricts your chord choice considerably. Thus, begin an unfigured bass with soprano by studying the bass line in conjunction with the soprano, which provides valuable hints in chord choice. Look for cadences and short melodic patterns that have harmonic settings you have learned. Avoid vertical "third stacking" in which you haphazardly choose harmonies based on individual bass pitches. Only after you have grouped bass and soprano pitches into logical musical units should you begin to add inner voices and roman numerals. This exercise contains a few passing tones.

CHAPTER 9

The Impact of Melody, Rhythm, and Meter on Harmony, and Introduction to V7

Assignment for Interaction of Harmony, Melody, Meter, and Rhythm, First- and Second-Level Analysis and I and V (only)

ASSIGNMENT 9.1

LISTENING AND ANALYSIS

DVD 1
CH 9
TRACK 1

EXERCISE 9.1 Dictation and Second-Level Analysis

Notate the bass and the soprano lines and provide roman numerals for the following homophonic examples. Then, step back to determine which harmonies in a measure are more important than others by focusing on their metrical placement and on the soprano line. Finally, based on these decisions, bracket entire measures in the bass and provide a second-level analysis in which a single roman numeral represents the underlying harmony that controls each measure. Note that the penultimate measure often contains two harmonies, such as I followed by V, which leads to a final tonic.

A.

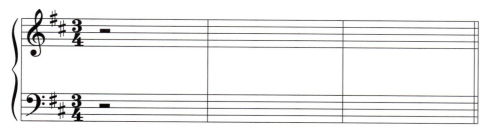

B.

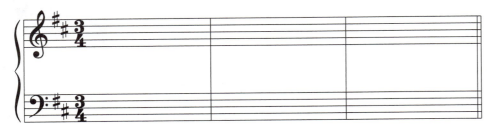

C.

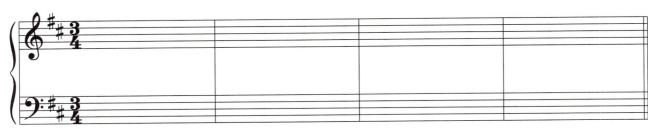

D.

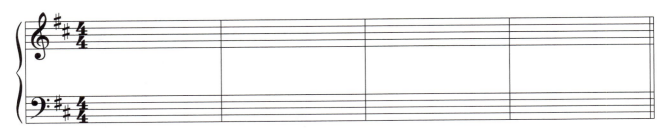

E.

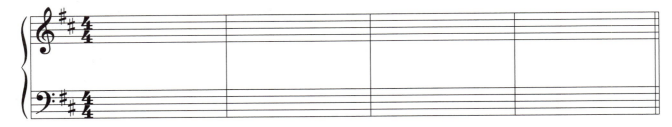

Assignments for V7

ASSIGNMENT 9.2

ANALYSIS

DVD 1
CH 9
TRACK 2

EXERCISE 9.2

Analysis of I, V, and V7

1. Label each tonic and dominant harmony. Distinguish between V and V7.
2. Specify whether each seventh is prepared (not a requirement) and indicate resolution by an arrow (a requirement).
   - If the seventh appears in the top voice, consider the possibility that it might be part of a longer, more slowly moving structural line that spans the entire melody, in which case it occurs at the supermetrical level (recall our studies of melodic fluency).
   - Remember, the seventh is resolved only by a change of harmony.
   - In freer textures, the resolution may occur in a different voice or even a different register.

A. Haydn, String Quartet in G major, op. 33, no. 5, *Largo*

(continues on next page)

B. Bach, Sonata for Flute and Continuo in E minor, BWV 1034, *Allegro*

C. Schumann, "In der Fremde" ("In Foreign Lands"), *Liederkreis*, op. 39, no. 1

Aus der Hei - - mat hin - ter den

Bli - tzen roth da kom - men die Wol - ken her.

D. Mozart, Serenade in D major "Posthorn," K. 320, *Andante grazioso*

E. Corelli, Church Sonata in G major, op. 1 no. 9, *Allegro*

EXERCISE 9.3 Error Detection

The following four-voice progressions that include root position I, V, and V7 contain one or two part-writing errors, including construction (spelling, spacing, doubling, etc.) and voice-leading problems (parallels, improper resolution of seventh, etc.). Label the key of each example, then identify and label each type of error. Focus especially on errors of the following types.

1. Incorrect treatment of tendency tones:
   A. The chordal seventh ($\hat{4}$) must resolve down by step.
   B. The leading tone ($\hat{7}$) must ascend, unless it occurs in an inner voice.
2. V7 follows V; the use of V after V7 is not allowed, given that V7 intensifies V.
3. Since harmonic rhythm usually aligns with metrical stress, chords should change from metrically weak to metrically strong beats (i.e., a new chord, or at least an intensification of a chord, such as V moving to V7, should appear on the following downbeat).

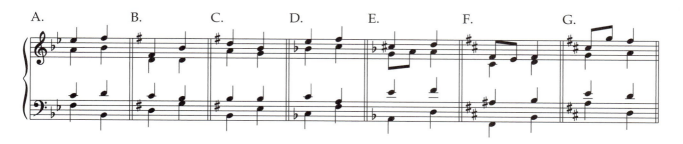

WRITING

EXERCISE 9.4 Completing V7 in Three and Four Voices

Identify the key and complete the V7 chords below (one or two chord members are missing). Examples A–G should be written in three voices. Thus, the V7 chords will necessarily be incomplete (lacking the fifth). Add the missing pitch(es). In examples H–N, you will write V7 chords in four voices. In these examples, there may be an opportunity to either double the root (and omit the fifth) or write a complete seventh chord. For examples H–N, indicate whether your chord is complete (C) or incomplete (I). The first one is done for you.

Sample solution

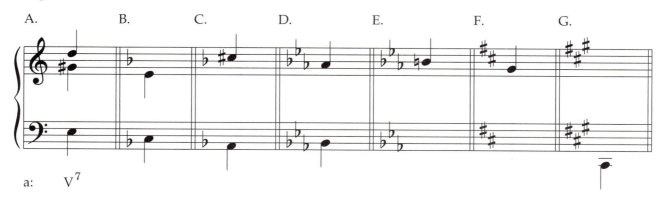

a: V^7

(continues on next page)

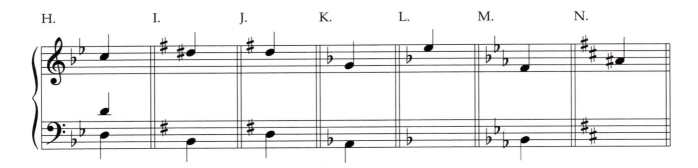

KEYBOARD

EXERCISE 9.5 Figured Bass

In keyboard style, realize the following figured bass by adding alto and tenor voices. Play in the parallel minor. Then, transpose to any two major keys and their parallel minor forms.

ASSIGNMENT 9.3

ANALYSIS

DVD 1
CH 9
TRACK 3

EXERCISE 9.6 Analysis of I, V, and V7

1. Label each tonic and dominant harmony. Distinguish between V and V7.
2. Specify whether each seventh is prepared (not a requirement) and indicate resolution by an arrow (a requirement).

   a. If the seventh appears in the top voice, consider the possibility that it might be part of a longer, slower moving structural line that spans the entire melody, in which case it occurs at the supermetrical level (recall our studies of melodic fluency).
   b. Remember, the seventh is resolved only by a change of harmony.
   c. In freer textures the resolution may occur in a different voice or even a different register.

A. Mozart, Symphony no. 22 in C major, K. 162, *Allegro assai*

This is the first of several orchestral scores that you will need to negotiate in this book. Do not panic; you can employ certain strategies when first encountering a full orchestral score. Focus on the instruments that are easiest to read and carry the most important harmonic and contrapuntal materials. Begin by looking at the strings, which are the backbone of the orchestra and are laid out in string-quartet style: cello and double bass carry the bass and therefore the harmonic underpinning, while the first violin carries the contrapuntal melody. The viola part is written in the alto clef.

You can then look to the woodwinds, which very often double the strings. High woodwinds (flutes and oboes) share material with the first and second violin parts, and the bassoon is aligned with the cellos and double basses. Occasionally the high woodwinds may have a separate melody from the upper strings, so examine these parts carefully. Remember, all the strings and many of the winds sound as written (though there are exceptions, such as B♭ clarinet and oboe d'amore in A). Most of the brass instruments are transposing (horns in F sound down a perfect fifth from the notated pitch, and trumpets in B♭ sound a major second lower than written); it is not until the nineteenth century that they arise as an independent force in the orchestra. In the 1700s and in the first half of the nineteenth century, brass instruments generally doubled other instruments. In this excerpt, Mozart is using brass instruments in C, thus the pitches you see are the pitches that sound (though horn in C actually sounds one octave lower than written).

B. Mozart, String Quartet in A major, K. 464, *Allegro*

This example contains a supermetrical passing seventh—the passing motion takes place over several measures. Label only root-position tonic and dominant harmonies. Then, trace the three-note melodic line that comprises the preparation of the seventh, the dissonant seventh, and its resolution.

EXERCISE 9.7 Error Detection

The following four-voice progressions that include root-position I, V, and V7 contain one or more part-writing errors, including construction (spelling, spacing, doubling, etc.) and voice-leading problems (parallels, improper resolution of seventh, etc.). Label the key of each example, then identify and label each type of error. Focus especially on the following types of errors:

1. Incorrect treatment of tendency tones:
   a. The chordal seventh ($\hat{4}$) must resolve down by step.
   b. The leading tone ($\hat{7}$) must ascend, unless it occurs in an inner voice.
2. V7 follows V; the use of V after V7 is not allowed, given that V7 intensifies V.
3. Since harmonic rhythm usually aligns with metrical stress, chords should change from metrically weak to metrically strong beats (i.e., a new chord, or at least an intensification of a chord, such as V moving to V7, should appear on the following downbeat).

WRITING

EXERCISE 9.8 Authentic Cadences and Figured Bass

Identify the key for each example, then write authentic cadences in four voices. You may write perfect or imperfect cadences. Specify the type of cadence and analyze with roman numerals. Be sure to obey the voice leading if given by a horizontal dash in the figured bass. Example A completed for you.

Sample solution

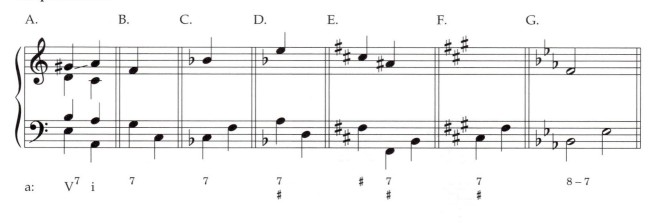

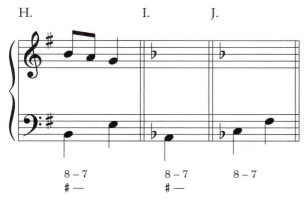

LISTENING

DVD 1
CH 9
TRACK 4

EXERCISE 9.9 Analysis and Dictation

The following excerpts do not have bass lines.

1. After listening to each example, notate the missing bass notes. Consider the given pitches to be helpful hints.
2. Identify I, V, and V7 using roman numerals.
3. Circle and label any tones of figuration in the melody.

A. Schubert, Trio, Minuet in G major, *20 Minuets*, D. 41, no. 20

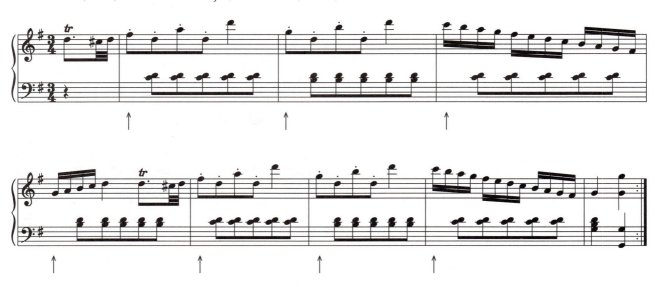

B. Haydn, German Dance in D major, *Seven German Dances*, Hob. IX:12

ASSIGNMENT 9.4

LISTENING

DVD 1
CH 9
TRACK 5

EXERCISE 9.10 Analysis and Dictation

The following excerpts do not have bass lines.

1. After listening to each example, notate the missing bass notes. Consider the given pitches to be helpful hints.
2. Identify I, V, and V7 using roman numerals.
3. Circle and label any tones of figuration in the melody.

A. Schubert, Waltz in B minor, *38 Waltzes, Ländler, and Ecossaises*, op. 18, no. 6, D. 145
The right-hand G in m. 4 is a dissonant upper neighbor to the harmony's F♯.

B. Haydn, String Quartet in C major, op. 50, no. 2, *Allegro* Hob. III:45

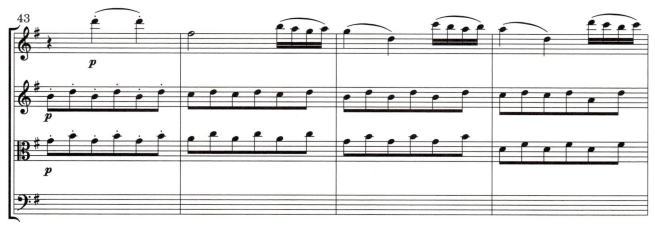

(continues on next page)

WRITING

EXERCISE 9.11 Authentic Cadences and Figured Bass

Identify the key for each example, then write authentic cadences in four voices. You may write perfect or imperfect cadences. Specify the type of cadence and analyze with roman numerals. Be sure to obey the voice leading if given by a horizontal dash in the figured bass.

KEYBOARD

EXERCISE 9.12 Unfigured Bass

Realize the two unfigured basses below in four voices. Use only root positions I, V, and V7. Analyze with roman numerals.

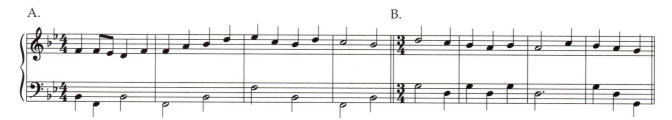

ASSIGNMENT 9.5

WRITING

EXERCISE 9.13 Writing Root-Position V7

Complete the tasks below in four voices. Begin by writing note-against-note outer voices, then, fill in tenor and alto.

A. Using a passing soprano line, write I–V7–I in D major and G minor.

B. Using a neighboring soprano line, write I–V7–I in E major and C minor.

EXERCISE 9.14 Figured Bass

Realize the two figured basses below in four voices. Write the soprano first, then add tenor and alto. Do a two-level analysis: the first level should include every harmonic change, and the second level should prioritize harmonies based on their metrical placement and on the subordinate passing and neighboring motions of the soprano.

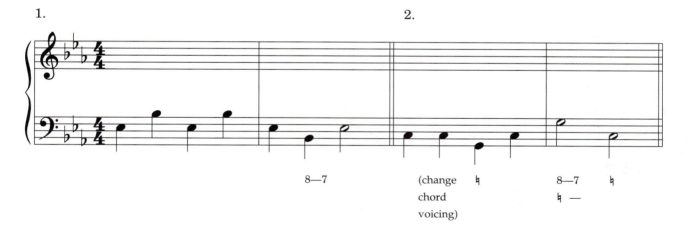

LISTENING

EXERCISE 9.15 Analysis/Dictation

These incomplete scores from the literature omit the bass lines. You are to:

1. Listen to each example and notate the missing bass notes. Note: In addition to I and V, you may encounter other chords. Listen for their appearance and notate their bass notes only, but do not analyze them.
2. Circle and label tones of figuration in the melody.

A. Mozart, Trio II, Serenade in B♭ major, K. 361

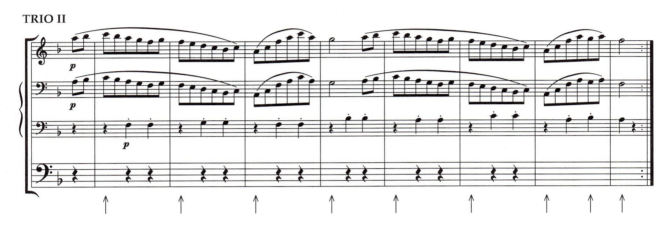

B. Schumann, "Jemand," *Myrten*, op. 25, no. 4

C. Schumann, String Quartet in A major, op. 41, *Scherzo*

ASSIGNMENT 9.6

LISTENING

DVD 1
CH 9
TRACK 7

EXERCISE 9.16 Dictation: Melodies with Accompaniments

Provide the following on the staves below:

1. Key and mode
2. Meter
3. Number of measures
4. cadence type at close of example
5. bass line and roman-numeral analysis

A.

B. Chopin, Etude in E, op. 10, no. 3, BI 74

C. Beethoven, Ecossaise in G

D. Haydn, String Quartet in E♭, op. 64, no. 6, Hob. III:64

WRITING

EXERCISE 9.17 Soprano Harmonization

1. Determine whether root-position I, V, or V7 chords are implied by the soprano lines below; add roman numerals.
2. Harmonize each soprano pitch with a single bass note to create note-against-note counterpoint.
3. Finally, fill in the alto and tenor voices.

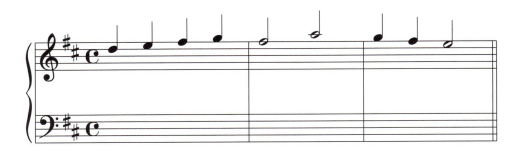

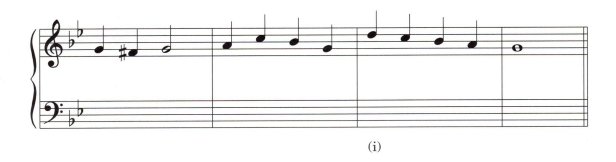

(i)

KEYBOARD

EXERCISE 9.18 Soprano Harmonization

Choose three soprano melodies from the four melodies given and harmonize each pitch by adding the three lower voices in keyboard style. Use only I, V, and V7. Circle all sevenths that occur in the soprano melodies and trace their resolutions. Transpose each melody to one other key of your choice.

ASSIGNMENT 9.7

WRITING

EXERCISE 9.19 Harmonization Using V and V7

After choosing a meter, use I, V, and V7 for the soprano fragments below. Remember, the chord progression V to V7 is not reversible. Write each exercise in a different major key and its relative-minor key.

A. $\hat{3}$–$\hat{4}$–$\hat{3}$ B. $\hat{5}$–$\hat{4}$–$\hat{3}$–$\hat{2}$–$\hat{1}$ C. $\hat{1}$–$\hat{7}$–$\hat{1}$–$\hat{2}$–$\hat{4}$–$\hat{3}$

D. $\hat{3}$–$\hat{2}$–$\hat{1}$–$\hat{7}$–$\hat{1}$ E. $\hat{2}$–$\hat{7}$–$\hat{1}$–$\hat{2}$–$\hat{3}$

EXERCISE 9.20 Harmonizing Melodies with Slow Harmonic Rhythm

Study the examples below, all of which are taken from Mozart's operas. Determine the key, then sing the melodies in order to plot which root-position tonic or dominant (seventh) chord is appropriate; the harmonic rhythm is usually one chord per measure. You need, then, only add the root of the chord. Submetrical figuration tones include chordal skips and leaps, arpeggiations, passing tones, and neighboring tones. Label each.

A. Mozart, "Voi, che sapete", from *Le Nozze di Figaro (The Marriage of Figaro)*, K. 492, act 2

B. Mozart, "Batti, batti, o bel Masetto" from *Don Giovanni*, K. 527, act 1

C. Mozart, "In quegli anni" from *Figaro*, act 4

Tempo di Minuetto

Men - tre an - cor ta - ci - to guar - do quel do - no,
While I was lost in a - maze - ment and won - der,

men - tre an - cor guar - do quel do - no,
lost in a - maze - ment and won - der,

D. Mozart, Introduction, *Die Zauberflöte (The Magic Flute)*, K. 620

Tamino *(runs in, pursued by a serpent.)*

Zu Hül - fe! zu Hül - fe! sonst bin ich ver - lo - ren! zu
O help me, pro-tect me, my pow - ers for - sake me! O

Hül - fe! zu Hül - fe! sonst bin ich ver - lo - ren!
help me, pro-tect me, my pow - ers for - sak - en!

LISTENING

DVD 1
CH 9
TRACK 8

EXERCISE 9.21 Outer-Voice Dictation

Notate the outer voices of the four-voice homophonic examples. Provide a roman numeral analysis.

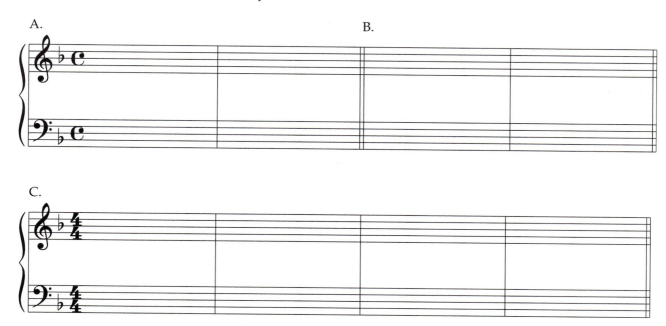

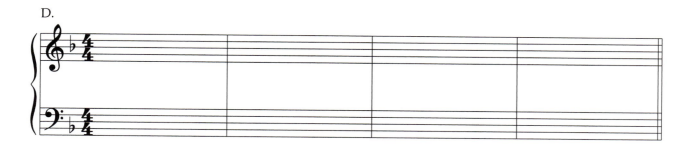

E.

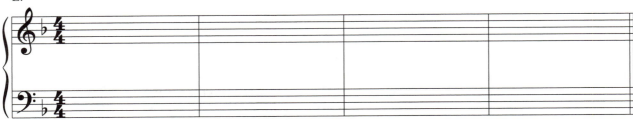

F.

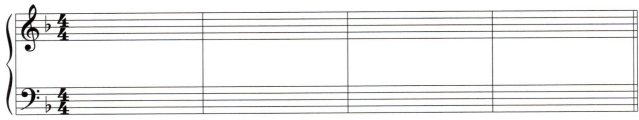

Additional Exercises

WRITING

EXERCISE 9.22 Writing V7–I Cadences

The following soprano fragments are represented by their scale degrees. Harmonize each in four voices using only I and V(7); label each cadence and analyze each chord, using roman numerals and figured bass.

A. $\hat{4}$–$\hat{3}$ (D major and relative minor and A major and relative minor)
B. $\hat{2}$–$\hat{1}$ (G major and relative minor and E♭ major and relative minor)
C. $\hat{7}$–$\hat{1}$ (E major and relative minor and B♭ major and relative minor)
D. $\hat{5}$–$\hat{5}$ (C major and relative minor and A♭ major and relative minor)

LISTENING

EXERCISE 9.23 Outer-Voice Dictation

Notate the outer voices of the four-voice homophonic examples. Provide a roman numeral analysis.

A.   B.

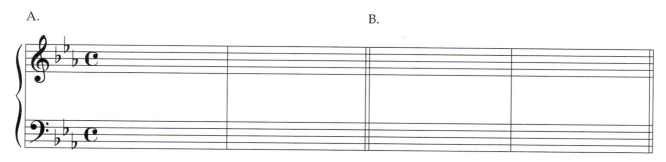

C.   D.

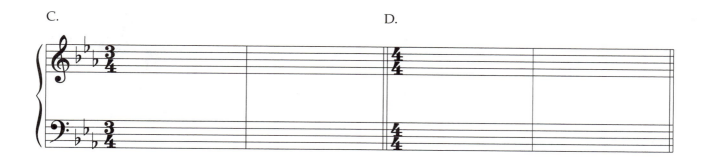

E.

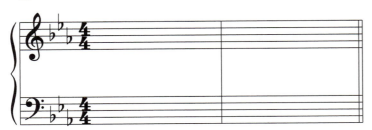

EXERCISE 9.24 Harmonizing Melodies with Slow Harmonic Rhythm

Study the examples below, all of which are taken from Mozart's operas. Determine the key, then sing the melodies in order to plot which root-position tonic or dominant (seventh) chord is appropriate. You need, then, only add the root of the chord. Submetrical figuration tones include chordal skips and leaps, arpeggiations, passing tones and neighboring tones Label each.

A. Mozart, "Tutto e disposto . . . Aprite un po' quegli occhi" from *Le Nozze di Figaro (The Marriage of Figaro)*, K. 492, act 4

B. Mozart, Finale, *Die Zauberflöte (The Magic Flute)*, K. 626, act 1

C. Mozart, Finale, *Flute*, act 2

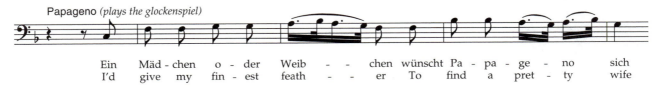

D. Mozart, "Se vuol ballare, Signor Contino," from *Figaro*, act 1, no. 3

Allegretto

CHAPTER 10

Contrapuntal Expansions of Tonic and Dominant: Six-Three Chords

Exercises for I6 and V6 and Second-Level Analysis

ASSIGNMENT 10.1

ANALYSIS

EXERCISE 10.1

Use two levels to analyze the following examples that contain $\frac{5}{3}$ and $\frac{6}{3}$ tonic and dominant triads. (Recall that level one is descriptive and provides an analysis of every chord, using roman numerals and figured bass. Level two is interpretive, and identifies what chords are more important than others by using roman numerals for structural chords, and contrapuntal functions (P, N, CS), for expanding harmonies.) Below is a sample solution.

Sample solution

Hasse, Trio Sonata no. 1 in E minor for Two Flutes and Basso Continuo, *Largo*

A. Mozart, String Quartet in D minor, K. 173, *Menuetto*

B.

C. Schubert, "Auf dem Flusse," *Winterreise*, D. 911
The E in the right hand of m. 3 is a nonchord tone that postpones the D♯ that follows.

LISTENING

DVD 1
CH 10
TRACK 2

EXERCISE 10.2

Listen to the following examples that contain tonic and dominant triads, their expanding $^6_3$ inversions, and V7 in root position. The meter signature is given, and dashes indicate chord changes. Specify roman numerals and figured bass for each chord. Then, supply a second-level analysis that summarizes the harmony underlying each progression.

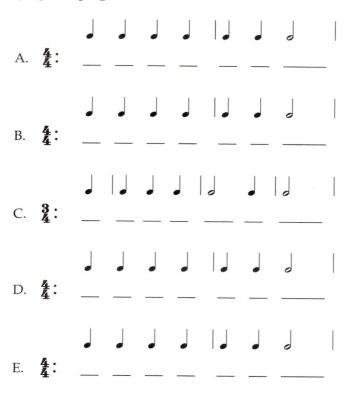

WRITING

EXERCISE 10.3 I, I6, V, V7, and V6

Study the soprano fragments to determine a suitable bass line. Begin and end with root position I and V, but use first inversions when possible within. Analyze and add inner voices.

A. In D major and G minor: $\hat{3}$–$\hat{1}$–$\hat{7}$–$\hat{1}$
B. In F major and A minor: $\hat{1}$–$\hat{2}$–$\hat{3}$–$\hat{2}$–$\hat{1}$
C. In A♭ major and C minor: $\hat{5}$–$\hat{5}$–$\hat{4}$–$\hat{3}$

EXERCISE 10.4 Figured Bass

1. Study the figured bass below, adding a soprano that moves primarily by step and creates mostly imperfect consonances with the bass (i.e., thirds and sixths).
2. Analyze, including a second-level analysis, then fill in inner voices.

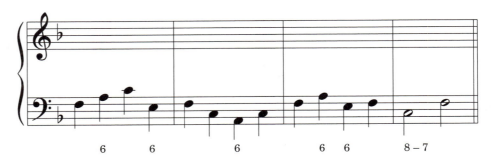

KEYBOARD

EXERCISE 10.5 Figured and Unfigured Bass

Play the outer voices as given, and determine the implied harmonies, adding roman numerals and second-level analysis. Then, add inner voices, playing soprano, alto, and tenor in the right hand and bass in the left hand. In Exercise B, you will need to determine the implied harmonies without the aid of a given figured bass.

A.

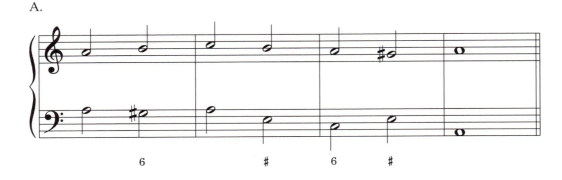

B.

ASSIGNMENT 10.2

ANALYSIS

DVD 1
CH 10
TRACK 3

EXERCISE 10.6

Using two levels, analyze the following examples that contain $\frac{5}{3}$ and $\frac{6}{3}$ tonic and dominant triads. Begin by determining the general harmonic rhythm so that you will be able to distinguish between chord tones and nonchord tones.

A. Vivaldi, Concerto Grosso in G major, op. 9, no. 10, Ryom 300, Ricordi 125, *Allegro molto*

B.

LISTENING

DVD 1
CH 10
TRACK 4

EXERCISE 10.7 Bass line Dictation

Listen to, memorize, and notate the bass lines in the following examples, and provide a two-level harmonic analysis.

A.   B.   C.

D.   E.   F.

DVD 1
CH 10
TRACK 5

EXERCISE 10.8 Two-Voice Dictation

You will hear short (four- to six-chord) outer-voice counterpoints. Notate the two voices and provide roman numerals based on their harmonic implications.

A.   B.   C.   D.   E.

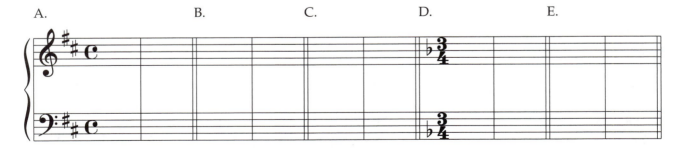

EXERCISE 10.9 Two-Voice Dictation: 2 + 2 = 4

You will hear how the two-voice counterpoint of the bass and soprano provides the skeleton for the added inner voices of alto and tenor. The result is a four-voice texture, the harmonies of which are essentially by-products of the confluence of voices. You will hear the outer-voice counterpoint for one beat, immediately followed by the added inner voices, their combination resulting in four-voice harmony. You are to notate the outer voices only, using both their counterpoint and the addition of the inner voices to label the harmonies.

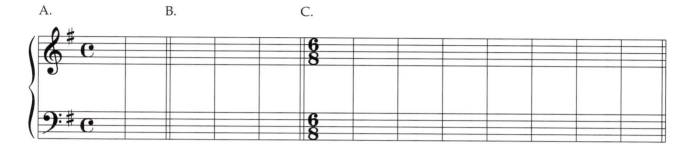

DVD 1
CH 10
TRACK 6

EXERCISE 10.10 Outer Voice Notation and Analysis

1. Listen to the four-voice examples and notate their outer voices below. To do this, listen to the entire example and determine the opening and closing harmonies. Then, start filling in the second level by distinguishing between harmonic progressions and contrapuntal expansions. Finally, memorize and notate one melodic line at a time. (Do not notate individual pitches as they are played; this is an inefficient and dangerous means of taking dictation because the pitches are not within a larger musical context.) A few pitches are provided.
2. Based on the harmonic implications of the outer voices, provide a two-level roman numeral analysis.

B.

WRITING

EXERCISE 10.11 Figured Bass

1. Study the figured bass below, adding a soprano that moves primarily by step and creates mostly imperfect consonances with the bass (i.e., thirds and sixths).
2. Analyze, including a second-level analysis.
3. Fill in inner voices.

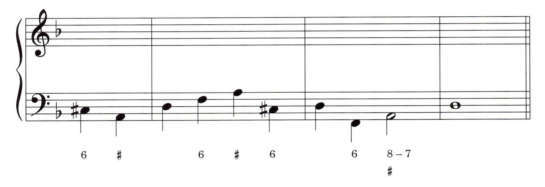

KEYBOARD

EXERCISE 10.12 Melody Harmonization

The two melodies below offer the chance to incorporate first-inversion tonic and dominant chords in four-voice keyboard style. Harmonize Example B in both a major key and its relative minor. You may write in a few bass notes and roman numerals to aid your playing. Be able to sing either outer voice while playing the other three voices.

A.

B.

Exercises for vii°6 and IV6

ASSIGNMENT 10.3

ANALYSIS

DVD 1
CH 10
TRACK 7

EXERCISE 10.13 Expanded I and V

Your harmonic vocabulary now includes I, I6, V, V7, V6, and vii°6. Provide a two-level harmonic analysis.

A. Beethoven, "Freudvoll und leidvoll" ("Joyful and Sorrowful"), op. 84, no. 2
Once again, accented tones of figuration occur on beat two of each measure; you need not analyze these for now.

B. Mozart, Piano Sonata in F major, K. 280, *Allegro assai*

WRITING

EXERCISE 10.14 Matching and Composition

In the left-hand column, labeled "Bass harmonies," is a summary of the progressions and prolongations that we have encountered. In the right-hand column is a series of soprano scale degree patterns. Match the soprano patterns with the appropriate bass progression (there will be some multiple solutions). Then, in B minor, choose a meter and string together three of the patterns to create a convincing progression. Add alto and tenor. Analyze using roman numerals and include a second-level analysis.

Bass Harmonies	Soprano Scale Degrees
1) I–V$_7$–I	A) $\hat{3}$–$\hat{4}$–$\hat{5}$–$\hat{4}$–$\hat{3}$
2) I–V$_6$–V$_7$–I	B) $\hat{5}$–$\hat{5}$–$\hat{4}$–$\hat{2}$–$\hat{1}$
3) I–V–V$_6$–I	C) $\hat{3}$–$\hat{2}$–$\hat{1}$–$\hat{7}$–$\hat{1}$
4) I–V$_6$–I–I$_6$–V$_7$–I	D) $\hat{1}$–$\hat{2}$–$\hat{3}$
5) I–vii°$_6$–I$_6$–V$_7$–I	E) $\hat{3}$–$\hat{2}$–$\hat{5}$–$\hat{3}$
6) I–IV$_6$–I$_6$–V$_7$–I	F) $\hat{3}$–$\hat{1}$–$\hat{7}$–$\hat{1}$
7) I–V–IV$_6$–V$_6$–I	G) $\hat{1}$–$\hat{2}$–$\hat{3}$–$\hat{1}$–$\hat{2}$–$\hat{1}$
8) I$_6$–V$_6$–I	H) $\hat{1}$–$\hat{7}$–$\hat{1}$

KEYBOARD

EXERCISE 10.15 Unfigured Bass

Determine a logical chord progression for the harmonic implications of the unfigured bass below; iv6 and vii°6 are important possibilities. Add inner voices and play in keyboard style. Be able to sing either outer voice while playing the remaining three voices.

LISTENING

EXERCISE 10.16 Two-Voice Dictation

Notate the two voices and provide roman numerals based on their harmonic implications.

A.   B.   C.

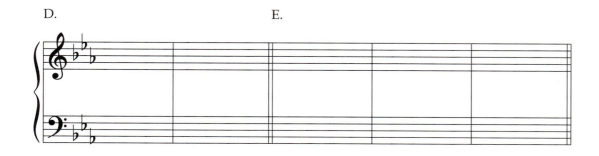

D.   E.

ASSIGNMENT 10.4

ANALYSIS

DVD 1
CH 10
TRACK 9

EXERCISE 10.17

Using two levels, analyze the examples below.

A. Verdi, "Au sein de la puissance" from *Les Vêpres Siciliennes* (*Sicilian Vespers*), act III

B. C. P. E. Bach, Sonata no. 5 in A minor for Flute and Keyboard, WQ 128, H555

LISTENING

DVD 1
CH 10
TRACK 10

EXERCISE 10.18 Two-Voice Dictation: 2 + 2 = 4

You will hear how the two-voice counterpoint of the bass and soprano provides the skeleton for the added inner voices of alto and tenor. The result is a four-voice texture, the harmonies of which are essentially by-products of the confluence of voices. You will hear the outer-voice counterpoint for one beat, immediately followed by the added inner voices, their combination resulting in four-voice harmony. You are to notate the outer voices only, using both their counterpoint and the addition of the inner voices to label the harmonies.

DVD 1
CH 10
TRACK 11

EXERCISE 10.19 Two-Voice Notation and Analysis

You will hear a mix of two- and four-voice examples. Notate the pitches of the two-voice examples and the outer voices of the four-voice examples. Remember to listen for context and attempt to memorize lines. Analyze with two levels.

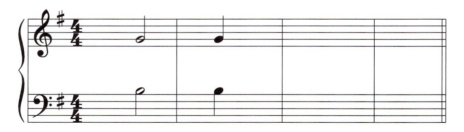

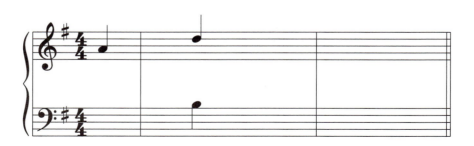

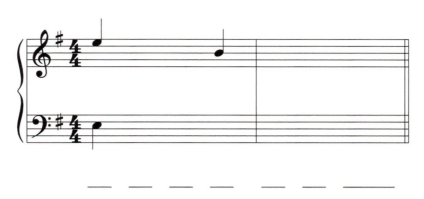

WRITING

EXERCISE 10.20 Figured Bass

Realize the figured bass below by adding inner voices and analyzing with two levels.

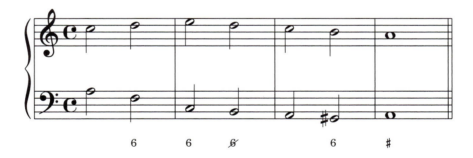

EXERCISE 10.21 Melody Writing over an Accompaniment

1. Analyze the implied harmonies of the accompaniment.
2. Continue the accompaniment based on the harmonic implications of the given bass.
3. Write a florid melody.

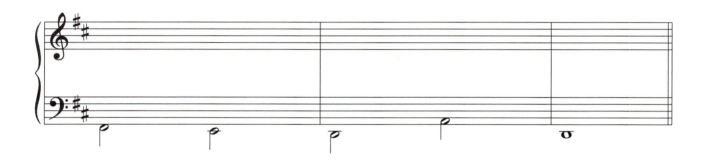

ASSIGNMENT 10.5

DVD 1
CH 10
TRACK 12

LISTENING

EXERCISE 10.22 Variation and Contrapuntal Expansion
of a Harmonic Model

You will now hear contrapuntal expansions of a I–V–I harmonic progression. The
model bass line will be fleshed out in six variations that maintain the metric placement of the given harmonies implied by the bass notes. Complete the following tasks.

1. Notate the bass and soprano voices of the contrapuntal chords that embellish the given harmonic structure.
2. Provide a two-level harmonic analysis. Your harmonic vocabulary now includes I, I6, IV6, V, V7, V6, and vii°6.

Model

       I   V   I

Var. 1   Var. 2

Var. 3   Var. 4

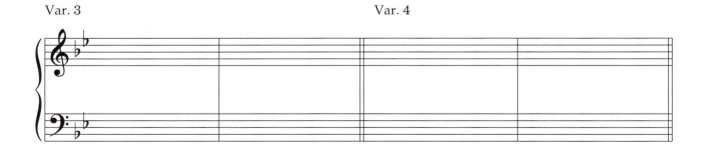

Var. 5   Var. 6

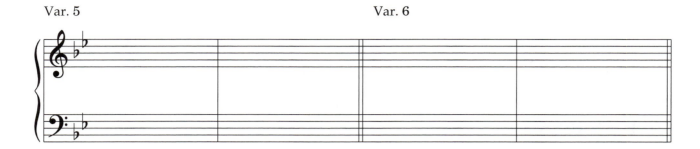

WRITING

EXERCISE 10.23 Figured Bass

Realize the figured bass below by adding a soprano melody, analyzing, and adding inner voices.

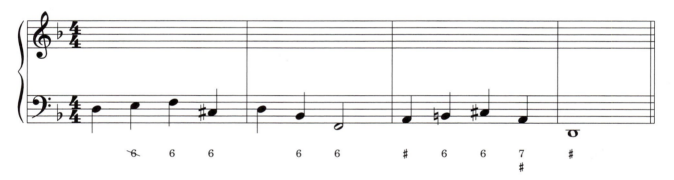

EXERCISE 10.24 Soprano Harmonization

For the soprano fragment, include as many contrapuntal expansions of tonic and dominant as possible. First, study the melody, noting whether I or V controls each measure. Then, write the bass and fill-in inner voices. Analyze with two levels, making sure that you have noted all contrapuntal harmonies by their appropriate letter names (e.g., N and P).

Extra credit:

Harmonize the melody again using a different solution.

KEYBOARD

EXERCISE 10.25

Sing the following operatic excerpts, then realize their figured basses in keyboard style. Finally, combine the two activities and accompany yourself while singing. Be aware that the key signatures do not represent the keys.

A. Handel, *Samson*, act. I, scene 2

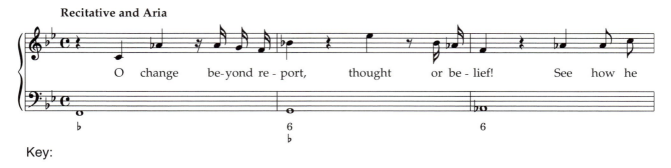

Key:

B. Handel, *Susanna*, act III, scene 2

Key:

Additional Exercises

LISTENING

DVD 1
CH 10
TRACK 13

EXERCISE 10.26 Potpourri

A. You will hear short (four- to six-chord) outer-voice counterpoints. Notate the two voices and provide roman numerals based on their harmonic implications.

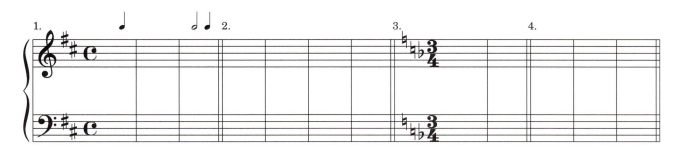

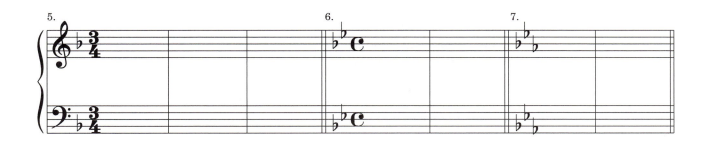

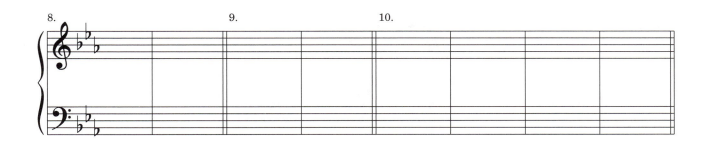

DVD 1
CH 10
TRACK 14

B. Two-Voice Dictation: 2 + 2 = 4. You will hear the outer-voice counterpoint for one beat, immediately followed by the added inner voices, their combination resulting in four-voice harmony. You are to notate the outer voices only, using both their counterpoint and the addition of the inner voices to label the harmonies.

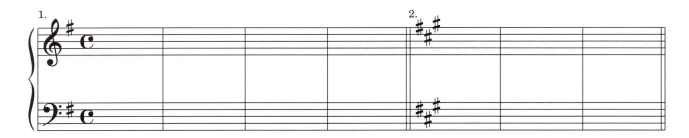

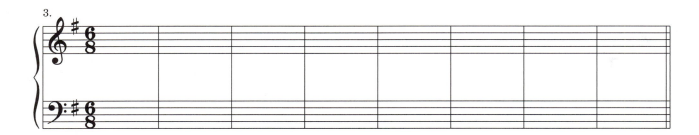

DVD 1
CH 10
TRACK 15

EXERCISE 10.27 Analysis/Dictation

Notate the bass lines and provide a two-level harmonic analysis from the incomplete scores from the literature.

A. Haydn, String Quartet in B minor, op. 64, no. 2, Hob. III:68, *Presto*

B. Bach, Flute Sonata in A minor, BWV 1033, *Adagio*

C. Brahms, "Muss es eine Trennung geben?" ("There Must Be a Parting?"), *Romanzen aus L. Tiecks Magelone* ("Romances from Tieck's Magelone"), op. 33, no. 12
   Add eighth-note bass pitches on beats 1 and 4.

EXERCISE 10.28 Variation and Contrapuntal Expansion of a Harmonic Model

You will now hear contrapuntal expansions of a I–V–I harmonic progression. The model bass line will be fleshed out in six variations that maintain the metric placement of the given harmonies implied by the bass notes. Complete the following tasks:

1. Notate the bass and soprano voices of the contrapuntal chords that embellish the given harmonic structure.
2. Provide a two-level harmonic analysis. Your harmonic vocabulary now includes I, I6, IV6, V, V7, V6, and vii°6.

Model

Var. 1   **Var. 2**

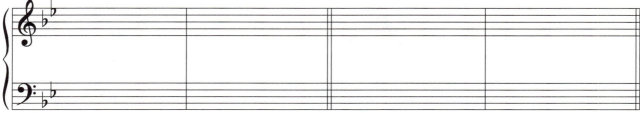

Var. 3   **Var. 4**

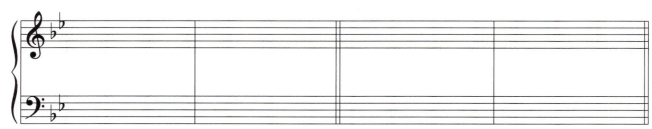

Var. 5   **Var. 6**

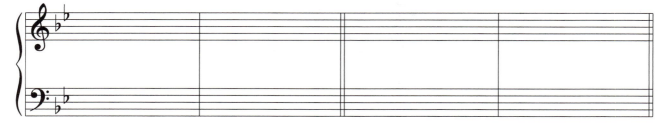

WRITING

EXERCISE 10.29 Soprano Harmonization

Harmonize each pitch of the melody below using the chords we have studied.

EXERCISE 10.30 Melody Harmonization

Harmonize the melody using a single harmony per measure, except in mm. 5 and 7, where you will write two harmonies in each measure. You need add only a single bass note, but make sure you include a complete roman numeral and figured bass analysis.

rhythm:

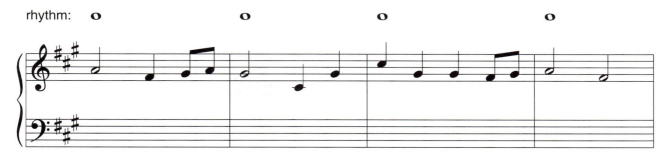

Key:

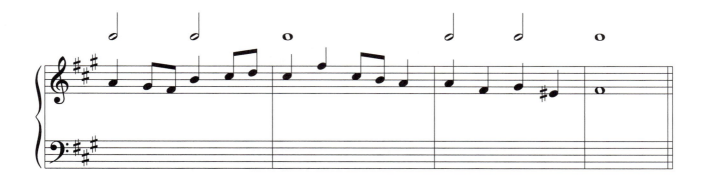

KEYBOARD

EXERCISE 10.31 Unfigured Bass

Determine a logical chord progression for the harmonic implications of the unfigured bass below. Two important possibilities are IV6 and vii°6. Add inner voices and play in keyboard style. Be able to sing either outer voice while playing the remaining three voices.

EXERCISE 10.32 Expansions of Harmonic Pillars

Based on the instructions beneath the staff and the rhythms above, expand the root-position tonic and dominant chords in the four-measure excerpt.

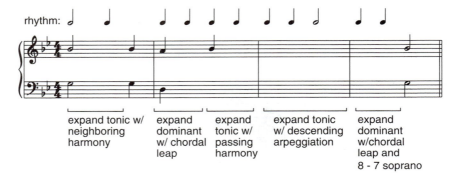

CHAPTER 11

More Contrapuntal Expansions: Inversions of V7 and Introduction to Leading Tone Seventh Chords

Exercises for V7 and Its Inversions

ASSIGNMENT 11.1

ANALYSIS

DVD 1
CH 11
TRACK 1

EXERCISE 11.1

In the following excerpts from Mozart piano sonatas, the tonic is expanded with inversions of V7. Provide a first- and second-level analysis. Some chords may be incomplete, but it is possible to determine their identity from the context.

A. Sonata in C major, K. 279, *Andante*

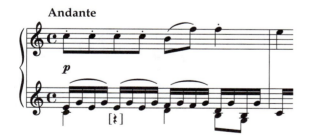

B. Sonata in F major, K. 547a, *Allegretto*

C.   Sonata in C major, K. 279, *Andante*

D.   Sonata in D major, K. 576, *Adagio*

E.   Sonata in G major, K. 283, *Allegro*

F.   Sonata in B♭ major, K. 281, *Allegro*

G.   Sonata in C major, K. 309, *Allegro*

LISTENING

EXERCISE 11.2 Notation of Bass Lines

Listen to each example, studying the given upper voices and then notate the bass line and provide a two-level harmonic analysis.

A. Mendelssohn, *Lieder ohne Wörte (Songs Without Words)*, Book 7, op. 85, no. 5

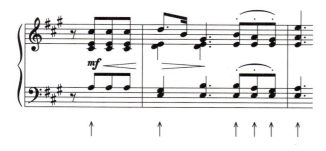

B. Mozart, Trio, Symphony in G major, K. 124

C. Mozart, Trio, String Quartet in B♭ major, K. 172

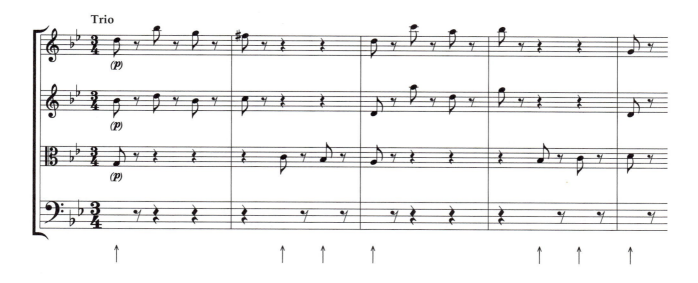

D. Mozart, Trio, Symphony in A major, K. 114

E. Grieg, "Ingrid's Complaint," *Peer Gynt Suite* no. 1.

WRITING

EXERCISE 11.3

Complete the tasks as required:

A. Add RNs and inner voices based on outer-voice implications.   B. Add SATB.

$$\text{I} \qquad \text{V} \text{—} \qquad {}^4_2 \qquad \text{I}^6$$

C. Harmonize in three different ways; provide a two-level analysis.

EXERCISE 11.4 Writing Inversions of V7

Complete the following tasks in four voices and an appropriate meter. Play your solutions, being able to sing the bass voice while playing the upper voices.

A. In D major and A minor, expand tonic using V^6_5 as a neighbor.

B. In F major and D minor, expand tonic using a passing V^4_3; close with a PAC.

C. In G major and F♯ minor, expand tonic using an incomplete neighboring V^4_2; close with a HC.

ASSIGNMENT 11.2

ANALYSIS

DVD 1
CH 11
TRACK 3

EXERCISE 11.5

In the excerpts below, the tonic is expanded with inversions of V7. Provide first- and second-level analyses. Some chords may be incomplete, but it is possible to determine their identity from the context.

A. Loeillet, Sonata for Oboe in A minor, op. 5, no. 2, *Second Movement*

B. Tchaikovsky, "The Sick Doll," *Children's Pieces*, op. 39

C. Beethoven, Piano Sonata no. 2 in A major, op. 2, no. 2, *Largo appassionato*

When you do your second-level analysis, focus on m. 3, because it is possible to interpret it as dominant or tonic. Your choice will affect its performance considerably. For example, if you view the dominant to control the measure, the tonic will not be played in a way as to indicate a return to that function; rather, it will sound as if it is harmonizing a soprano passing tone that links statements of the dominant. If you view the tonic as in control, then you might slightly delay and/or intensify through dynamics its return, thus breaking any connection between the preceding and following dominant.

D. Beethoven, Rondo, Violin Sonata in D major, op. 12, no. 1.
As in Exercise C, m. 3 may be variously interpreted as a dominant or tonic in your second-level analysis

E. Schumann, "An meinem Herzen, an meiner Brust" ("At My Heart, at My Breast"), *Frauenliebe und Leben* ("A Woman's Life and Love"), op. 42, no. 7

WRITING

EXERCISE 11.6 Writing Inversions of V7

Using only inversions of V7 to expand the tonic, find a suitable meter and rhythmic setting (based on the criterion that expanding harmonies be placed on weak beats) and write the given soprano or bass line and an appropriate outer-voice counterpoint. Add roman numerals and include a second-level analysis. Add the inner voices.

A. Given the following soprano line in A major: $\hat{3}$–$\hat{4}$–$\hat{3}$–$\hat{2}$–$\hat{3}$–$\hat{5}$–$\hat{4}$–$\hat{3}$–$\hat{2}$–$\hat{1}$

B. Given the following bass line in B minor: $\hat{1}$–$\sharp\hat{7}$–$\hat{1}$–$\hat{4}$–$\hat{3}$–$\hat{2}$–$\sharp\hat{7}$–$\hat{1}$

EXERCISE 11.7 Inversions of V7 and Figured Bass

Realize the figured bass below in four voices and provide a two-level harmonic analysis.

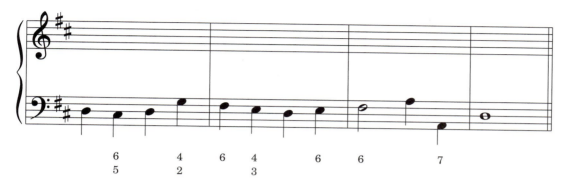

LISTENING

DVD 1
CH 11
TRACK 4

EXERCISE 11.8 Two-Voice Dictation: Unmetered Paradigms

Notate the pitches of the missing voice (either bass or soprano). Then, based on the harmonic implications of the two voices, provide roman numerals (your choices are I, I6, V, V6, and V7, and its inversions).

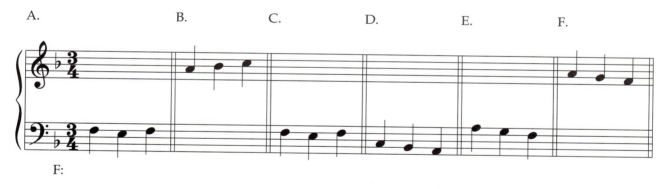

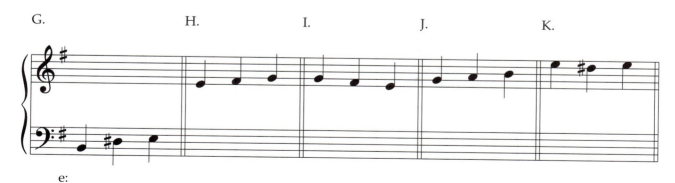

DVD 1
CH 11
TRACK 5

EXERCISE 11.9 Two-Voice Dictation: 2 + 2 = 4

You will hear how the two-voice counterpoint of the bass and soprano provides the skeleton for the added inner voices of alto and tenor. The result is a four-voice texture, the harmonies of which are essentially by-products of the confluence of voices. You will hear the outer-voice counterpoint for one beat, immediately followed by the added inner voices, their combination resulting in four-voice harmony. You are to notate the outer voices only, using both their counterpoint and the addition of the inner voices to label the harmonies.

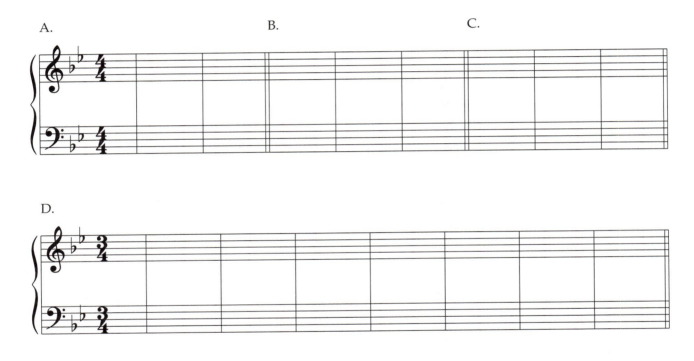

KEYBOARD

EXERCISE 11.10 Voicing Inverted Dominant Seventh Chords

Below are right-hand voicings for root-position and inverted dominant seventh chords in F major. Note that root position is the only form that contains four (rather than three) possible voicings because root position may omit the fifth (as shown by the asterisk); inverted seventh chords, however, must be complete; angle brackets illustrate the "gap" that occurs between various voicings because the missing note lies in the bass. Transpose to keys up to and including two sharps and two flats.

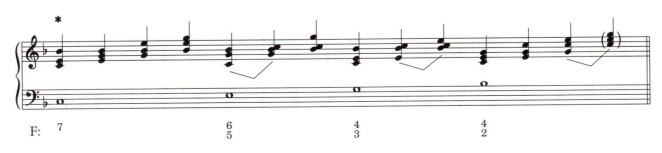

ASSIGNMENT 11.3

WRITING

EXERCISE 11.11 Figured Bass and Contrapuntal Expansions

1. Realize the figured bass in keyboard style.
2. Analyze, then sing either outer voice while playing the other three voices.

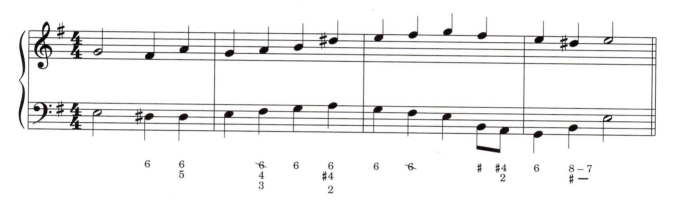

EXERCISE 11.12 Figured Bass

Realize the following figured bass in four voices and provide a two-level harmonic analysis.

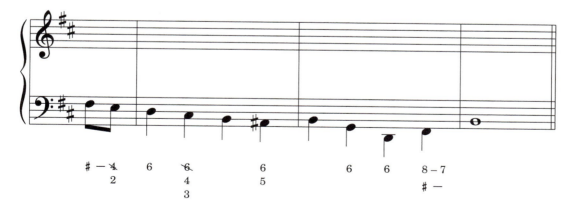

EXERCISE 11.13 Two-Voice Dictation: Metered Paradigms

Notate the outer voices, then, based on the harmonic implications of the two voices, provide roman numerals (your choices are I, I6, V, V6, and V7, and its inversions).

A.   B.   C.   D.

D:

E.   F.   G.

c:

DVD 1
CH 11
TRACK 7

EXERCISE 11.14 Dictation from the Literature

Notate the bass lines of the following contrapuntal progressions and include a single-level harmonic analysis. Some of the exercises provide a few pitches to guide you.

A. Chopin, Waltz in B minor, op. 69, no. 2, op. posth., BI 95, no. 2

B. Sammartini, Recorder Sonata no. 1 in G minor, *Allegro*

C. Beethoven, Piano Sonata No. 6 in F major, op. 10, no. 2, *Allegro*

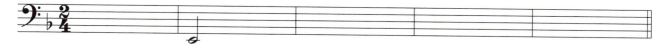

D. Beethoven, String Quartet in C♯ minor, op. 131, *Andante*

E. Chopin, Nocturne in E minor, op. 72, no. 1, op. posth., BI 11

F. Rossini, "Ehi Fiorello" from *Il Barbiere di Sivigila (The Barber of Seville)*, act I, scene 3

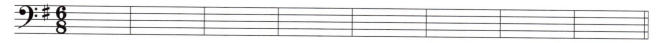

EXERCISE 11.15 Dictation of Figurated Examples

The chords in this exercise are presented as horizontal melodies, and you must aurally stack the chordal members to create a vertical harmonic structure. Notate the bass. Focus on the "sonic dimension" in this exercise rather than the outer-voice counterpoint. That is, listen not only for underlying tonic or dominant progressions but exactly how they are expanded in time.

A.

B.

C.

D.

Exercises for Leading Tone Seventh Chords

ASSIGNMENT 11.4

PERFORMING

EXERCISE 11.16 Singing Leading Tone Seventh Chords

Using solfège or numbers, sing (or perform on your instrument), the following minor-key patterns that contain vii°7 and the major-key pattern that contains viiø7.

A.

B.   C.

D.

ANALYSIS

DVD 1
CH 11
TRACK 9

EXERCISE 11.17

Using two levels, analyze the examples below that contain either the vii°7 or the viiø7 chords. Label preparation and resolution of the seventh.

A. Mozart, Piano Sonata in F major, K. 332, *Allegro*
In what key is this passage?

(continues on next page)

B. Mozart, Piano Sonata in F major, K. 332, *Allegro assai*
In what key is this passage?

C. J. Strauss, Overture, *Die Fledermaus*

LISTENING

EXERCISE 11.18 Two-Voice Dictation, Including vii°7 and viiø7

Notate the two-voice counterpoint, then, based on the harmonic implications, provide roman numerals (in addition to vii°7 and viiø7 your choices include I, I6, V,

V6, and V7 and its inversions). Examples A–D are very short and unmetered. Examples E–H are slightly longer and metered.

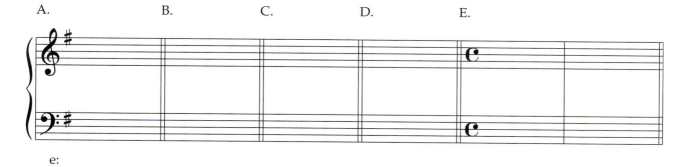

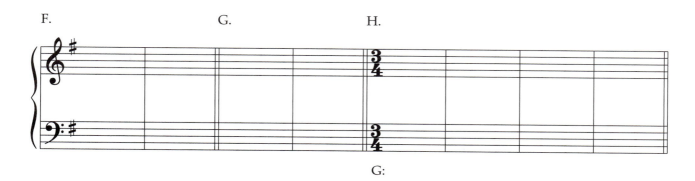

EXERCISE 11.19 Two-Voice Dictation: 2 + 2 = 4

Follow the instructions given for Exercise 11.9.

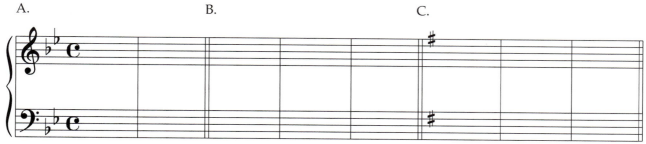

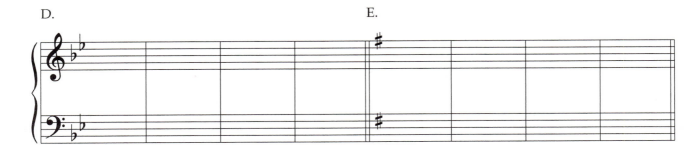

D.

E.

KEYBOARD

EXERCISE 11.20 Progression Incorporating vii°7

Play the two-measure progression that incorporates vii°7. Transpose it by ascending perfect fourths until you reach G minor. Part of the first transposition is given; the final chord of m. 2 is a link that transforms the tonic into the dominant of the upcoming key. Sing bass or soprano while playing.

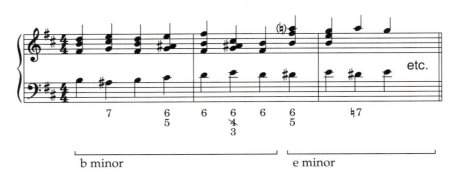

ASSIGNMENT 11.5

ANALYSIS

DVD 1
CH 11
TRACK 11

EXERCISE 11.21

Analyze the examples below using two levels. Ignore pitches in parentheses.

A. Gluck, "Pantomime" from *Alceste*

B. Beethoven, Piano Sonata No. 5 in C minor, op. 10, no. 1 *Allegro*
The metrically accented dissonances that occur in the right hand in mm. 14–16 are called "suspensions" and will be taken up in Chapter 13.

C. C.P.E. Bach, Sonata no. 5 in A minor for Flute and Continuo, WQ 128 H555

LISTENING

EXERCISE 11.22 Analysis and Dictation

Analyze the following examples, in which tonic is expanded by V7 and vii°7. Listen to the recording, which may or may not play what is notated. If what you hear is what you analyzed, then write "OK." If, however, there are discrepancies between the notated score and what you hear, correct the analysis to reflect the played version.

EXERCISE 11.23 Dictation of vii°7

You will hear examples that use vii°7. Notate the outer voices of Exercises A and B and provide roman numerals. Exercises C–G, from the literature, are more figurated; notate only the bass voice and analyze. When the bass voice is figured (i.e. it contains broken chord or arpeggiations) notate only the lowest pitch.

A.   B.

C. Mozart, String Quartet in G major, K.156, *Adagio*

D. Haydn, String Quartet in D major, op. 20, no. 4, K.157, *Andante*

E. Mozart, String Quartet No. 1 in C major, Hob. III:34, *Un poco adagio affettuoso*

F. Chopin, Sonata in B♭ minor, op. 35, BI 128, *Doppio movimento*

G. Handel, Concerto Grosso in G minor, op. 6, no. 6, HWV 324, *Allegro*

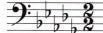

WRITING

EXERCISE 11.24 Figured Bass

Realize the figured bass below and analyze. Then, add and label unaccented tones of figuration in the upper voices that include passing tones, neighboring notes, and chordal skips and leaps.

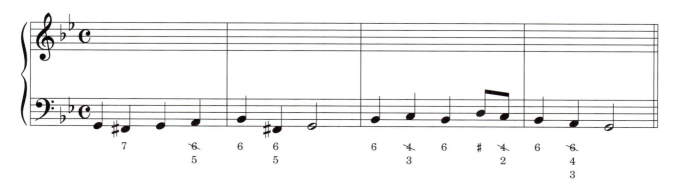

EXERCISE 11.25 Writing Harmonic Paradigms

There are many ways to expand the tonic and dominant. Here you are to combine a number of these paradigms in a logical manner into what will become a larger four- to eight-measure musical unit.

A. Choose a key, a mode, a meter, and a basic rhythmic pattern. Since, for example, in $\frac{6}{8}$, the pattern quarter–eighth or dotted eighth–sixteenth is very common, you might wish to restrict your rhythmic vocabulary to those two patterns in order to maintain rhythmic consistency.

B. Provide a general harmonic sketch. You may wish to make a list of various types of expansions and progressions. For example, a good way to get from I to I6 is by passing (use vii°6 or V_3^4), neighboring (V_2^4), or even arpeggiating (use IV6 and arpeggiate down to I6).

C. Sketch out harmonies beginning with the cadence. If you envision a longer example, one that encompasses eight measures, then you may wish to subdivide it into two four-measure units. Thus, the first unit will probably close with a half cadence.

D. Focus on individual measures and determine which chord will be the most important. For example, in $\frac{3}{4}$, you may wish to move from root-position tonic in the first measure to first inversion in the second measure.

E. Determine local expansions. For example, you may wish to sustain the tonic for two beats in your first $\frac{3}{4}$ measure, and then include a passing chord that links the first-measure tonic with the second-measure, first-inversion tonic.

F. Create a soprano melody. You may include submetrical passing and neighboring notes on weak parts of beats. Resolve all dissonance.

G. Add the inner voices; you may include a few nonharmonic tones.

KEYBOARD

EXERCISE 11.26 Melodic Fragment Harmonization

Determine a possible key for each of the unmetered melodic fragments below. Choose a meter and rhythmic setting and harmonize each in four voices using inversions of V7 or vii7 to create contrapuntal expansions of the tonic.

EXERCISE 11.27 Bass Harmonization

Harmonize three of the four bass fragments. Follow the instructions for Exercise 11.26. You may write out the soprano voice.

A.   B.   C.   D.

Additional Exercises

KEYBOARD

EXERCISE 11.28 Keyboard Reduction

Play the opening of Haydn's song and analyze it to reduce it to a four-voice homophonic texture. Play your four-voice reduction.

Haydn, "Das strickende Mädchen" ("The knitting maiden"), *XII Lieder für das Clavier*, Book 1, Hob. XXVIa:1

1. Und   hörst   du, __ klei - - ne
2. In   dei   - -   nen __ Au - - gen
3. So   man - -   chen. Tag,   so

Phyl - - lis, nicht   der   Vög - lein ____ sü ____   Bes ____
herrscht ____   der Gott   der   Lieb ____ und ____ zau - bert ____
man - - ches Jahr   schlich   ich ____ dir ____ ein - sam ____

EXERCISE 11.29

Sing the tunes below, then realize the figured bass in keyboard style. Combine the two activities by accompanying yourself as you sing.

Handel, *Semele*, Act I, scene 2

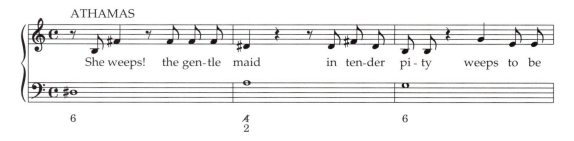

ATHAMAS

She weeps!   the gen-tle   maid   in ten-der pi - ty   weeps to be

6                        $\frac{4}{2}$ 6

Handel, *Giulio Cesare*, Act 2 scene 2

Ich fühl es wohl   zu mei - nem tief - sten Un - glück,   dass

ihr im Her-zen ra-send schon die Flam-me ent - lo-dert;

ANALYSIS

**DVD 1
CH 11
TRACK 14**

EXERCISE 11.30 Analytical Snapshots

Each short excerpt below contains expansions of the tonic and the dominant using inversions of V7. Expect to encounter vii°6, IV6, and V6 as well. Analyze each using two levels.

A. Beethoven, Piano Sonata in G major, op. 31, no. 1

B. Mendelssohn, "Song Without Words," op. 4, op. 85, in D major

C. Haydn, String Quartet in B♭ major, op. 33, no. 4, Hob. III:40, *Allegretto*

D. Beethoven, "Der Abschied" ("The Farewell"), WoO 124

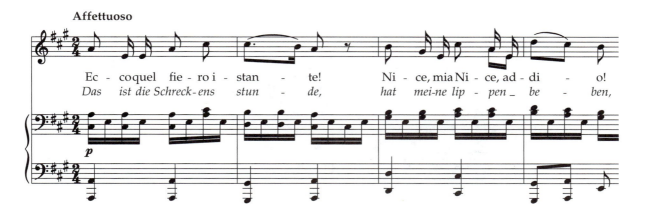

LISTENING

EXERCISE 11.31 Analysis and Dictation of Progressions Using Inversions of V7

Add bass lines to the examples below and include a two-level harmonic analysis.

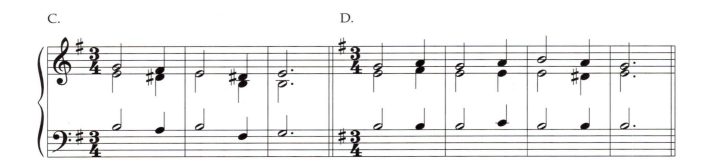

DVD 1
CH 11
TRACK 16

EXERCISE 11.32 Dictation of Contrapuntal Expansions

Each of the examples below contains contrapuntal expansions of I and V. Notate the bass and provide a first-level roman numeral analysis. The chords available are I, I6, IV6, V, V7, $_5^6$, $_3^4$, $_2^4$, and vii°6.

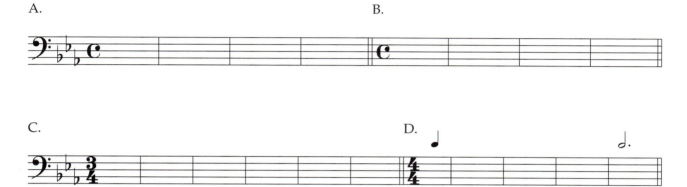

Listening guidelines

Begin by listening to the entire example, focusing on the large musical context (opening harmony, general shape of melody and the underlying harmonies, and final cadence). Then, in the second and third playings, focus on complete smaller units, such as a two-measure tonic expansion and the chords involved. Use the fourth playing to check your work and fine-tune your harmonic choices (e.g., if $\hat{2}$ occurs in the bass, determine whether it is V_3^4 or vii°6). Do not worry if you are still having trouble distinguishing between V6 and V_5^6 or vii°6 and V_3^4; these are details; it is sufficient to perceive the underlying contrapuntal function and notate the correct bass note.

EXERCISE 11.33 Paradigm Dictation

You will hear eight short progressions, each containing from three to five chords. They are not presented in a metric or rhythmic context. On a separate sheet of manuscript paper, notate only the outer voices and provide roman numerals. Try to memorize each exercise in one or two hearings. All examples contain one flat in their key signatures.

DVD 1
CH 11
TRACKS
17/18

EXERCISE 11.34 Variation and Contrapuntal Expansion of a Harmonic Model

You will hear contrapuntal expansions of two I–V–I progressions. Each of the two progressions below will be fleshed out with various contrapuntal expansions that maintain the harmonic rhythm of the model progressions. Complete the following tasks:

1. Notate the bass and soprano voices of the contrapuntal chords that embellish the given harmonic structure.

2. Provide a two-level harmonic analysis. Your harmonic vocabulary now includes I, I_6, IV_6, V, V_6, V_7, V_5^6, V_3^4, V_2^4, $vii°_6$, $vii°_7$, $vii°_5^6$, and $vii°_3^4$.

WRITING

EXERCISE 11.35 Writing Complete Progressions

Write the following progressions in four-part keyboard style (manuscript paper on back side of page).

- Use any meter, remembering to place contrapuntal harmonies on weak beats.
- You may use a variety of rhythmic values.
- Your solution should be four measures long.
- Provide a second-level analysis.

A. Write in D major:

Soprano note:	$\hat{3}$	$\hat{4}$	$\hat{5}$	$\hat{4}$	$\hat{3}$	$\hat{2}$	$\hat{1}$
Roman numeral:	I	V_3^4	I_6	V_5^6	I	V_7	I

B. Write in G minor (remember to raise $\hat{7}$ for the leading tone):

Soprano note:	$\hat{1}$	$\hat{7}$	$\hat{1}$	$\hat{2}$	$\hat{4}$	$\hat{3}$	$\hat{2}$	$\hat{1}$	$\hat{7}$	$\hat{1}$
Roman numeral:	i	V_3^4	i_6	V_6	V_5^6	i	V_2^4	i_6	vii°$_6$	i

A.

B.

CHAPTER 12

The Pre-Dominant Function and the Phrase Model

Exercises for ii and IV

ASSIGNMENT 12.1

ANALYSIS

EXERCISE 12.1

Analyze the following examples using two levels.

A. Verdi, "Anch' io dischiuso un giorno," from *Nabucco*, act 2

B. Corelli, Violin Sonata in D major, op. 5, no. 6, *Largo*
Although there are numerous incomplete chords and a key signature that does not represent the key accurately at this point in the movement, both the context and figured bass will provide chordal implications.

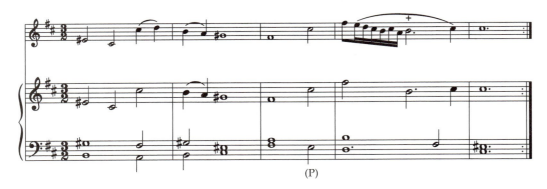

(P)

C. Mozart, Symphony in D, K. 81, *Andante*

D. Corelli, *Giga*, Chamber Sonata in E♭, op. 2, no. 11

Be aware of the key signature since it represents the key of this inner movement, but not the piece as a whole.

DVD 1
CH 12
TRACK 1

EXERCISE 12.2 Aural Identification of Pre-Dominants

Provide the roman numeral (RN) of the pre-dominant that occurs in each short (six-to eight-chord) example. Your choices are ii (root position in major only), ii6 and IV (major and minor modes), and iv6 (in minor only, as part of half cadence). Then, given the key for each example, write the names of the pitches of the pre-dominant harmony in ascending order from the bass note. To hear the PD, work backward from the dominant of the cadence and listen for the bass motion: 4̂–5̂, 2̂–5̂, and 6̂–5̂ are possible lines, then listen to the melody to figure out the exact chord.

Sample Solution:

A. RN: __iv_ Key: d minor: _GB♭D_   G. RN: ____ Key: f minor: _____
B. RN: ____ Key: D Major: _____   H. RN: ____ Key: F Major: _____
C. RN: ____ Key: d minor: _____   I. RN: ____ Key: G Major: _____
D. RN: ____ Key: D Major: _____   J. RN: ____ Key: g minor: _____
E. RN: ____ Key: d minor: _____   K. RN: ____ Key: G major: _____
F. RN: ____ Key: f minor: _____   L. RN: ____ Key: g minor: _____

DVD 1
CH 12
TRACK 2

EXERCISE 12.3 Dictation and Analysis

The upper voices are given. Notate the bass and provide roman numerals and second-level analysis. Begin by listening to the examples and by studying the harmonic implications provided by the upper voices.

A.   B.

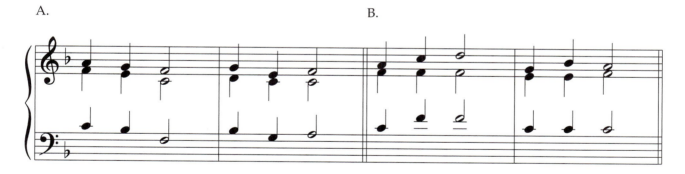

C.   D.

WRITING

EXERCISE 12.4 Error Detection

The following exercise contains a number of voice-leading errors. After providing a roman numeral analysis (two levels), circle and label voice-leading and spelling problems.

EXERCISE 12.5

Complete the tasks below in four voices. Add missing roman numerals.

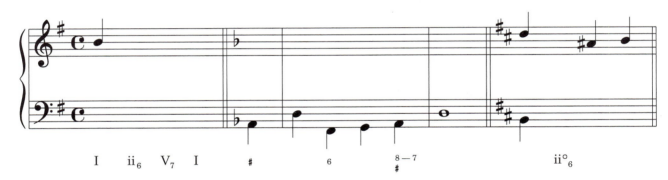

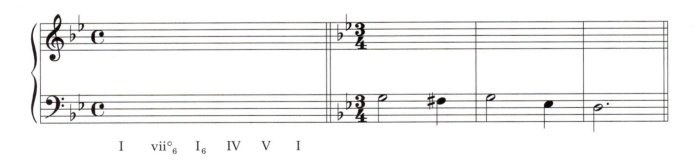

KEYBOARD

EXERCISE 12.6 Paradigms

Play the following progressions in all major and minor keys that contain one and two sharp and flats.

A. Soprano: $\hat{3}$–$\hat{2}$ —$\hat{7}$—$\hat{1}$ B. $\hat{5}$–$\hat{4}$–$\hat{2}$–$\hat{1}$ C. minor only: $\hat{3}$– $\hat{4}$—$\hat{5}$

     Harmony: I –ii6–V7—I   I–IV–V–I   i– iv6–V

ASSIGNMENT 12.2

LISTENING

DVD 1
CH 12
TRACK 3

EXERCISE 12.7 Two-Voice Dictation

Notate the bass and soprano voices and provide roman numerals given their harmonic implications.

DVD 1
CH 12
TRACK 4

EXERCISE 12.8 Two-Voice Dictation: 2 + 2 = 4

You will hear how the two-voice counterpoint of the bass and soprano provides the skeleton for the added inner voices of alto and tenor. The result is a four-voice texture, the harmonies of which are essentially by-products of the confluence of voices. You will hear the outer-voice counterpoint for one beat, immediately followed by the added inner voices, their combination resulting in four-voice harmony. You are to notate the outer voices only, using both their counterpoint and the addition of the inner voices to label the harmonies.

A.   B.   C.

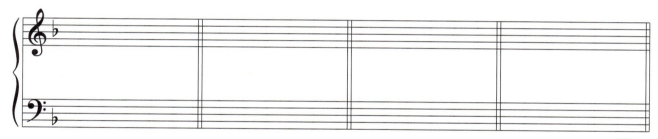

WRITING

EXERCISE 12.9 Figured Bass

Realize the following figured bass, first composing the soprano in good counterpoint with the bass, and then adding inner voices. Analyze with two levels.

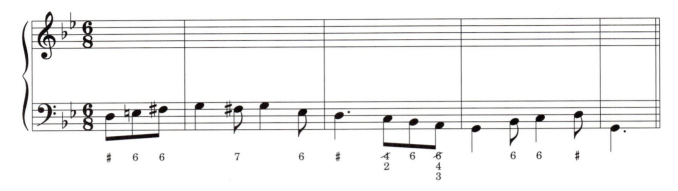

KEYBOARD

EXERCISE 12.10 Reduction

Each example below represents the fleshing out of a two-voice counterpoint. Play each example, then reduce the texture to simple four-voice homophony by determining each measure's governing harmony, omitting repeated notes and nonchord tones. Look for a melodically fluent soprano voice. Play your reduction in four voices.

Exercises for Extending the PD (iv–ii complex), the Phrase Model, and T–PD–D–T Within Tonic Prolongations

ASSIGNMENT 12.3

LISTENING

DVD 1
CH 12
TRACK 5

EXERCISE 12.11 Dictation and Analysis

The upper voices are given in the following examples from the literature. Notate the bass and provide roman numerals and second-level analysis. Begin by listening to the examples and by studying the harmonic implications of the upper voices.

A. Haydn, String Quartet in G major, op. 76, no. 1, Hob. III: 75, *Menuetto*

B. Haydn, String Quartet in D major, op. 76, no. 5, Hob: III, 79, *Menuetto*

C. Beethoven, String Quartet no. 6 in B♭ major, op. 18, no. 6, *Adagio ma non troppo*

DVD 1
CH 12
TRACK 6

EXERCISE 12.12 Notation of Pre-Dominants

Memorize each progression's basic harmonic structure, focusing on the bass. Then, notate the bass line and provide roman numerals.

A.

B.

C.

D.

E.

F.

WRITING

EXERCISE 12.13 Pre-Dominants and Figured Bass

Realize the figured bass as follows:

1. Compose a soprano that works in good counterpoint with the bass (consider, e.g., what a good soprano line would be for the opening $\hat{1}$–$\hat{7}$–$\hat{1}$, or the $\hat{3}$–$\hat{2}$–$\hat{1}$ in m. 3, or the $\hat{1}$–$\hat{2}$–$\hat{3}$ in mm. 5 and 7).
2. Add inner voices.
3. Analyze with two levels.

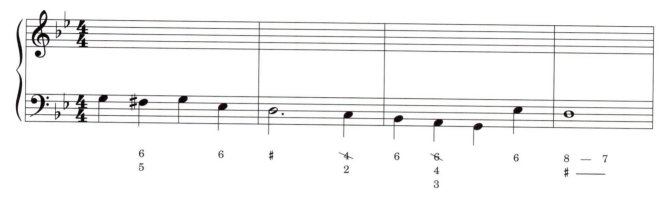

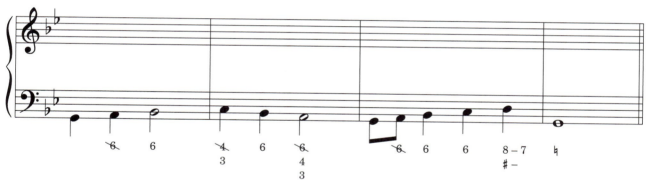

ASSIGNMENT 12.4

LISTENING

DVD 1
CH 12
TRACK 7

EXERCISE 12.14 Homophonic Dictation

Use roman numerals to label the underlying harmonic progression and the cadence type in the following phrase models. There is usually one chordal function per measure; be aware that the pre-dominant and dominant may occupy the same measure.

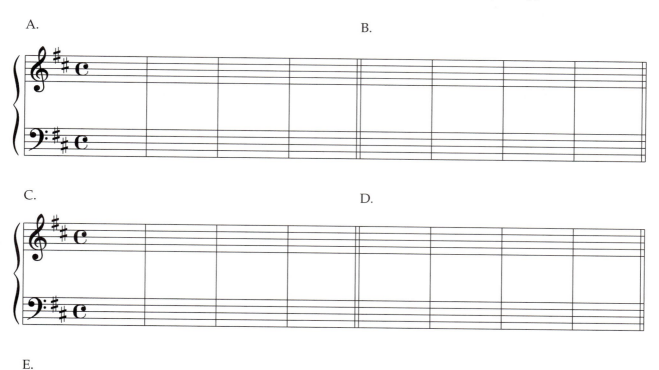

A.

B.

C.

D.

E.

WRITING

EXERCISE 12.15 Multiple Settings of Soprano Tune

Write three different, logical bass lines for the soprano melody on a separate sheet of manuscript paper. Analyze. Extra credit: add inner voices.

KEYBOARD

EXERCISE 12.16 Unfigured Bass

Realize the unfigured bass in four-voice keyboard style. Be able to sing one of the outer voices while playing the other three voices. Analyze.

ASSIGNMENT 12.5

LISTENING

DVD 1
CH 12
TRACK 8

EXERCISE 12.17 Figurated Dictation from the Literature

Use roman numerals to label the underlying harmonic progression in the phrase models. Also, label the cadence type. Horizontal lines indicate harmonic placement and vertical lines indicate measures.

A. Schumann, "Tief im Herzen trag' ich Pein" ("Deep in My Heart I Suffer"), *Spanisches Liebeslieder (Spanish Love Songs)*, op. 138, no. 2

$\frac{3}{4}$: ____ | ____ | ____ __ | ____ __ | ____ | |

B. Haydn, *Menuetto*, String Quartet in B♭ major, "Der Frosch," op. 50, no. 6, Hob. III:49. *Allegretto.*

$\frac{3}{4}$: ____ | ____ | ____ | ____ | |

C. Bach, "Wo soll ich fliehen hin," Cantatas 163 and 148, BWV 163 and 148

$\frac{4}{4}$: __ | __ __ __ | ____ __ | __ __ __ | ____ | |

D. Schubert, "Litanei auf das Fest aller Seelen" ("Litany for the Feast of All Souls"), D. 343

$\frac{4}{4}$: ____ ____ | __ __ __ |

E. Loeillet, Trio Sonata in B♭ major, Op. 2, no. 9, *Largo*

$\frac{3}{4}$: ____ __ | ____ __ | ____ __ | ____ |

KEYBOARD

EXERCISE 12.18

Sing the tunes from the excerpts below, then realize the figured bass in keyboard style. Finally, combine the two activities by accompanying yourself while you sing. Be aware that the key signature may not reflect the key of the excerpt.

A. Handel, "Mein Kelch ist voll" ("My Cup is Full,") from *Joshua*, act 3, scene 1

Mein Kelch ist voll, welch' se-gen voll-Ge-schenk! wie sag' ich würd gen-Dank dem Herrn und dir!

6

B.   Handel, "Of My Ill-Boding Dream," from *Semele*, act 3, scene 8

PERFORMANCE

EXERCISE 12.19

Reduce the textures in the Mozart symphonic excerpts below. Analyze, verticalize (into a four-voice homophonic texture), and then perform each example as follows: if you are a pianist, simply play your four-voice realization. If you are a melodic instrumentalist, arpeggiate each example. If necessary, refer to the discussion in Chapter 11 for a detailed procedure. Play each reduction in the key in which it is written; for extra credit, transpose to one other key of your choice.

A.   Mozart, Symphony in D major, K. 97, *Allegro*

B. Mozart, *Andante*, Symphony in C major, K. 96

WRITING

EXERCISE 12.20

Harmonize the following tunes, each of which requires a pre-dominant harmony. Begin by determining the harmonic rhythm, and don't forget the phrase model. Use either a simple homophonic accompaniment or a broken-chord figuration.

A. English

B. American

C.   Brahms, "Vergebliches Ständchen"

D.   Gluck, "Schweizer Heimweh"

E.   Haydn, Sonata in C major, *Allegro con brio*

F.   Mozart, Piano Trio in G major, K. 564, *Allegretto*

CHAPTER 13

Accented and Chromatic Dissonances

Assignments for Accented Tones of Figuration (APT, CPT, AN, CN, AIN, APP, SUSP, ANT, and PED)

ASSIGNMENT 13.1

ANALYSIS

DVD 1
CH 13
TRACK 1

EXERCISE 13.1

The following examples contain both accented and unaccented tones of figuration, which may occur in any voice. Begin by providing roman numerals. Then use the shorthand method presented in the text to label all tones of figuration. The chords employed are restricted to those we have already encountered [except in examples of suspension chains. For these, simply provide figured bass labels of type (9–8 and 7–6)]. Label the components of suspensions (preparation "P," suspension "S," and resolution "R."). Example A has been solved for you.

A. Haydn, Piano Sonata no. 50 in D major, Hob. XVI: 37, *Presto non troppo*

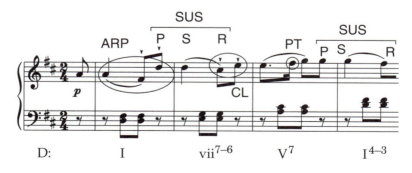

B.   Bach, Chorale, "Ermuntre dich, mein schwacher Geist," BWV 454

C.   Bach, Chorale, "Christe, du Beistand deiner Kreuzgemeine," BWV 275

D.   Beethoven, *Menuetto*, Piano Sonata in B♭, op. 22

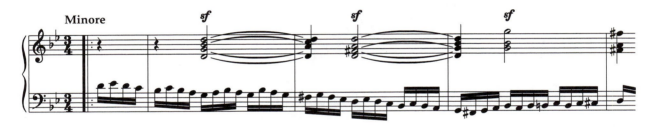

E.   Brahms, "Du mein einzig Licht," *Deutsches Volkslieder*, WoO 33, no. 37

EXERCISE 13.2 Error Detection

Label errors in suspension writing and in other accented and unaccented figurations as well as errors in chord spelling and voice leading. Note: Assume that there are no appoggiaturas or anticipations in this exercise. Analyze using two levels of roman numerals. Measure 1 and part of measure 2 in Exercise A provide a sample solution.

LISTENING

DVD 1
CH 13
TRACK 2

EXERCISE 13.3 Dictation

The short progressions below either expand the tonic or are cadential motions. Each contain tones of figuration. Notate the outer voices and provide roman numerals; label any figurations. The choices are PT (passing tone), CS (chordal skip), APT (accented passing tone), N (neighbor note), SUS (suspension), and APP (appoggiatura).

A.   B.

C.   D.

ASSIGNMENT 13.2

ANALYSIS

DVD 1
CH 13
TRACK 3

EXERCISE 13.4

The following examples employ both accented and unaccented tones of figuration, which may occur in any voice. Begin by providing roman numerals. Then use the shorthand method presented in the text to label all tones of figuration. The chords employed are restricted to those we have already encountered [except in the cases of suspension chains. For these, simply provide figured bass labels of type (9–8 and 7–6)]. Label the components of suspensions (preparation "P," suspension "S," and resolution "R").

A. Thomas Roseingrave (1688–1766), Gavotte in D major for Flute and Continuo

B. Beethoven, Piano Sonata in C minor, op. 10, no. 1, *Adagio molto*

C. Schumann, "Chiarina," *Carnaval*, op. 9

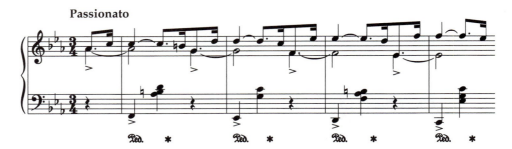

D. Mozart, String Quartet in G major, K. 156, *Tempo di Menuetto*

KEYBOARD

EXERCISE 13.5 Adding Suspensions to Harmonic Paradigms

Below is a series of harmonic paradigms in four voices. Play each two times, the first time as written without suspensions, and then, following the figured bass, with the suspensions.

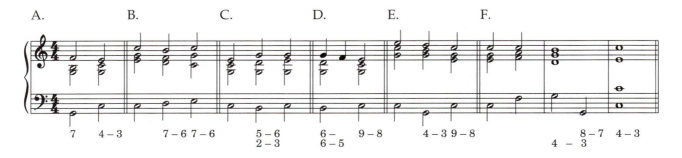

WRITING

EXERCISE 13.6 Writing Suspensions: Realignment

Analyze the following progressions using two levels. Then, on a separate sheet of manuscript paper, add suspensions to the progressions. Measures 1–2 of Exercise A are completed for you. Given that the resolutions will occur on the weak second and fourth beats, the note values will need to change from half notes to primarily quarter notes. Add one or two suspensions per measure. Hint: Look for descending stepwise motion, then suspend the upper note to create an accented dissonance that will naturally descend. You may also add chordal leaps to prepare suspensions. These faster notes create another submetrical level of activity, so use them sparingly.

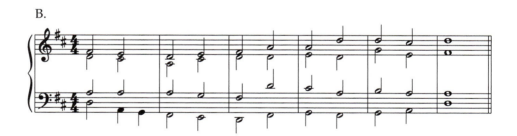

LISTENING

DVD 1
CH 13
TRACK 4

EXERCISE 13.7 Dictation

You will hear short progressions that are *either* expansions of tonic *or* cadential motions, each of which contains tones of figuration. Notate the outer voices and provide roman numerals; label any figurations. The choices are PT (passing tone), CL (chordal leap), APT (accented passing tone), N (neighbor note), SUS (suspension), and APP (appoggiatura).

A.   B.   C.

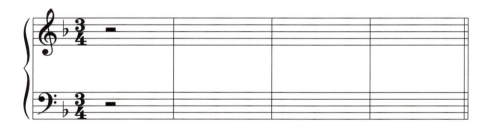

D.

ASSIGNMENT 13.3

ANALYSIS

DVD 1
CH 13
TRACK 5

EXERCISE 13.8

The following examples employ both accented and unaccented tones of figuration which may occur in any voice. Begin by providing roman numerals. Then label all tones of figuration using the shorthand method presented in the text. For all examples, label the components of suspensions (preparation "P," suspension "S," and resolution "R").

A.   Schubert, Waltz in C♯ minor, *36 Originaltänze*, op. 9, D. 365

B.   Mozart, *Menuetto*, Sonatina in C major, K. 545

C.   Haydn, Piano Sonata No. 11 in B♭ major, Hob. XVI: 2, *Largo*

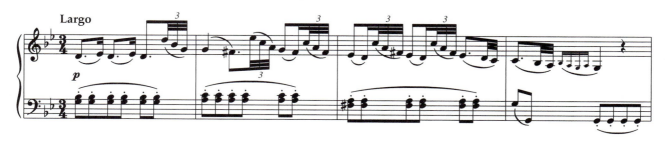

D.   Beethoven, Piano Sonata in A♭ major, op. 26

WRITING

EXERCISE 13.9 Writing Suspensions

Add suspensions according to the given figured bass. When suspensions occur in an outer voice, you must realign the given pitch, since it will be displaced by the suspension. Fill in the inner voices and analyze.

A.   B.

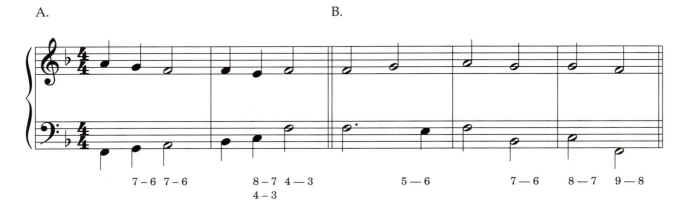

7 – 6 7 – 6   8 – 7 4 – 3   5 — 6   7 — 6   8 — 7   9 — 8
                    4 – 3

LISTENING

DVD 1
CH 13
TRACK 6

EXERCISE 13.10 Analysis Dictation

You will hear embellishments of the homophonic excerpts below. Renotate the scores to reflect what you hear. Exercises A and B contain a maximum of two embellishments. Exercises C–E contain three or more embellishments. Embellishments are PT, CL, APT, NT, SUS, and APP. Begin by analyzing each with roman numerals.

KEYBOARD

EXERCISE 13.11 Adding Suspensions to a Figured Bass

Realize the following figured bass in four voices. Then, add at least two suspensions in appropriate places (it is possible to insert *c.* 6 suspensions). Analyze.

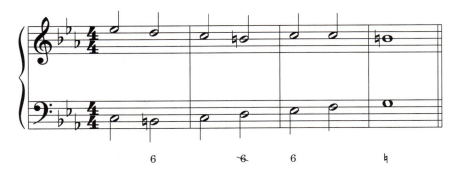

ASSIGNMENT 13.4

ANALYSIS

DVD 1
CH 13
TRACK 7

EXERCISE 13.12

The following examples employ both accented and unaccented tones of figuration that may occur in any voice. Begin by providing roman numerals (except for passages that contain chains of suspensions that create six-three chords). Then use the shorthand method presented in the text to label all tones of figuration. The chords employed are restricted to those we have already encountered, except for chords within parallel $\frac{6}{3}$ passages. For all examples, label the components of suspensions (preparation "P," suspension "S," and resolution "R").

A. Loeillet, Sonata in G major for Two Flutes and Basso Continuo, op. 1, no. 2, *Grave*

B. Haydn, Piano Sonata No. 39, in D major, Hob. XVI: 24, *Adagio*

C. Corelli, Trio Sonata in B minor, op. 1, no. 6, *Adagio*

KEYBOARD

EXERCISE 13.13 Suspensions in Context

The example below illustrates the most common upper-voice suspensions. Play as written (in keyboard style) and in the parallel minor. Then transpose to G major and E major and their parallel minors. Be able to sing either outer voice or the alto while playing the other voices.

WRITING

EXERCISE 13.14 Elaborating Homophonic Textures

The excerpts from Bach's chorales below have been stripped of their tones of figuration. Each excerpt appears twice. Add *nonaccented* tones of figuration in the first appearance. [These include PT (single and double), NN, CL, ANT, and ARP.] Add only *accented* tones of figuration in the chorale's second appearance. These include APT, SUSP (single, double, and figurated), and APP. Label each type of figuration. Adhere to the following guidelines:

1. One or two figurations per measure is enough; it is easy to overload the voices with tones that obscure or even contradict the harmony. Since leaping dissonances in the inner voices confuse the harmony, it is generally safest to

avoid them. Reserve such incomplete neighbors, including the appoggiatura, for the soprano, and even then, use them sparingly. The best way to make sure that you have not produced a garish mess is to play your solutions at the piano.

2. It is easy to create problematic parallels when adding passing tones and chordal leaps. Check to make sure you have not fallen into this trap.

A. "Dies sing die heil'gen zehn Gebot," BWV 298

1

2

B. "Für Freuden lasst uns springen," BWV 313

1

2

C. "Christus, der uns selig Macht," *St. John Passion*, BWV 245

1

VI

(continues on next page)

2

VI

LISTENING

DVD 1
CH 13
TRACK 8

EXERCISE 13.15 Dictation

Each of the following longer four-voice examples contains from two to five tones of figuration. Notate the outer voices and provide roman numerals.

A.

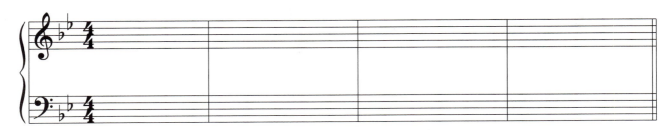

B.

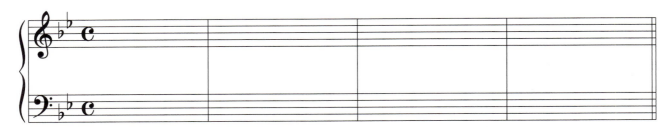

C.

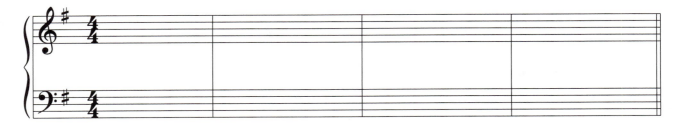

ASSIGNMENT 13.5

WRITING

EXERCISE 13.16 Writing Tones of Figuration

Complete the following tasks; include roman numeral and figured bass analysis, and label each tone of figuration.

A. Set the following melody in four voices in G minor: $\hat{3}$–$\hat{2}$–$\sharp\hat{7}$–$\hat{1}$. Add two suspensions.

B. In F major write a progression that

1. expands tonic with a voice exchange
2. includes a bass suspension
3. ends with a PAC and a suspension

C. In G minor, write a progression that includes at least

1. one accented passing tone
2. one appoggiatura
3. one 7–6 suspension

D. In D minor, write a progression that includes at least

1. one diminished seventh chord that expands the tonic
2. two different suspension types
3. one chordal leap and one passing tone

KEYBOARD

EXERCISE 13.17 Figured Bass

Realize the following figured bass in four voices. Analyze. You may write out the soprano voice.

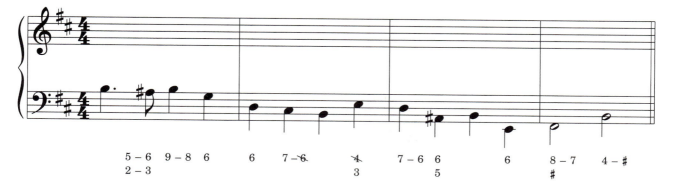

EXERCISE 13.18

Notate the bass and florid soprano of the two examples from Mozart's string quartets. Analyze with roman numerals and label tones of figuration.

A. Mozart, String Quartet in G major, K. 80, *Adagio*

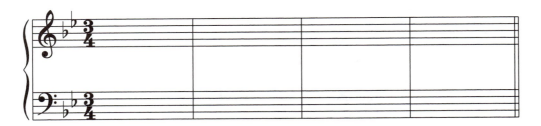

B. Mozart, String Quartet in G major, K. 156, *Presto* (but played *Moderato*)

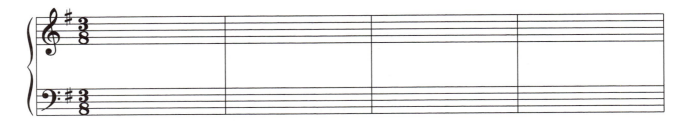

Additional Exercises

WRITING

EXERCISE 13.19 Adding Suspensions

The two-chord examples below will *not* permit the addition of suspensions because each of the voices in the second chord is higher than that of the preceding chord. Rewrite each example by inserting a revoiced second chord that is higher than the first chord and will prepare a suspension in the final chord. Notice that not only will such revoicings permit suspensions, but also, as in the case of Example D, will help to avoid the marked parallel fifths.

Sample solutions

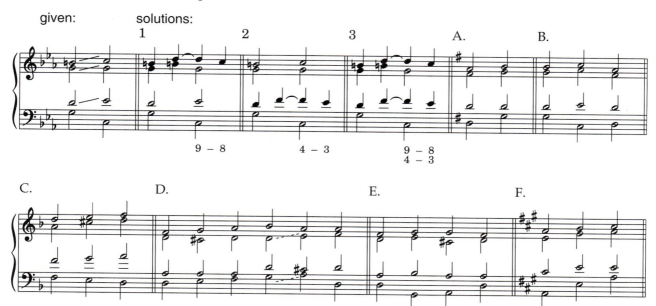

EXERCISE 13.20 Figured Bass

Realize the suspension-filled figured basses below. Analyze using two levels.

A.

B.

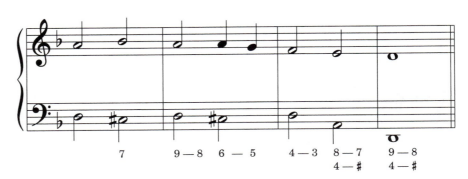

CHAPTER 14

Six-Four Chords

Exercises for Six-Four Chords and Another Use of IV

ASSIGNMENT 14.1

ANALYSIS

DVD 2
CH 14
TRACK 1

EXERCISE 14.1

Listen to each of the following homophonic examples. Provide a two-level roman numeral analysis. Your expanded harmonic vocabulary now includes:

In major keys	Function(s)	In minor keys
I, I^6	Tonic	i, i^6
ii, ii^6	PD	ii^{o6}
IV, IV^6	PD, or expand tonic	iv, iv^6
V, V^6, V^7	D, or expand tonic	V, V^6, V^7
V$^6_5$, V$^4_3$, V$^4_2$	D, or expand tonic	V$^6_5$, V$^4_3$, V$^4_2$
vii^{o6}	expand tonic	vii^{o6}, vii^{o7}, vii$^{o6}_5$, vii$^{o4}_3$
$^6_4$ chords	Passing, pedal, cadential, arpeggiating	$^6_4$ chords

A.

B.

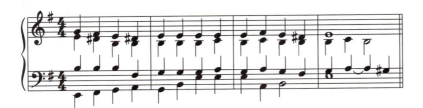

C.

D. "Amazing Grace"

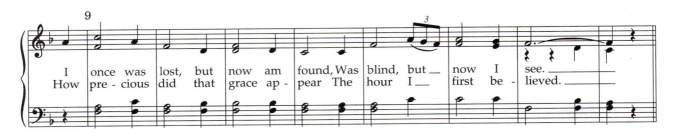

E. Mozart, Piano Sonata in B♭ major, K. 570, *Andante*

EXERCISE 14.2 Error Detection

Analyze the following error-ridden example with roman numerals and figured bass. Errors are not restricted to six-four chords. Identify errors with numbers keyed to your detailed explanations of what is wrong.

LISTENING

DVD 2
CH 14
TRACK 2

EXERCISE 14.3 Notation of Bass Lines

Notate the bass lines below the given upper voices. Determine the chords implied by the given voices before listening to the example. Add a first- and second-level harmonic analysis.

A.

B.

C.

D.

E.

ASSIGNMENT 14.2

DVD 2
CH 14
TRACK 3

ANALYSIS

EXERCISE 14.4

Listen to each of the following homophonic examples. Provide a two-level roman numeral analysis.

A. Schubert, "Der Lindenbaum" *Winterreise*, op. 89, no. 5, D. 911

B. Schumann, "Der Himmel hat eine Träne geweint," op. 37, no. 1

C.   Brahms, Symphony no. 1 in C minor, op. 68, *Allegro non troppo*

WRITING

EXERCISE 14.5

Complete the exercises below to create four-voices in chorale style accompanied by a complete roman numeral analysis. (Put key signatures with your RNs). You must determine an appropriate meter signature and rhythmic setting, given the presence of six-four chords.

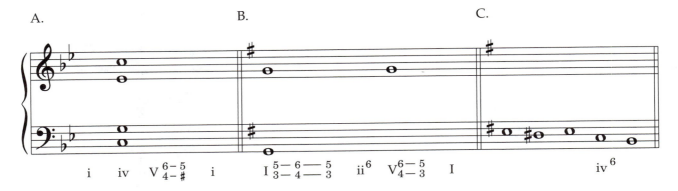

A.

B.

C.

$$i \quad iv \quad V^{6-5}_{4-\#} \quad i \qquad I^{5-6-5}_{3-4-3} \quad ii^6 \quad V^{6-5}_{4-3} \quad I \qquad iv^6$$

D.

E.

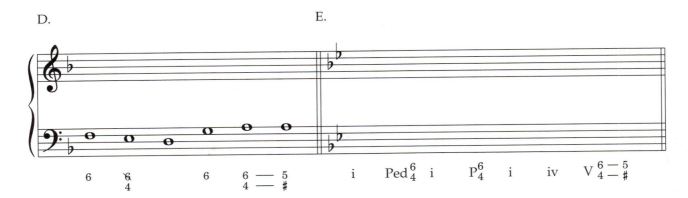

$$6 \quad 6 \atop 4 \qquad 6 \quad 6-5 \atop 4-\# \qquad i \quad Ped^6_4 \quad i \quad P^6_4 \quad i \quad iv \quad V^{6-5}_{4-\#}$$

KEYBOARD

EXERCISE 14.6

The unfigured bass below incorporates six-four chords. Realize it in four-voice keyboard style. Analyze. Be aware of six-four chords.

LISTENING

DVD 2
CH 14
TRACK 4

EXERCISE 14.7 Two-Voice Dictation

Notate the two voices and, based on the harmonic implications of these voices (bass and soprano), analyze using roman numerals.

A.

B.

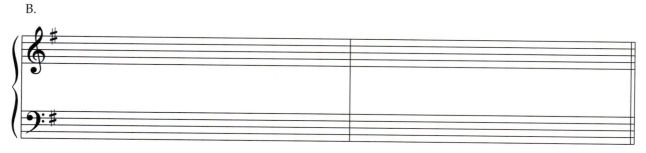

(continues on next page)

C.

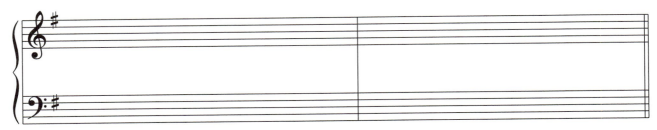

D.   E.

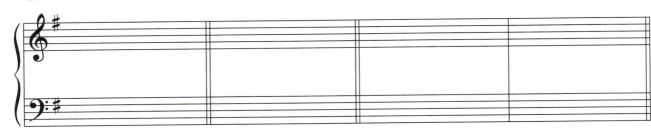

DVD 2
CH 14
TRACK 5

EXERCISE 14.8 Two-Voice Dictation: 2 + 2 = 4

You will hear how the two-voice counterpoint of the bass and soprano provides the skeleton for the added inner voices of alto and tenor. The result is a four-voice texture, the harmonies of which are essentially by-products of the confluence of voices. You will hear the outer-voice counterpoint for one beat, immediately followed by the added inner voices, their combination resulting in four-voice harmony. You are to notate the outer voices only, using both their counterpoint and the addition of the inner voices to label the harmonies.

A.   B.   C.

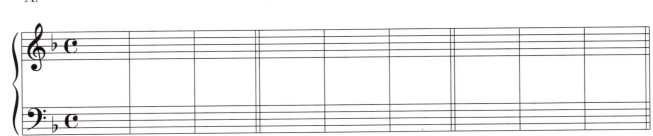

ASSIGNMENT 14.3

LISTENING

DVD 2
CH 14
TRACK 6

EXERCISE 14.9 Two-Voice Dictation

Notate the two voices and, based on their harmonic implications (as bass and soprano), analyze using roman numerals.

A.   B.   C.

D.   E.

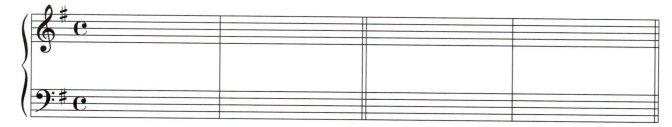

EXERCISE 14.10 Dictation

Notate outer voices and provide a two-level analysis for examples that contain six-four chords.

A.

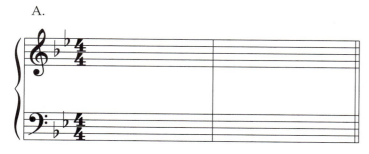

B.

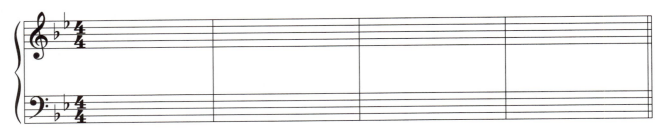

C.

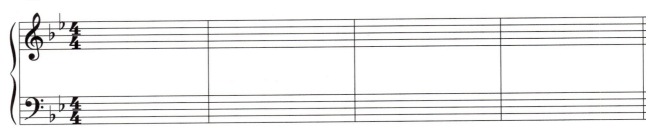

D.

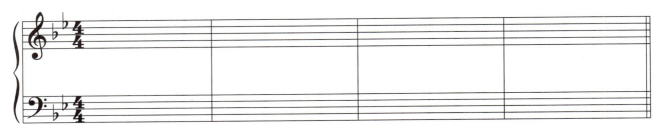

WRITING

EXERCISE 14.11

Harmonize the following sopranos in four voices; analyze. For Examples A, B, and C, include one six-four chord; for D, E, and F, include at least two. Choose the meters for each example, be aware of the metric placement of six-fours.

A. $\hat{3}$–$\hat{2}$–$\hat{1}$ in D minor   B. $\hat{5}$–$\hat{6}$–$\hat{5}$ in A minor   C. $\hat{5}$–$\hat{6}$–$\hat{5}$–$\hat{4}$–$\hat{3}$–$\hat{2}$–$\hat{1}$ in B minor
D. $\hat{1}$–$\hat{2}$–$\hat{3}$–$\hat{4}$–$\hat{5}$–$\hat{6}$–$\hat{5}$–$\hat{3}$–$\hat{2}$–$\hat{1}$ in A major

EXERCISE 14.12 Figured Bass

Realize the figured bass below in four voices. It contains numerous six-four chords as well as other new devices. Analyze and be able to sing either outer voice while playing the other voices. Note: Measure 1 contains a triple suspension. You are used to the $\frac{5}{2}$ bass suspension that resolves to V6; here the added figure, 4, indicates resolution to a V_5^6 chord.

ANALYSIS

DVD 2
CH 14
TRACK 7

EXERCISE 14.13

Below are excerpts from the literature. Analyze with two levels.
A. Beethoven, Symphony no. 9, in D minor, op. 125, *Adagio molto e cantabile*

B. Verdi, "Anchi' io dischiuso un giorno" *Nabucco*, act 2

(continues on next page)

C.   Mozart, *Allegretto*, Piano Sonata in C major, K. 309

ASSIGNMENT 14.4

WRITING

EXERCISE 14.14 Writing Six-Four Chords

Complete the tasks below.

A. In E minor, expand tonic with a Ped $^6_4$ and end with a PAC that incorporates a Cad $^6_4$ chord.

B. In E♭ major, expand the tonic with a P $^6_4$ and end with a HC.

C. In G minor, expand the tonic with a iv6; follow this with a P $^6_4$. Complete the progression with a PAC that includes a suspension and a Cad $^6_4$.

D. In B♭ major, write a four-measure progression that divides into two phrases as follows: close the first half with a HC (use a Cad $^6_4$); close the second with a PAC. Add one suspension in each phrase.

EXERCISE 14.15

Realize the figured bass below in four voices; analyze with roman numerals.

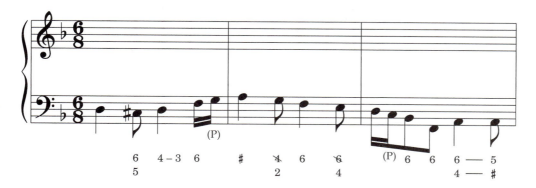

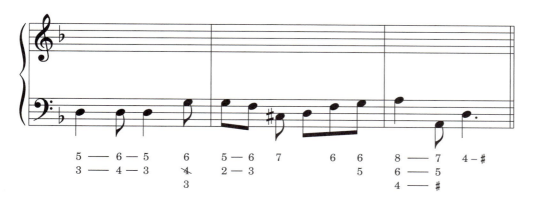

LISTENING

DVD 2
CH 14
TRACK 8

EXERCISE 14.16

For Examples A and B, add the bass line beneath the given upper voices of the following examples. For Examples C–G, no upper voices are given; add the bass line. Include a first- and second-level harmonic analysis.

A.   Schumann, "Die beiden Grenadier," op. 49. no. 1

B.   Mozart, "Non ti fidar, o misera" from *Don Giovanni*, K. 527, act 1, scene 3

C.   "Wayfaring Stranger"

D.   Verdi, "Ah Si, ben mio, coll' essere" from *Il Trovatore*, act 3, scene 2

E.   Mozart, *Andante*, Symphony in D major, K. 133

upbeat

F.   Bach, Chorale, "His Bitter Passion's Story"

upbeat

G.   Haydn, Piano Sonata in D major, Hob. XVI: 24, *Adagio*

ASSIGNMENT 14.5

KEYBOARD

EXERCISE 14.17

Sing the tune from Beethoven's song, then realize the figured bass in keyboard style in order to accompany yourself.

EXERCISE 14.18 Illustrations

In four voices, play the following progressions. You may write out a bass line to assist in your preparation.

A. A progression in E minor, $\frac{4}{4}$, that

1. expands the tonic with a passing six-four chord
2. closes with a cadential six-four chord and PAC
3. contains a 4–3 suspension

B. A progression in C minor, $\frac{4}{4}$, that considerably expands the tonic using the following chords in any order:

1. a diminished seventh chord
2. a passing V^4_3
3. a descending bass arpeggiation incorporating iv^6

C. A progression in B minor, $^6_8$, that

1. contains one bass suspension
2. contains a passing six-four chord and one chordal leap
3. closes with a cadential six-four chord

WRITING

EXERCISE 14.19 Composition

The phrase below closes with a half cadence. Analyze the remaining harmonies then write a second phrase ("consequent phrase") that closes on the tonic. The added phrase should continue the basic texture and harmonic rhythm set up in the first phrase.

ANALYSIS

DVD 2
CH 14
TRACK 9

EXERCISE 14.20

Analyze each example and label the function of each subdominant. (The subdominant either extends the tonic or functions as a predominant.

A. Tchaikovsky, "Old French Song," *Children's Album*, Op. 3, no. 16

B. Leclair, Trio Sonata in D major, op. 2, no. 8, *Allegro assai*

LISTENING

DVD 2
CH 14
TRACK 10

EXERCISE 14.21 Dictation

You will hear examples in which the subdominant extends the tonic. Notate bass
and soprano in Exercises A–D, then analyze with roman numerals and figured
bass. Notate only the bass and analyze for Exercise E.

A.

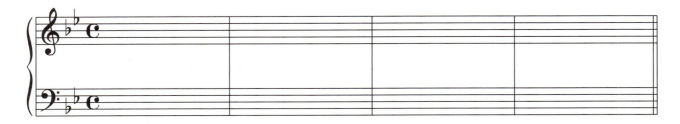

C.

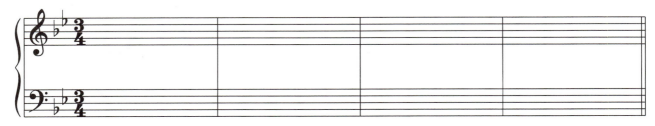

D.

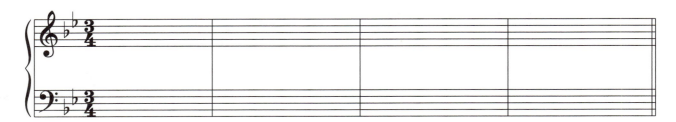

E.   "Red River Valley"

Additional Exercises

WRITING

EXERCISE 14.22

Realize the following figured bass in four voices. Analyze.

EXERCISE 14.23 Multiple Settings of Soprano Fragments

On a sheet of manuscript paper, write three different, logical bass lines for the two soprano fragments. Analyze. Extra credit: Add inner voices.

A.

B.

KEYBOARD

EXERCISE 14.24

Realize in four voices the figured bass below that incorporates IV in root position. Analyze.

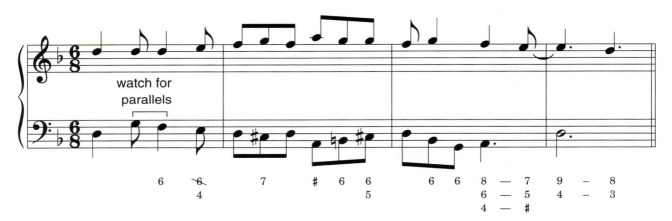

watch for
parallels

CHAPTER 15

Invertible Counterpoint and Compound Melody

ASSIGNMENT 15.1

PERFORMING

EXERCISE 15.1 Singing and Playing Invertible Counterpoint

Sing one voice while playing the other in the short exercises below. Then swap the pitches in each voice to create invertible counterpoint. Now repeat the exercise, this time singing and playing the opposite voices. Analyze the implied harmonies in each exercise. Note: All these exercises expand the tonic. Play each exercise in major and in the parallel minor and transpose to two other keys of your choice. Exercise A is completed for you.

E.

ANALYSIS

EXERCISE 15.2 Compound Melodies

1. Analyze the underlying harmonies, circling and labeling all nonharmonic tones. When you encounter a harmony we have not covered, simply write the letter name of the chord's root and its appropriate figured bass.
2. Make a three or four-voice rhythmic reduction. Maintain good voice leading between the outer voices. It may be difficult to use consistently good voice leading in the inner voices because composers writing compound melody often treat the alto and tenor quite freely, sometimes dropping one of the voices and then having it reenter the texture. Exercise A is completed for you.

A.

B.   Corelli, Violin Sonata in B♭ major, op. 5, no. 2, *Allegro*

C.   Bach, Gigue, Partita no. 2 for Solo Violin in D minor, BWV 1004

COMPOSITION

EXERCISE 15.3

Complete the following compound melody excerpt.

1. Determine the appropriate harmonies from the given bass.
2. Add the upper voices. Maintain the basic pattern.
3. Write a new phrase (but one that maintains the general mood and texture of the original phrase) that ends on a half cadence.
4. Play the new phrase, followed by the given phrase. The result is a large antecedent-consequent structure.

ASSIGNMENT 15.2

ANALYSIS

EXERCISE 15.4 Analysis of Incomplete Harmonies

Use roman numerals to analyze the passages based on the harmonic implications presented by the incomplete chords. Label all tones of figuration, including passing and neighbor tones and suspensions. Note: You will encounter only chords we have studied.

WRITING

EXERCISE 15.5

Beethoven, like nearly all common-practice musicians, vigorously (if grudgingly) studied theory and counterpoint. Below is an exercise in invertible counterpoint that he completed under the tutelage of a famous teacher named Albrechtsberger. Study Beethoven's solution and label intervals and suspensions; then on a separate sheet of manuscript paper, recopy his solution in the key of A major so that the counterpoint appears above the cantus firmus. In a sentence or two, remark on the quality of Beethoven's counterpoint.

ASSIGNMENT 15.3

ANALYSIS

EXERCISE 15.6 Analysis of Compound Melodies

1. Analyze the underlying harmonies, circling and labeling all nonharmonic tones. When you encounter a harmony we have not covered, simply write the letter name of the chord's root and its appropriate figured bass.
2. Make a voice-leading reduction of the outer voices by using stems for structural notes and unstemmed pitches for passing and neighboring motions.
3. If more than the two outer voices are present, add the inner parts. You need not worry about strict voice leading because inner voices are treated quite freely, sometimes dropping out and reentering the texture.

A. Bach, Prelude, Cello Suite No. 2 in D minor, BWV 1008

B. Bach, Bourrée I, Cello Suite No. 3 in C major, BWV 1009

C. Bach, *Allemande*, Cello Suite No. 2 in D minor, BWV 1008

D_7

D.   Bach, Gigue, Cello Suite No. 2 in D minor, BWV 1008

EXERCISE 15.7   Analysis of Incomplete Harmonies

Use roman numerals to analyze the passages based on the harmonic implications of the voices. Label all tones of figuration, including passing and neighboring tones and suspensions. Note: You will encounter only the chords we have studied.

A.   Bach, Minuet, French Suite No. 3 in B minor, BWV 814

B.   Haydn, Piano Sonata No. 30 in D major, Hob. XVI: 19, *Moderato*

C. Haydn, Piano Sonata No. 5 in G major, Hob. XVI. 11, *Presto*
     What contrapuntal technique from this chapter is used in mm. 9–12?

EXERCISE 15.8 Instrumental Application: Reduction and Elaboration

These embellished examples—all taken from Bach's solo violin and cello works—differ from previous instrumental application exercises in that compound melody is involved (i.e., there are more voices implied than there are instruments playing). Analyze, verticalize (into a three- or four-voice homophonic texture), and then perform each example as follows. If you are a pianist, simply play your homophonic realization. If you are a melodic instrumentalist, arpeggiate each example. If necessary, refer to the discussion in Chapter 11 for a detailed procedure. Play each reduction in the key in which it is written, then transpose to one other key of your choice.

The sample solution shows how Corelli's vivace can be verticalized to create four voices.

Sample Solution

Corelli, Violin Sonata, op. 5, no. 2, *Vivace*

A. Bach, *Gavotte en Rondeau*, Violin Partita in E major, BWV 1006

B.   Bach, *Courante*, Cello Suite no. 1 in G major, BWV 1007

   1.

   2.

C. Bach, Violin Sonata in A minor, BWV 1003, *Allegro*

continue pattern to AC or HC

CHAPTER 16

The Motive

ASSIGNMENT 16.1

ANALYSIS

DVD 2
CH 16
TRACK 1

EXERCISE 16.1 Comparison of Motivic Repetitions

In each of the following examples a motive and one or more repetitions have been boxed. Label the transformation used for each motivic repetition based on the initial statement. Repetitions may be literal (not so common) or transformed (common). Transformations include embellishment (e.g., tones of figuration, interpolation, etc.), transposition, sequence, inversion, retrograde, retrograde inversion, augmentation and diminution, fragmentation, change of interval, imitation, and occasionally, two or more transformations simultaneously.

A.   Bach, Gigue, English Suite No. 4 in F major, BWV 809

(continues on next page)

B.   Bach, Organ Fugue in C major, BWV 545

C.   Haydn, String Quartet in D major, op. 33, no. 6

D.   Bach, Gigue, English Suite No. 4 in F major, BWV 809

E.   Haydn, (Finale) String Quartet in F major, op. 55, no. 2, *Presto*

ANALYSIS

EXERCISE 16.2

DVD 2
CH 16
TRACK 2

In each example below one (or in some cases a second) motive has been circled. Identify as many repetitions (transformations) as possible in the rest of each example.

A. Brahms, Capriccio in G minor, op. 116

(continues on next page)

B.   Haydn, String Quartet in B♭ major, op. 55, no. 3, *Vivace assai*

C.   Haydn, Trio, Piano Sonata in D major, Hob. XVI: 14

(continues on next page)

D. Bach, Fugue in C minor, *Well-Tempered Clavier*, Book II, BWV 820

1.

(continues on next page)

2.

ASSIGNMENT 16.3

ANALYSIS

DVD 2
CH 16
TRACK 3

EXERCISE 16.3 Intermovement Motivic Relationships

Excerpts from two or more movements taken from single works appear below with hints that will lead you to discover motivic relationships that occur between the movements.

A. Mozart, Piano Sonata in C minor, K. 457 *Molto allegro* and *Allegro assai*
These two movements contain numerous relationships, some of which lie directly on the surface, including the rising broken-chord figure that opens the sonata's first movement (Example A1) and its inversion a falling figure, that opens the last movement (Example A2); even the rhythmic figure (long-short-short) reappears in both figures. Other types of relationships occur as well and are somewhat hidden, since they span longer stretches of music, and their members are not stated as adjacent pitches. However, they too are marked by melodic fluency, registral prominence, and musical parallelism (i.e., they are members of a pattern). Identify a single motive that underlies the openings of the first and last movements.

A1.

A2.

B.   Corelli, Trio Sonata no. 8 in B minor

> Corelli subtly works in gestures that are not literal transformation, but nonetheless preserve the gestural content of an initial motive.

B1. Preludio

B2. Allemanda

B3. Tempo di Gavotta

C. Corelli, Trio Sonata no. 6 in G minor
The first appearance of the motive is beamed.

C1. Allemanda

C2. Corrente

C3. Giga

ASSIGNMENT 16.4

ANALYSIS

EXERCISE 16.4 Motivic Saturation: Analysis of Bach's Two-Part Invention in C major, BWV 772

DVD 2
CH 16
TRACK 4

Listen to and/or play through Bach's invention. On your score, the main theme, called the "subject," is labeled "S." The subject is divided into two smaller motives, a rising stepwise fourth (labeled "x") and a falling third motive (labeled "y"). The highest pitch of the subject, F, belongs to both motives. The "countersubject" (labeled "CS") accompanies the subject. Bach repeats the subject and its motivic components in many ways. On your score, circle all statements of the subject (and its motives x and y) and the countersubject. Answer the following questions in the space provided (use another sheet of paper if necessary).

(continues on next page)

A. In a sentence or two, compare and contrast the contour (melodic shape) of the S and the CS.

B. Is the counterpoint in mm. 1–2 invertible in the strict sense? Explain in a sentence or two.

C. What is the origin of the sequence (right hand) in mm. 3–4?

D. What is the origin of the left hand in the same bars?

E. What is the origin of the sequence (right hand) in mm. 5–6?

F. Compare mm. 7–8 with 1–2.

G. What is the origin of the figure sequenced in mm. 9–10?

H. Compare mm. 15–18 with mm. 9–10. What is the same and what is different?

I. Label all melodic sequences.

J. Use roman numerals to analyze the following measures: 1–3 (downbeat); 7–9 (downbeat).

ASSIGNMENT 16.5

ANALYSIS

EXERCISE 16.5 Analysis of Implied Harmonies and Motives

Use roman numerals to analyze the following phrase. Harmonies change usually twice each measure. Then, determine what short pitch/rhythmic event stated at the beginning of the piece may best be labeled a motive: circle and label it; then trace its repetitions throughout the piece, labeling each according to how it is transformed. Consider that the motive may occur at different levels of the musical structure.

EXERCISE 16.6 Basic Motivic Elaboration

Below are short, slowly moving melodies and a bass line that implies a harmonic structure. Choose one (or two contrasting) melodic/rhythmic motives and incorporate it or them within the melody. You might want to focus on neighbors, passing, and broken-chord figures, two of which may be combined to form a single longer motive.

ASSIGNMENT 16.6

WRITING

EXERCISE 16.7 Outer-Voice Elaboration

Below is an outer-voice contrapuntal framework, both voices of which you will flesh out with one or two motives. The result will be a rhythmically interesting and unified composition, one in which the two voices participate equally. Complete the following steps, in order.

1. Based on the harmonic implications of the two voices, analyze, using roman numerals.
2. Choose one or at most two of the motives given in Exercise 16.6 (or create your own), adding them in various contexts based on the implied harmonies of the exercise.

LISTENING

EXERCISE 16.8 Hearing Motivic Elaborations

Each example below is an elaboration of a basic 1:1 contrapuntal structure. Listen to each example then notate only the outer-voice 1:1 skeleton, omitting all elaborating pitches and motives. Analyze. Then, in a sentence or two, describe the *single* main motivic component used in each exercise (e.g., "the motive is a passing, dotted rhythmic figure").

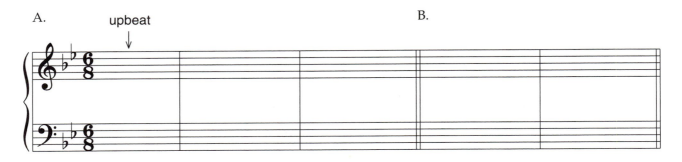

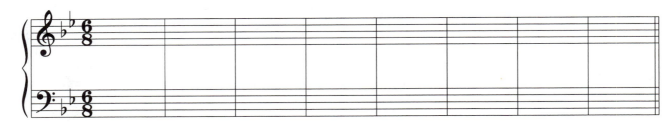

ASSIGNMENT 16.7

WRITING

EXERCISE 16.9 Outer-Voice Elaboration

Below are two outer-voice contrapuntal frameworks, both voices of which you will flesh out with one or two motives. The result will be rhythmically interesting and unified compositions in which the two voices participate equally. Complete the following steps in order.

1. Based on the harmonic implications of the two voices, analyze, using roman numerals.
2. Choose one or at most two motives, adding them in various contexts based on the implied harmonies of the exercise.

A.

B.

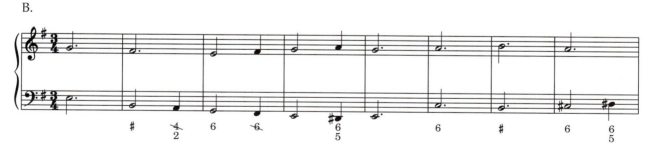

CHAPTER 17

The Phrase Model Refined: Perception, Animation, and Expansion

Assignments for Listening to Complete Phrases

ASSIGNMENT 17.1

LISTENING

DVD 2
CH 17
TRACK 1

EXERCISE 17.1 Dictation

Listen to each complete phrase four times (a few pitches are given).

- First playing: focus on the underlying harmonic progression. Keep the meter in mind, noting the progression from tonic (usually expanded) to predominant and dominant within the phrase. Add roman numerals and the bass of the harmonic changes that occur after the tonic expansion.
- Second playing: notate the bass line for the tonic expansion, and any structural melodic notes (e.g., the first pitch and the two or three pitches involved in the cadence).
- Third playing: complete the melody.
- Fourth playing: try to reserve this playing for checking your work.

Beat within
measure: 1   3

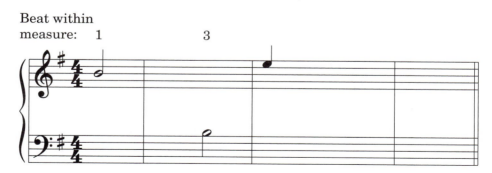

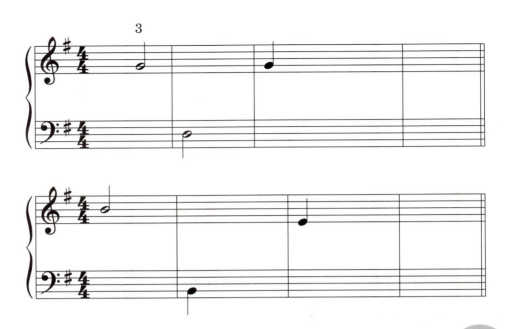

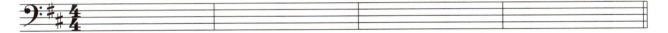

EXERCISE 17.2 Figurated Textures

This exercise incorporates a melody over a figurated accompaniment. Notate the bass and provide roman numerals.

A.

B.

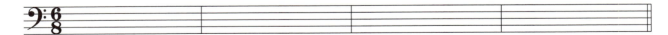

C.

ASSIGNMENT 17.2

LISTENING

DVD 2
CH 17
TRACK 3

EXERCISE 17.3 Dictation

Listen to each complete phrase four times (a few pitches are given).

- First playing: focus on the underlying harmonic progression. Keep the meter in mind, noting the progression from tonic (usually expanded) to predominant and dominant within the phrase. Add roman numerals and the bass of the harmonic changes that occur after the tonic expansion.
- Second playing: notate the bass line for the tonic expansion, and any structural melodic notes (e.g., the first pitch and the two or three pitches involved in the cadence).
- Third playing: complete the melody.
- Fourth playing: try to reserve this playing for checking your work.

A.

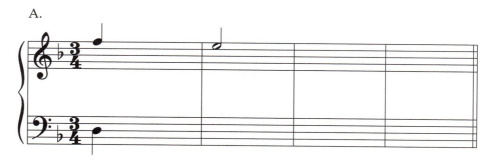

Beat within
measure: 3

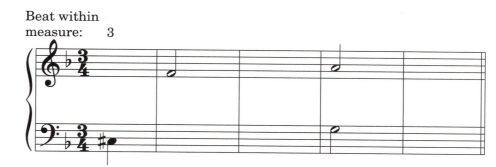

C.

D.

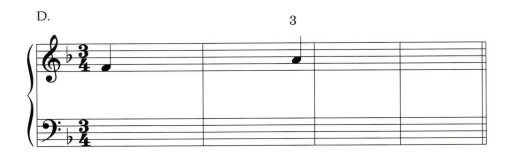

EXERCISE 17.4 Figurated Textures

This exercise incorporates a melody over a figurated accompaniment. Notate the bass and provide roman numerals.

A.

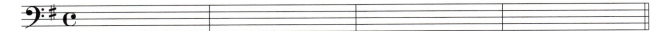

B.

Assignments for Pre-Dominant Seventh Chords

ASSIGNMENT 17.3

ANALYSIS

EXERCISE 17.5

The examples below feature figured bass with soprano melody. Each contains non-dominant seventh chords. Analyze all chords in each example.

A. Bach, *Geistliche Lied*

B. Handel, "Lascia ch'io pianga" from *Rinaldo*

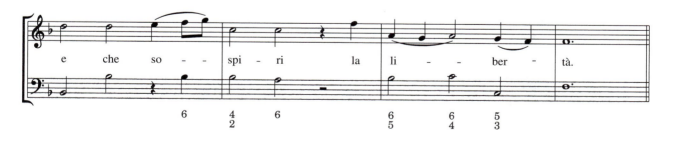

C. Bach, *Geistliche Lied*

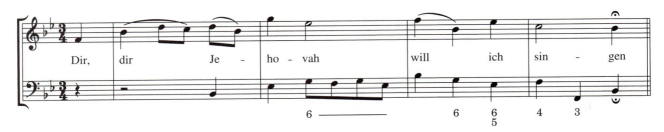

KEYBOARD

EXERCISE 17.6 Model Progressions Using Pre-Dominant Seventh Chords

Play the four-voice models below as written and in major and minor keys up to and including two sharps and two flats. Be able to sing either outer voice while playing the other three voices. Circle the seventh of each pre-dominant seventh chord, then draw a line to its preparation and resolution pitches. Provide roman numerals with inversions, for models C and D.

A.

$$\text{F:}\quad \text{I}\qquad \text{ii}^{6}_{5}\quad \text{V}^{8-7}\quad \text{I}$$

B.

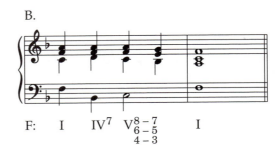

$$\text{F:}\quad \text{I}\qquad \text{IV}^{7}\quad \text{V}^{8-7}_{6-5}\quad \text{I}$$
$$\phantom{\text{F:}\quad \text{I}\qquad \text{IV}^{7}\quad}{}_{4-3}$$

C.　　　　　　　　　D.

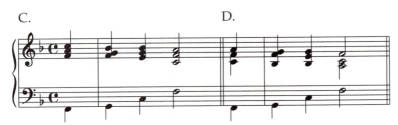

LISTENING

DVD 2
CH 17
TRACK 5

EXERCISE 17.7 Dictation of Pre-Dominant Seventh Chords

Notate outer voices and provide roman numerals for the examples that contain pre-dominant sevenths.

A.

B.

C.

ASSIGNMENT 17.4

WRITING AND PLAYING

EXERCISE 17.8 Pre-Dominant Seventh Chords in Context

Complete the progressions below in four voices, then play them on the piano. Transpose each exercise to a different key of your choice.

A.

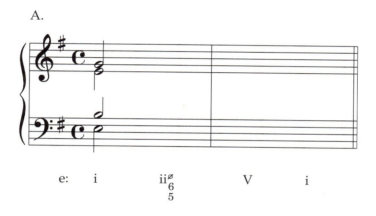

$$e: \quad i \qquad ii^{\varnothing}_{\substack{6\\5}} \qquad V \qquad i$$

B.

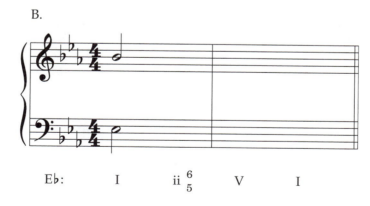

$$E\flat: \qquad I \qquad ii^{\substack{6\\5}} \qquad V \qquad I$$

C.

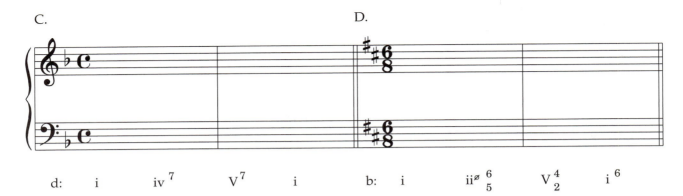

d: i   iv⁷   V⁷   i   b: i   ii∅ $_5^6$ V $_2^4$ i⁶

E.

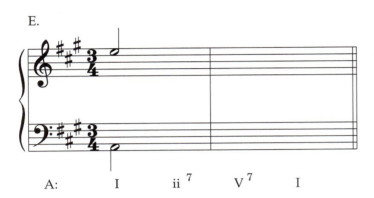

A: I   ii⁷   V⁷   I

Note: You should use an incomplete seventh chord for either the ii7 or the V7 harmonies in Example E.

LISTENING

DVD 2
CH 17
TRACK 6

EXERCISE 17.9 Bass Dictation from the Literature

Notate the bass line and provide roman numerals; focus on the type of nondominant seventh used.

A. Beethoven, "Rule Britannia," *Fünf Variationen* in D major, WoO 79

B. Schumann, "Auf einer Burg" ("In a castle"), *Liederkreis*, op. 39, no. 7

C. Haydn, Piano Sonata in E major, Hob. XVI:37, *Allegretto*

D. Mozart, "Rex tremendae majestatis," *Requiem*, K. 626

E. Handel, Chamber Sonata no. 22, *Adagio*

ANALYSIS

DVD 2
CH 17
TRACK 7

EXERCISE 17.10

Below are two excerpts from Mozart's first symphony, written at the age of 8. The first excerpt comes from the opening of the piece and contains a single progression. The second excerpt is drawn from later material and contains two complete harmonic progressions in two different keys. Determine the key for each progression; analyze using roman numerals; then, in a sentence or two, compare the three progressions.

1. Mozart, Symphony no. 1 in E♭ major, K. 16

2.

2. Mozart, K. 16, continued

Assignments for EPMs, Contrapuntal Cadences, and Expanded PDs

ASSIGNMENT 17.5

WRITING

EXERCISE 17.11 Figured Bass

Realize the following figured bass example in four-voice keyboard style. Provide a two-level analysis.

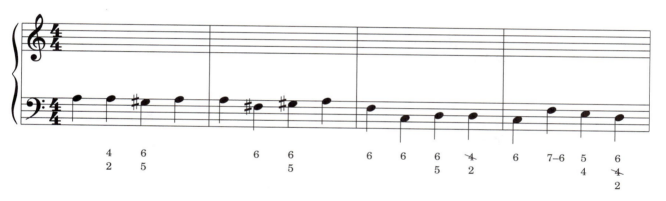

ANALYSIS

EXERCISE 17.12 Analysis of Expanded Pre-Dominant Functions

1. Label tonic, pre-dominant, and dominant functions, focusing on expanded pre-dominants.
2. Next, determine how each expanded function is accomplished. For example, do you find literal repetition, change of inversion, passing or neighboring chords, or EPMs? Label the chords and summarize what occurs in the pre-dominant area.
3. Finally, provide roman numerals for the entire passage.

A.

B.   Mendelssohn, *Lieder ohne Wörte* ("Song Without Words"), no. 45 in C major, op. 102
Notice the tonic pedal that occurs in mm. 1 and 2. What harmonic progression is implied above the pedal? Label accordingly.

B.

C.   Mozart, Menuetto, Symphony no. 30 in D major, K. 202

DVD 2
CH 17
TRACK 8

KEYBOARD

EXERCISE 17.13 Figured Bass Recitative

Sing the following tune from one of Handel's operas. You must determine the key from the context since there is no key signature. Then, realize the figured bass. Finally, be able to accompany your singing with your figured bass realization.

Handel, "Ye worshippers" from *Judas Maccabeus*, HWV 63 act 2, no. 49

ASSIGNMENT 17.6

LISTENING

EXERCISE 17.14 Variation and Contrapuntal Expansion of a Harmonic Model

DVD 2
CH 17
TRACK 9

You will hear contrapuntal expansions of a T-PD-D-T harmonic progression. The model bass line below will be fleshed out in variations that maintain the metric placement of the given harmonies implied by the bass notes. Complete the following tasks:

1. Notate the bass and soprano voices of the contrapuntal chords that embellish the given harmonic structure.
2. Provide a two-level harmonic analysis. Your harmonic vocabulary now includes I, I6, IV6, V, V6, V7, V_5^6, V_3^4, V_2^4, vii°6, vii°7, vii° $_5^6$, and vii° $_3^4$, and the pre-dominants ii, ii6, ii7, ii_5^6, ii_3^4, IV, IV6, IV7, IV_5^6. Don't forget EPMs and contrapuntal cadences.

Model

Variation 1   Variation 2

Variation 3

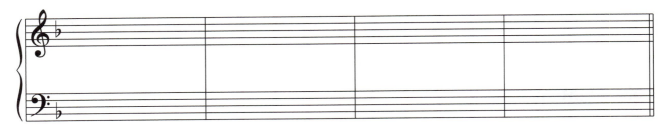

Variation 4

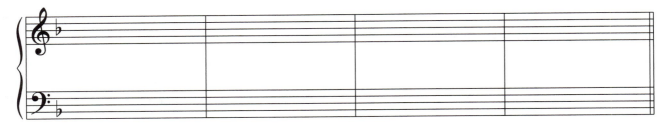

ASSIGNMENT 17.6

WRITING

EXERCISE 17.15 Embedded Phrase Models (EPMs) and Contrapuntal Cadences

Complete these tasks and analyze using two levels.

A. In D minor, write a short progression that contains two tonic expansions, each of which uses a different EPM.

B. Set the following soprano melody in B minor: $\hat{5}$–$\hat{4}$–$\hat{4}$–$\hat{3}$–$\hat{2}$–$\hat{7}$–$\hat{1}$. Include ii$^4_2$ and $^6_5$.

KEYBOARD

EXERCISE 17.16 Figured Bass

Realize the figured bass below in four voices. Be able to analyze the progression and to sing either outer voice while playing the three other voices. Bracket and label phrases, EPMs, expanded pre-dominants, and contrapuntal cadences.

ASSIGNMENT 17.7

EXERCISE 17.17 Writing Extended Pre-Dominants

Complete the following tasks in four voices; provide a two-level analysis.

A. In D major, write a four-measure progression that
   1. expands the tonic with an EPM; close with an IAC
   2. expands the PD at the cadence through voice exchange
   3. includes at least one suspension

B. In C minor, write a four-measure progression that:

   1. includes a bass suspension
   2. includes a tonic expansion with a bass that descends a sixth from $\hat{1}$ to $\hat{3}$
   3. expands the PD with a six-four chord
   4. concludes with an IAC

EXERCISE 17.18 Variation and Contrapuntal Expansion of a Harmonic Model

You will now hear contrapuntal expansions of a T-PD-D-T harmonic progression. The two-voice model below will be fleshed out in variations that maintain the metric placement of the given harmonies in the model. Complete the following tasks:

1. Notate the bass and soprano voices of the contrapuntal chords that embellish the given harmonic structure.
2. Provide a two-level harmonic analysis. Your harmonic vocabulary now includes I, I6, IV6, V, V6, V7, V_5^6, V_3^4, V_2^4, vii°6, vii°7, vii° $_5^6$, and vii° $_3^4$, and predominants: ii, ii6, ii7, ii_5^6, ii_3^4, IV, IV6, IV7, and IV_5^6. Don't forget EPMs and contrapuntal cadences.

Model

expansions 1 – 4 are 2 measures.
expansions 5 – 6 are 4 measures.

Variation 1   Variation 2

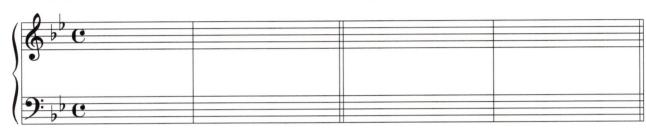

Variation 3   Variation 4

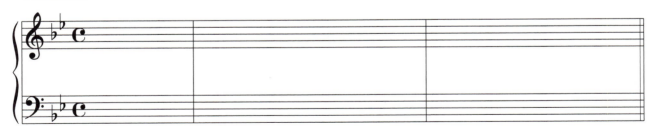

Variation 5

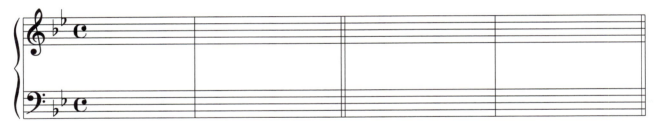

Variation 6   upbeat

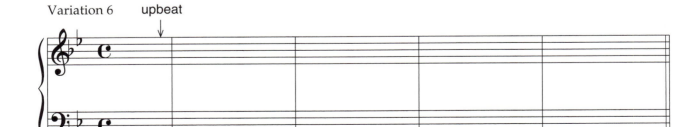

Assignments That Also Include Subphrases and Composite Phrases

ASSIGNMENT 17.8

WRITING

EXERCISE 17.19 Composition Project

Below are two models, each of which can be fleshed out into a two-phrase musical unit. Such a musical unit is called a period. We will explore periods in detail in Chapter 20.

A. Choose one of the models. Begin with good outer voices in a major key of your choice and label the implied harmonies. Label tonic, pre-dominant, and dominant expansions.

B. Flesh out the texture in four voices and, if you desire, figurate your texture.

C. Elaborate your melody with suspensions, arpeggios, passing notes, and embellishing skips.

D. Along the same lines, elaborate the inner voices appropriately.

Model 1

mm:	1	2	3	4		5	6	7	8
	I	I	PD-D	IAC		I	I	PD-D(7)	PAC

Model 2

mm:	1	2	3	4		5	6	7	8
	I	I	I	PD-D (HC)		I	I	PD-D(7)	I (PAC)

ANALYSIS

EXERCISE 17.20 Phrases and Subphrases

DVD 2
CH 17
TRACK 10

Determine whether the examples below contain single phrases with one or more subphrases, or if there are multiple phrases. Support your answer in one or two sentences. Bracket phrases beneath the bass clef and subphrases above the treble clef. Remember, phrases are self-standing musical units that contain harmonic motion (i.e., a traversing of tonic and dominant functions) and end with a cadence. Subphrases combine to create phrases (usually in proportional pairs) and therefore are components of phrases. Yet, subphrases are in many ways self-standing, given that they may contain miniature harmonic motions (e.g., EPMs) and even weak cadential gestures (e.g., contrapuntal cadences). Be aware that musical flow may come to a stop because of a caesura, but does not necessarily mean that you have encountered a subphrase. Note there will often be more than one possible interpretation in these examples.

A.   Haydn, Piano Sonata no. 19 in E minor, Hob. XVI:47, *Allegro*

B.   Mozart, "Bei Männern," (from *The Magic Flute*), K. 620, act I, scene 7

Bei Män-nern, wel - che Lie - be füh len,-fehlt auch ein_ gu - tes Her - ze nicht

C.   Haydn, Sonata no. 35 in Ab major, Hob. XVI:34, *Moderato*

D.   Beethoven, *Klavierstück*, WoO 82

ASSIGNMENT 17.9

EXERCISE 17.21 Variation and Contrapuntal Expansion of a Harmonic Model

DVD 2
CH 17
TRACK 11

You will now hear contrapuntal expansions of a T-PD-D-T harmonic progression. The bass line model will be fleshed out in variations that maintain the metric placement of the implied harmonies in the model. Complete the following tasks:

1. Notate the bass and soprano voices of the contrapuntal chords that embellish the given harmonic structure.
2. Provide a two-level harmonic analysis. Your harmonic vocabulary now includes I, I6, IV6, V, V6, V7, V^6_5, V^4_3, V^4_2, vii°6, vii°7, vii° $^6_5$, and vii° $^4_3$, and predominants ii, ii6, ii7, ii^6_5, ii^4_3, IV, IV6, IV7, and IV^6_5. Don't forget EPMs and contrapuntal cadences.

Model

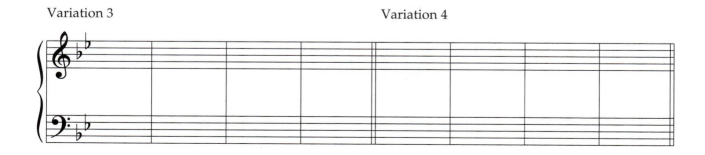

Variation 5   Variation 6

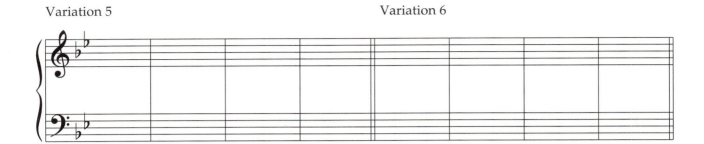

ANALYSIS

EXERCISE 17.22 Subphrases and Composite Phrases

Analyze each example, determining whether the composer has created extended phrases through a single large-scale progression or through a series of linked subordinate harmonic motions.

A. Haydn, Piano Sonata No. 32 in G minor, Hob. XVI: 44, *Allegretto*

B. Schubert, "Die Sterne"

Wie blit-zen die Ster-ne so   hell durch die   Nacht!_____

bin   oft schon dar-ü-ber vom Schlum-mer er-wacht._____

C.   Haydn, Piano Sonata in E♭ Major, Hob. XVI:52, *Presto*

Additional Exercises

LISTENING

DVD 2
CH 17
TRACK 13

EXERCISE 17.23 Dictation

Listen to each phrase four times. On the first playing, focus on the underlying harmonic progression. Keep the meter in mind, noting the changes from tonic to predominant to dominant within the phrase. Then, add roman numerals and the bass of the harmonic changes that follow the tonic expansion. On the second playing, notate the rest of the bass line and structural melodic notes. On the third playing, complete the melody. Check your work on the fourth playing.

A.

B.

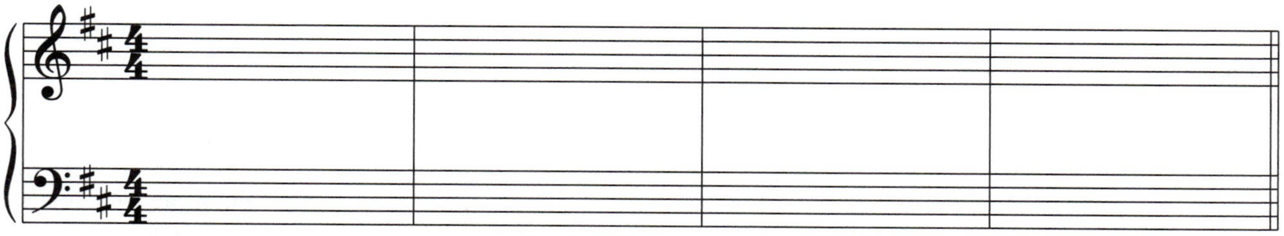

C.

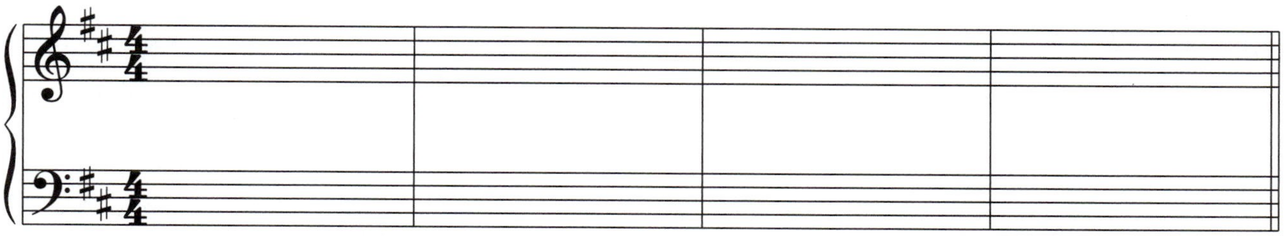

D.

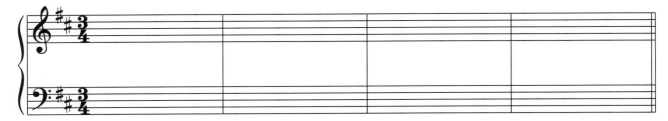

E.

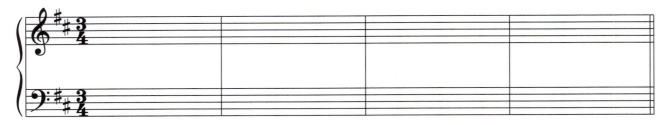

F.

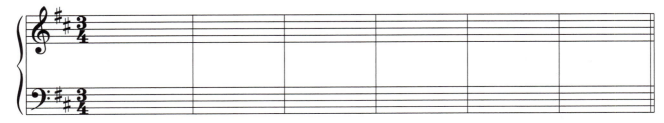

PERFORMING

EXERCISE 17.24

The following arpeggiations create progressions that incorporate EPMs and expanded pre-dominants. Listen to how often harmonies change; then analyze the progressions with roman numerals and either sing or play them on your instrument. (If you play the examples, you must transpose them to one other key of your choice.)

A.

B.

C.

WRITING

EXERCISE 17.25 Unfigured Bass and Melody Harmonization

Determine the best harmonizations for the examples below, using only the chords we have studied. Add the missing outer voice first. Include a two-level analysis. Add inner voices. Finally, add tones of figuration as required below (you may alter the rhythms in the given voices to add suspensions and other metrically accented tones of figuration). In each exercise, include and label the following:

Two different suspensions
Two unaccented passing tones
One accented passing tone
One neighbor or appoggiatura

A.

B.

EXERCISE 17.26 Figured Bass

Realize the following figured bass, first composing the soprano and then adding inner voices. Analyze with two levels.

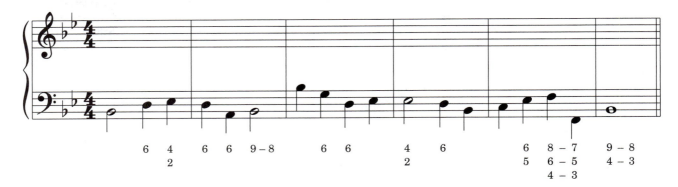

CHAPTER 18

The Submediant: A New Diatonic Harmony and Further Extensions of the Phrase Model

Exercises for Standard Functions of the Submediant

ASSIGNMENT 18.1

LISTENING

DVD 2
CH 18
TRACK 5

EXERCISE 18.1 Bass Line Dictation

Notate bass lines of the progressions that contain the submediant harmony; provide roman numerals. Since this exercise continues to develop tonal memory, begin by listening and memorizing before notating pitches. Focus on the deeper-level harmonic functions. For example, since a tonic prolongation will often begin the exercise, ask yourself how long tonic is prolonged before it yields to a new harmonic function. Do not focus on details (such as the type of contrapuntal chords used to expand the tonic) until the last hearing, during which you are encouraged to refine your answer. Always begin with the large picture, which should include questions such as "How long is the excerpt?" "Is it a progression, a prolongation, or both?" and "Where does the tonic prolongation end?"

A.

B.

C.

D.

WRITING

EXERCISE 18.2 Figured Bass

Complete the soprano voice for the figured bass, then add the inner voices. Provide a two-level analysis. (Since you will need to consider the harmonies as you complete the soprano, add the roman numerals at the same time.)

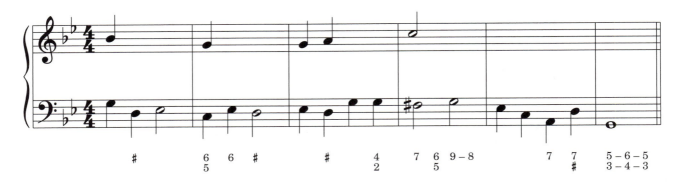

ANALYSIS

EXERCISE 18.3

Analyze the excerpts below, each of which contains the submediant harmony.

A.   Mozart, "Rex tremendae majestatis," *Requiem*, K. 626

B. Chopin, Nocturne in C minor, BI 108

KEYBOARD

EXERCISE 18.4 Harmonizing the Ascending Scale

We know that by combining two or more harmonic paradigms we can create longer progressions. One such progression is a complete stepwise octave ascent. We will learn one harmonization for the ascending soprano and one for the ascending bass. Study the figures and realize in four voices. Paradigms are bracketed. Be able to sing either outer voice while playing the other three voices.

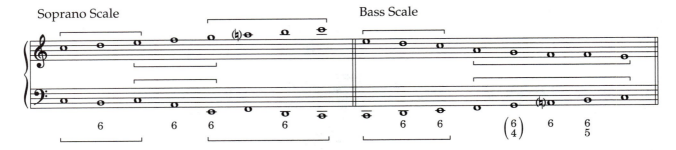

ASSIGNMENT 18.2

LISTENING

EXERCISE 18.5 Outer-Voice Dictation

DVD 2
CH 18
TRACK 3

Notate bass and soprano voices of progressions that include the submediant harmony. A few pitches are provided. Analyze using two levels.

A.

B.

ANALYSIS

DVD 2
CH 18
TRACK 4

EXERCISE 18.6

Below are three different harmonizations by Bach of the opening of the chorale tune "Jesu meine Freude" from his *St. Matthew Passion* (BWV 244). Analyze each setting, then write a paragraph comparing and contrasting them. Which do you like best and why?

A.

B.

C.

Weg mit al - len Schit - zen!
Weg ihr eit - len Eh - ren,

Weg, weg mit al - len Schit - zen
Weg, weg ihr eit - len Eh - ren

Weg, weg, weg, weg mit al-len Schit - zen
Web, weg, weg, weg ihr eit-len Eh - ren

Weg, weg, weg, weg mit al-len Schit - zen
Weg, weg, weg, weg ihr eit-len Eh - ren

WRITING

EXERCISE 18.7 Illustration

In any minor key, write a progression that includes the following tasks, which appear in order of composition:

1. A tonic prolongation that includes one suspension figure
2. A descending bass arpeggiation that includes the submediant
3. A pre-dominant that is expanded by voice exchange
4. A dominant that includes one suspension figure

ASSIGNMENT 18.3

ANALYSIS AND LISTENING

EXERCISE 18.8

The bass lines are omitted from the literature excerpts below. Based on listening and with the assistance of the upper voices, notate the missing voice and add roman numerals.

A. Schubert, Impromptu in G♭ major, op. 90, D. 899

B. Haydn, Symphony no. 104 in D major, "London," Hob. I: 102, *Andante*

C.   Haydn, String Quartet in E♭ major, "Fantasia," op. 76, no. 6, Hob. III: 80, *Adagio*

(CPT)

D.   Mascagni, "O Lola" from *Cavalleria Rusticana*, scene i

LISTENING

EXERCISE 18.9 Dictation of Figurated Excerpts Using the Submediant

DVD 2
CH 18
TRACK 6

Notate the bass of each example that contains one or two appearances of the submediant. Provide roman numerals, and label the harmonic function for each statement of the submediant.

A.

B. (Contains intro.)

C. (Contains intro.)

WRITING

EXERCISE 18.10

In any major key (except C) write a progression that includes the following tasks. Begin by logically ordering the tasks so that your progression makes harmonic sense. (Write your progression on the next page)

1. A deceptive harmonic progression
2. A bass suspension
3. A tonic expansion using a passing figure in the bass
4. A pre-dominant seventh chord
5. A descending fifth progression using vi

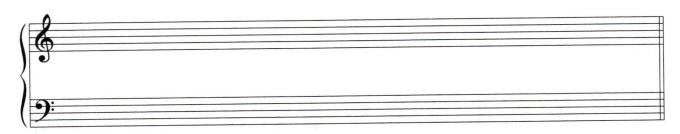

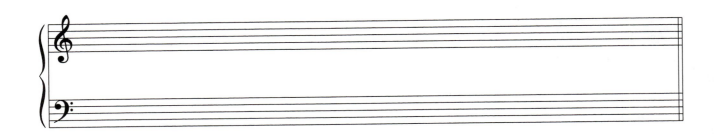

Exercises for Contextual Analysis and Step-Descent Basses

ASSIGNMENT 18.4

WRITING

EXERCISE 18.11 Harmonizing Melodic Fragments Using the Submediant

Choose an appropriate meter and rhythmic setting. Then harmonize the soprano fragments below by using at least one submediant harmony in each example; analyze. For Exercise C you must determine a suitable meter and rhythmic setting (you may change the given rhythms); add barlines.

A.

B.

C.

ANALYSIS

EXERCISE 18.12 Step-Descent Bass

DVD 2
CH 18
TRACK 7

Listen to each excerpt, determining first whether there is a direct, tetrachordal descent to V, or whether there is an indirect descent of a fifth. Finally, analyze using two levels.

A.　Handel, "Thou Art Gone Up on High," *Messiah*, HWV 56

Is there a textual motivation for the contour of the vocal line? What effect does this contour create with the bass?

A.

B.　Handel, Sarabande, Suite in G minor, HWV 253

In this example the descent occurs on the downbeat chords. The intervening weak-beat chords elaborate it. The elaboration may be viewed as essential, given the voice-leading problems that would result if they were absent.

B.

C.　Corelli, Concerto Grosso no. 8 in G minor, op. 6, *Vivace*

LISTENING

DVD 2
CH 18
TRACK 8

EXERCISE 18.13 Dictation

Notate the bass and soprano and provide roman numerals. Label the function for each occurrence of the submediant harmony. Your choices are bridge between T and PD, PD, part of the step-descent bass.

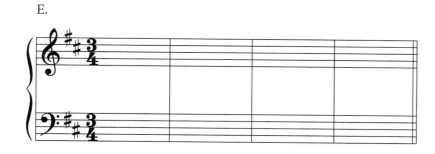

ASSIGNMENT 18.5

DVD 2
CH 18
TRACK 9

LISTENING

EXERCISE 18.14 Dictation from the Literature

Notate the bass and provide roman numerals. You need not notate repeated pitches.

A. Bach, "Ermuntre dich, mein schwacher Geist," *Christmas Oratorio*, no. 12, BWV 248

B. Carissimi, "Plorate, filii Israel" from *Jepthe*

C. Schubert, "Am Bach im Frühling" ("To the Brook in Springtime"), D. 361

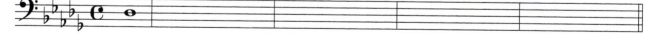

WRITING

EXERCISE 18.15 Writing the Step-Descent Bass

Complete the soprano line, adding roman numerals as you go. Then, add inner voices and complete your analysis by adding a second-level analysis.

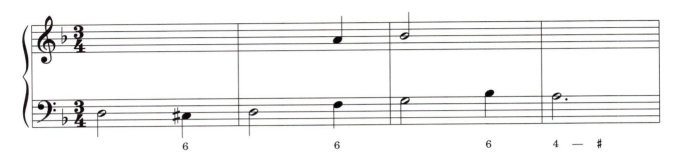

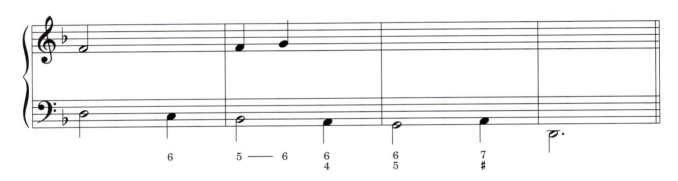

KEYBOARD

EXERCISE 18.16 Step-Descent Basses

Realize the contrapuntal models below in four voices. Be able to sing either outer voice while playing the other three. Transpose to C and B minor.

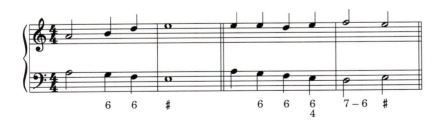

Additional Exercises

KEYBOARD

EXERCISE 18.17 Figured Bass

Create a good soprano line and add inner voices; you may write out the soprano.
Analyze, and be able to sing the bass while playing the other three voices.

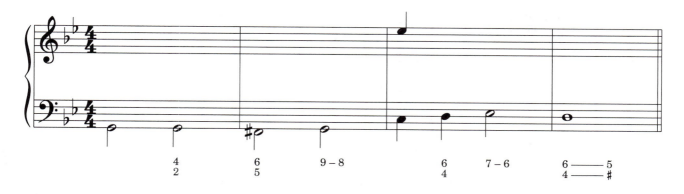

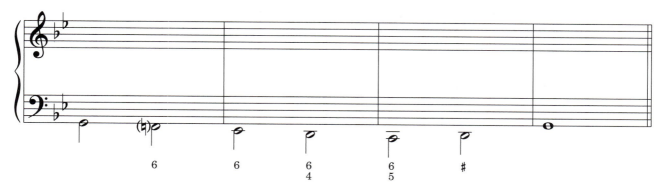

EXERCISE 18.18 Figuration

You will now create a figurated piece from the figured bass you realized in Exercise 18.17. Below is one realization of mm. 1–2 of Example 18.17, followed by common figurations used in Baroque keyboard music. Choose one that you like or develop your own. Then play Exercise 18.17 in the figurated style.

EXERCISE 18.19 Illustrations

Complete one of the two illustrations below in a meter of your choice (tasks need not appear in the order given). Hint: Study each carefully, for you might save time by combining one or more tasks (e.g., the following four individual tasks can be made into a single contrapuntal expansion of tonic: a suspension, an EPM, a bass arpeggiation, and a $^6_4$ chord).

1. In D minor:
   a. VI in a bass arpeggiation
   b. a direct step-descent bass V
   c. at least two suspensions
   d. a contrapuntal expansion using $ii\o^4_2$
   e. a $ii\o\,^6_5$ in the final half cadence

2. In B minor
   a. a lament bass that descends to $\hat{4}$
   b. a six-four chord
   c. at least one suspension
   d. a deceptive progression
   e. a iv7 in the final cadence

The Mediant, the Back-Relating Dominant, and Synthesis of Diatonic Harmonic Relationships

ASSIGNMENT 19.1

LISTENING

DVD 2
CH 19
TRACK 1

EXERCISE 19.1 Dictation

For the following progressions that feature III, notate the bass and analyze. (Remember, III is often preceded by its dominant, V/III.)

A.

B.

C.

D.

WRITING

EXERCISE 19.2

Exercise A provides roman numerals; add four voices. Exercises B and C require adding upper voices and roman numerals.

A.   B.   C.

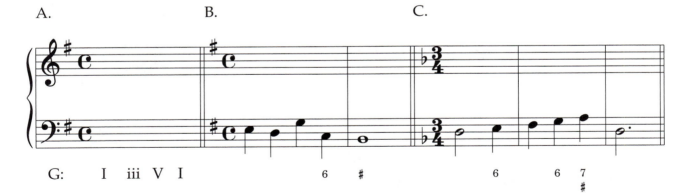

G: I   iii V I   6   #   6   6   7
                                                                                #

ANALYSIS

DVD 2
CH 19
TRACK 2

EXERCISE 19.3 Analytical Synthesis

The examples below share certain musical characteristics, such as harmonic progression. There are, of course, contrasting features as well. Listen to and analyze each excerpt. Then, in a paragraph, compare and contrast them.

1. Mozart, Piano Sonata in A minor, K. 310

   Do you hear m. 1 as a motion from I to I6 or as I to iii? Measure 2 begins with a six-four chord. Is it consonant or dissonant? (Hint: We have encountered this six-four chord many times before, but only in the context of V.)

2. Mozart, Piano Sonata in C major, K. 330, *Andante cantabile*

   Consider your analysis of six-four chords in light of what you did in the preceding example.

KEYBOARD

EXERCISE 19.4 Multiple Harmonizations

Harmonize the melodic fragment below in three different ways. Include at least one statement of the submediant or mediant in each harmonization. You may wish to set this melody in major and its relative minor.

ASSIGNMENT 19.2

LISTENING

DVD 2
CH 19
TRACK 3

EXERCISE 19.5 Dictation

For the following progressions that feature III, notate the bass and analyze. [Remember, III is often preceded by its dominant (V/III)].

A.   Wagner, "Bridal Chorus" from *Lohengrin,* act 3, scene 1

B.   Beethoven, Piano Sonata no. 25 in G major, op. 79, *Andante*

C.   Schubert, Impromptu in A♭ major, op. 90, D. 899, no. 4

WRITING

EXERCISE 19.6 Figured Bass

The following figured bass includes III and VI. Write a soprano voice, provide a first- and second-level analysis, and then add the inner voices.

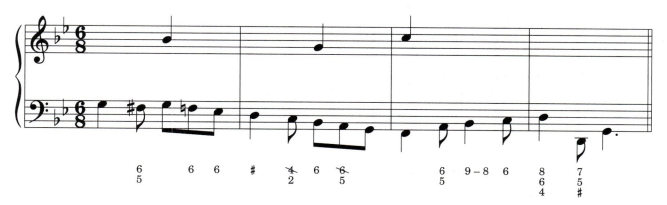

EXERCISE 19.7 Multiple Harmonization of a Soprano Melody

Harmonize the melody in two significantly different ways by adding a bass voice and roman numerals (you do *not* need to include inner voices). Use at least one example of the mediant and the submediant harmonies in each harmonization. Determine the mode; it is often possible to cast the tune in both a major key and its relative minor. Review the process of harmonizing a melody that was presented at the end of Chapter 17. Play each solution on the piano, singing either outer voice while playing the other voice.

ASSIGNMENT 19.3

LISTENING

DVD 2
CH 19
TRACK 4

EXERCISE 19.8 Analysis/Dictation

Analyze the following examples with a two-level analysis. All the examples are missing some or all of their bass lines; notate them. Mozart wrote the violin sonata at the age of 7.

A. Mozart, *Menuetto*, Symphony no. 35 in D major, K. 385

B. Mozart, Violin Sonata in D major, K. 7, *Adagio*

C.   Brahms, "Da unten im Tale" (Down in the Valley There), *Deutsche Volkslieder*, WoO 33, no. 6

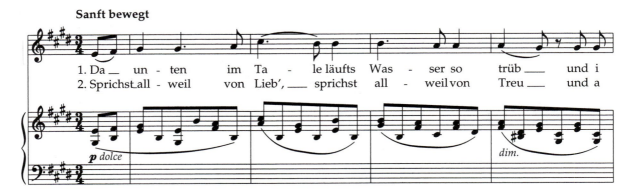

Sanft bewegt

1. Da ___ un - ten   im Ta - le läufts Was - ser so trüb ___ und i
2. Sprichst all - weil   von Lieb', ___ sprichst all - weil von Treu ___ und a

p dolce   *dim.*

kann dirs   nit sa - gen,   i hab'   di so   lieb.
bis - se - le Falsch - heit   is au   wohl da - bei!

D.   Schubert, "Ave Maria," D. 839

1. A -   - ve Ma - ri -   - a!   Jung -   - frau mild,
2. A -   - ve Ma - ri -   - a!   un -   - be - fleckt!
3. A -   - ve Ma - ri -   - a!   Rei -   - ne ˍ Magd!

(vii$^{\varnothing 6}_{5}$/V)

WRITING

EXERCISE 19.9 Multiple Harmonization of a Soprano Melody

Harmonize the melody in two significantly different ways by adding a bass voice and roman numerals (you do *not* need to include inner voices). Use at least one example of the mediant and the submediant harmonies in each harmonization. Review the process of harmonizing a melody that was presented at the end of Chapter 17. Play each solution on the piano, singing either outer voice while playing the other voice.

ASSIGNMENT 19.4

LISTENING

DVD 2
CH 19
TRACK 5

EXERCISE 19.10 Analysis/Dictation

Analyze the following examples with a two-level analysis. All the examples are missing some or all of their bass lines; notate them.

A.   Handel, "I Know That My Redeemer Liveth" from *Messiah*, HWV 56

B.   Tchaikovsky, "June," *The Seasons*, op. 37b, no. 6

(continues on next page)

WRITING

EXERCISE 19.11 Unfigured Bass and Soprano

Determine implied harmonies using roman numerals. Expect to encounter step descents, the mediant and submediant, and back-relating dominants. Add inner voices and a second-level analysis. Then, add tones of figuration to create a more fluid sound, distributing them between voices in order to create a balanced texture.

ASSIGNMENT 19.5

LISTENING

DVD 2
CH 19
TRACK 6

EXERCISE 19.12 Dictation

The following six exercises contain the upper voices of progressions that include various functions of III and VI. Notate the bass and choose one example to subject to two-level analysis. Begin by bracketing short, complete progressions. For example, a tonic expansion may be followed by a PD–D that may be followed by a deceptive motion. There may be more than a single motion to the cadence. Study the sample chord progression below.

I   vii°6   I6   ii6   V   vi   IV   vii°6   I   iii   IV   V   I
T_____EPM w/deceptive motion   another EPM   mediant leads to cadence
T_____PD   D   T

A.

B.

C.

D.

E.

F.

ANALYSIS

DVD 2
CH 19
TRACK 7

EXERCISE 19.13 Functions of the Dominant

Below are examples in which the dominant prominently appears. Determine whether the dominant is structural (i.e., it moves the harmonic progression forward) or whether it is a voice-leading chord (e.g., a passing chord in a bass descent to vi or a weak back-relating dominant).

A.

B.

C.

D.   Mozart, Piano Sonata in D major, K. 576, *Allegro*

(vii$^{\circ}_{6}$/ii)

E. Beethoven, *Menuetto*, Piano Sonata No. 7 in D major, op. 10, no. 3, *Allegro*
   Compare and contrast this example with the Mozart, in Example D.

(V_3^4/ii)

KEYBOARD

EXERCISE 19.14 Figured Bass and Back-Relating Dominants

Realize the figured bass below. Explain the function of each dominant harmony.

ASSIGNMENT 19.6

LISTENING

DVD 2
CH 19
TRACK 8

EXERCISE 19.15 Dictation

Notate the outer voices of the homophonic examples below that contain back-relating dominants. Provide a first-and second-level analysis. A few notes are given.

(continues on next page)

D.

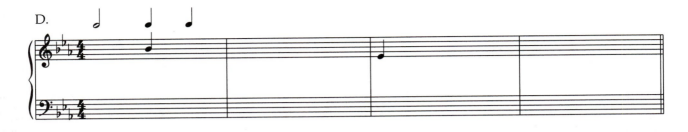

E.

WRITING

EXERCISE 19.16 Soprano and Bass Figures

Based on harmonic patterns that you've learned, and the implications of the figures with the soprano line, add a bass line, roman numerals, and the inner voices. The absence of figures implies root position. Include one example each of vi and iii.

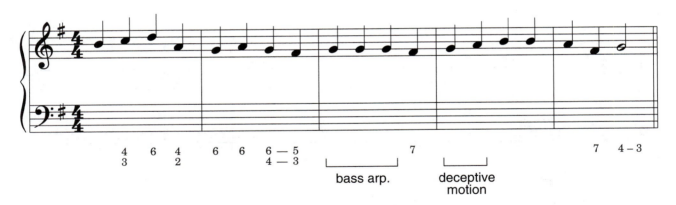

ANALYSIS

EXERCISE 19.17 Analytical Synthesis

The examples below share certain musical characteristics, such as harmonic progression. There are, of course, contrasting features as well. Listen to and analyze each excerpt. Then, in a paragraph, compare and contrast them.

A.   Schumann, "Arabesque," op. 18

B.   Schumann, "Kind im Einschlummern," *Kindersenen (Scenes from Childhood)*, op. 15, no. 12

KEYBOARD

EXERCISE 19.18 Expansions of a Harmonic Model

The following harmonic models present a standard tonic—pre-dominant—dominant—tonic progression. Expand each stage as required by the instructions. Analyze your work.

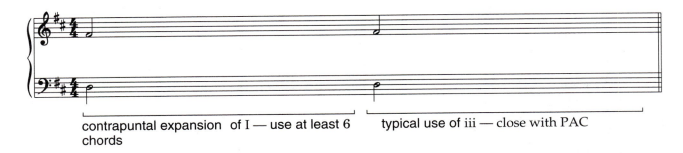

contrapuntal expansion of I — use at least 6 chords

typical use of iii — close with PAC

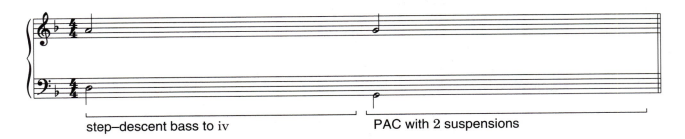

step–descent bass to iv

PAC with 2 suspensions

Additional Exercises

LISTENING

DVD 2
CH 19
TRACK 10

EXERCISE 19.19 Analysis/Dictation

Analyze the following examples with two-level analysis. All the examples are missing some or all of their bass lines; notate them.

A. Rossini, "Una voce poco fa" from *Il Barbiere di Siviglia (The Barber of Seville)*, act I, scene 9

B. Haydn, "Es vollbracht," *The Seven Last Words*, op. 51, no. 6, Hob. III: 55

EXERCISE 19.20 Dictation

Listen to the figurated exercises for flute with piano accompaniment. Notate the bass line of the piano and provide a roman numeral analysis.

A.

B.

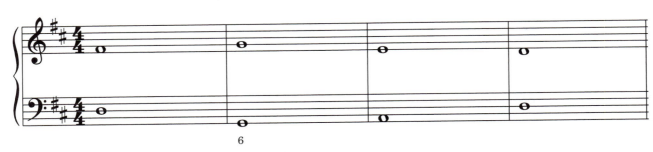

EXERCISE 19.21 Variation and Expansion

Each of the models below is followed by a series of variations and expansions that flesh out each model's basic progressions. Notate the outer voices and analyze each of the expansions.

Model A

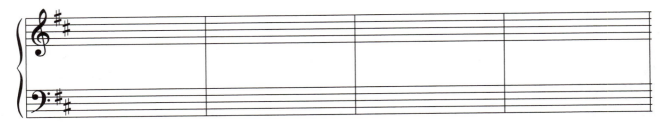

1.

(continues on next page)

2.

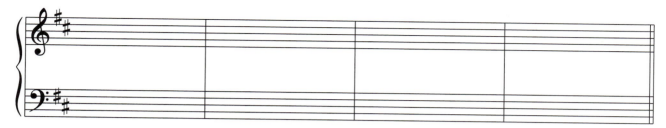

3.

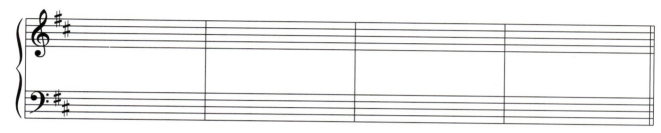

4.

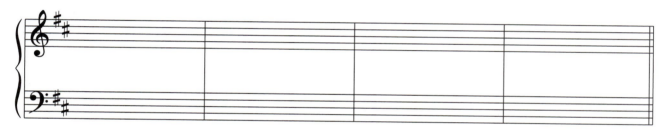

Model B

1.

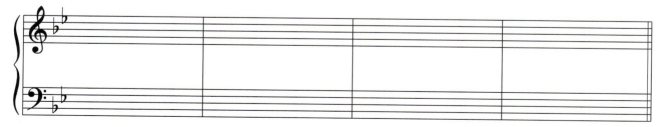

(continues on next page)

2.

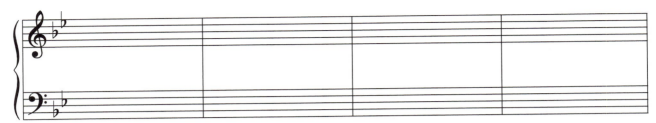

3.

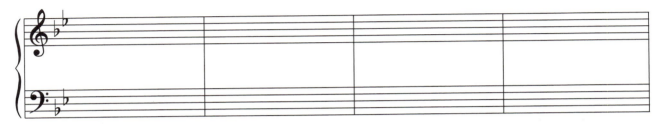

4.

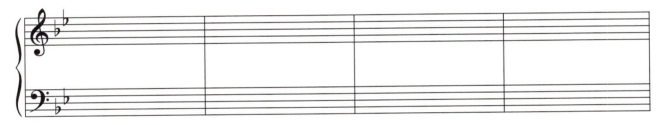

WRITING

EXERCISE 19.22 Paradigms

Below are short bass and soprano fragments, some of which include figured bass or other hints. Harmonize each in four voices and provide a first- and second-level analysis.

EXERCISE 19.23 Soprano and Bass Figures

Based on harmonic patterns you've learned and the implications of the figures and soprano line, add a bass line, roman numerals, and the inner voices. The absence of figures implies root position, and ties indicate a stationary bass. Include one example of vi and iii.

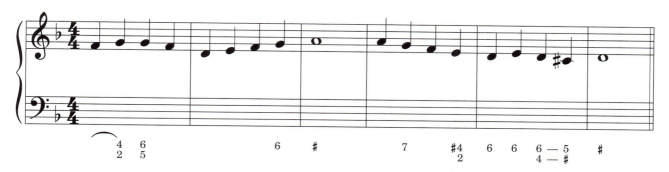

EXERCISE 19.24 Unfigured Bass

Label cadences and locate harmonic paradigms; add roman numerals. Label remaining harmonies, and then add a soprano melody and inner voices.

EXERCISE 19.25 Small Compositional Projects

Complete the following tasks in four voices.

A. Harmonize the soprano scale degrees $\hat{3}$–$\hat{3}$–$\hat{2}$–$\hat{1}$–$\hat{7}$–$\hat{2}$–$\hat{1}$–$\hat{7}$–$\hat{6}$–$\hat{5}$ in D major and G minor in two different ways.

B. In the key of C minor, write a four-measure phrase using a mixture of half and quarter notes in the soprano, each of which is harmonized, that contains
   1. a deceptive progression
   2. three different types of six-four chords

3. a voice exchange
4. two suspensions, one of which occurs in the bass

C. In B minor, write an eight-measure composition, comprising two four-measure phrases, that contains
1. a descending bass tetrachord
2. a typical use of the mediant
3. a half cadence
4. a phrygian cadence

KEYBOARD

EXERCISE 19.26 Continuation of Figurated Textures

Play the first half of the exercise as written. Complete the exercise by realizing the figured bass and continuing the pattern of figuration. Add appropriate tones of figuration.

EXERCISE 19.27 Descending Scale Harmonization

We now harmonize descending soprano scales (ascending scales were presented in Chapter 18). Study each model and realize it according to the figured bass. Note that the mediant appears in setting the descending line $\hat{8}$–$\hat{7}$. Be able to sing the scale while playing the other voices. Transpose each to another key of your choice.

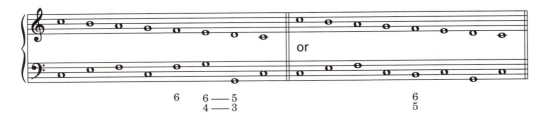

EXERCISE 19.28 Figured Bass and Singing from the Literature

Sing the tunes below and determine their key. Then, realize the figured bass in four voices and analyze. Finally, combine singing and realizing the figured bass at the keyboard.

A. Handel, "What Do I Hear," from *Saul*, HWV 53, act I, scene 3

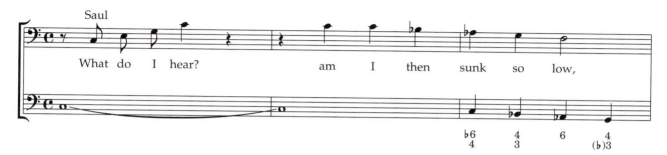

B. Stradella, "Pietà, Signore!" ("Have Pity, Lord"), S11-27 (by Fétis)

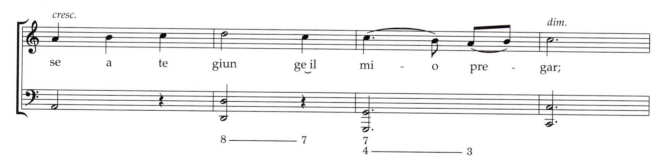

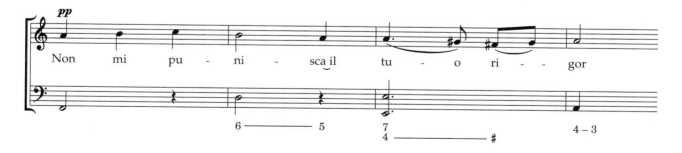

C.   Torelli, "Tu lo sai quanto t'amai" ("You Know How Much I Love You")

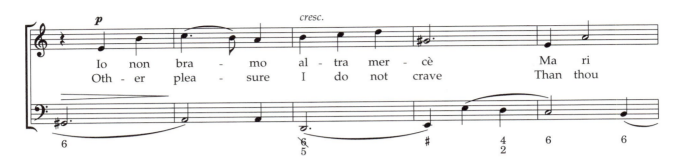

Io non bra - mo al - tra mer - cè   Ma ri
Oth - er plea - sure I do not crave   Than thou

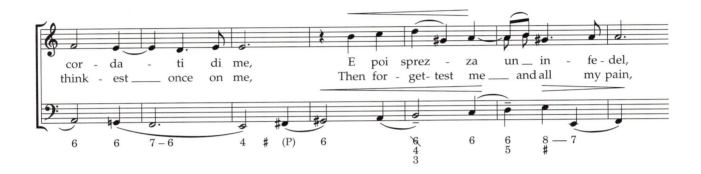

cor - da - ti di me,   E poi sprez - za un — in - fe - del,
think - est — once on me,   Then for - get - test me — and all my pain,

ANALYSIS

EXERCISE 19.29

The short excerpts below illustrate the concepts we have covered since Chapter 8. Analyze each example in its entirety, including labeling tones of figuration and a two-level roman numeral analysis.

A.   Beethoven, Violin Sonata in D major, op. 12, no. 1

B. Schumann, *Davidsbundlertänze*, no.11

C. Mozart, Symphony in A major, K. 114

D.   Corelli, *Gavotta*, Trio Sonata, op. 4, no. 5

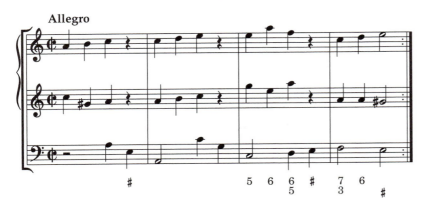

E.   Beethoven, *Adagio con molta espressione,* Violin Sonata in E♭ major, op. 12, no. 3

F.   Mozart, *Tema*, Piano Sonata in D major, K. 284.

G.   Mozart, *Andante*, Symphony in D, K, 95

H.   Leoncavallo, *I Pagliacci*, Prologue

I.   Puccini, *La Bohème*, act 2

charm - ing, a ve - ry charm-ing ___ lit - tle girl.
me da capo a pi - è da capo a pi - è.

DVD 2
CH 19
TRACK 14

EXERCISE 19.30 Analytical Synthesis

These examples share certain musical characteristics, such as similar harmonic progression. There are, of course, contrasting features as well. Listen to and analyze each excerpt. Then, in a paragraph, compare and contrast them.

A.   Grieg, "Spring Dance", op. 38, no. 5

The A♯ that appears in mm. 7–10 is the temporary leading tone of the harmony that controls these measures. A single harmony is extended in mm. 11–16.

B. Mahler, "Die zwei blauen Augen" ("The two blue eyes"), *Lieder eines fahrenden Gesellen (Songs of a Wayfarer)*, no. 4

CHAPTER 20

The Period

ANALYSIS

DVD 2
CH 20
TRACK 1

EXERCISE 20.1 Cadence and Phrase Model Review

1. Label each cadence in the excerpts below. Your choices are PAC, IAC, HC, PHRY, DC, and PLAG. The deceptive cadence (DC), as we learned, is more accurately described as a "deceptive progression" given that most deceptive progressions do not close phrases, but rather simply provide a pause, or caesura; they are part of a larger harmonic trajectory that continues to an authentic or half cadence. PLAG is more accurately described as "plagal motion," since in most cases it follows an authentic cadence and therefore functions to extend the tonic. Be aware that authentic cadences are of two types:
   a. Those that are strong (perfect, strongest) and imperfect (stronger)
   b. Those that are weak, defined by stepwise contrapuntal motions to tonic (contrapuntal cadences), which contain inverted dominant (or dominant-function) harmonies or inverted tonic harmonies.

2. Label each component of the phrase model (either T-PD-D (HC) or T-PD-D-T (AC), or T-PD-D (PHRY), or T-PD-D-T (DC). Don't forget that an EPM may occur within the tonic function.

A. Haydn, String Quartet in F minor, op. 20, no. 5, Hob. III: 35, *Adagio*

B.   Rossini, "L'amoroso e sincero Lindoro" ("Your Loving and Sincere Lindoro") from *Il Barbiere di Siviglia* (*The Barber of Seville*), act I, scene 6

C.   Beethoven, Piano Sonata no. 9 in E major, op. 14, no. 1, *Allegretto*

D.   Bach, Prelude in B♭ major, BWV 866 *Well-Tempered Clavier*, Book 1

E.   Scarlatti, Sonata in A minor, K. 149

EXERCISE 20.2 Analysis of Periods

Make formal diagrams of each example below and include a label and any comments that support your interpretation or illuminate motivic structures. Label each component of the phrase model [either T-PD-D (HC) or T-PD-D-T (AC), or T-PD-D (PHRY), or T-PD-D-T (DC)], except for continuous periods, whose tonal motion unfolds as a single progression. Don't forget that an EPM may occur within the tonic function. Note: Some examples may not be periods.

A.   Mozart, String Quartet no. 19 in C major, "Dissonant," K. 465, *Allegro assai*

B.   Chopin, Mazurka in D major, op. 33, no. 2, BI 115

C.   Beethoven, Romance in F major for Violin and Orchestra, op. 50, *Adagio cantabile*

(continues on next page)

LISTENING

EXERCISE 20.3 Period Structures and Dictation

For this exercise, notate missing soprano and/or bass voices (arrows indicate missing pitches) and provide a roman-numeral analysis and period diagram.

A.   Beethoven, Piano Sonata no. 1 in F minor, op. 2, no. 1, *Adagio*

B. Schubert, "Frühlingstraum," ("A Dream of Spring"), *Winterreise*, D. 911, no. 11
    What is unusual about the phrase lengths?

ASSIGNMENT 20.2

ANALYSIS

DVD 2
CH 20
TRACK 4

EXERCISE 20.4 Phrase and Subphrase Identification

Label phrases and subphrases using brackets. Label cadences as in Exercise 20.1. Label each component of the phrase model [either T-PD-D (HC) or T-PD-D-T (AC), or T-PD-D (PHRY), or T-PD-D-T (DC)]. Don't forget that an EPM may occur within the tonic function.

A. Mendelssohn, *Lieder ohne Wörte* (*Songs Without Words*), Book 5, no. 6 in A major, op. 62

B. Haydn, Piano Sonata No. 35 in A♭ major, Hob. XVI: 34, *Moderato*

C.   Chopin, Waltz in E minor, BI 56

EXERCISE 20.5 Analysis of Periods

Make period diagrams of each example below. Include a label and any comments that support your interpretation or illuminate motivic structures. Label each component of the phrase model [either T-PD-D (HC) or T-PD-D-T (AC), or T-PD-D (PHRY), or T-PD-D-T (DC)]. Don't forget that an EPM may occur within the tonic function. Do not analyze every chord.

A.   Lehar, Waltz from *The Merry Widow*

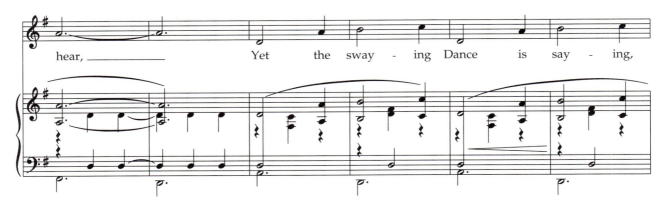

(continues on next page)

Love   me,   dear! _____

B.   Beethoven, *Scherzo,* Piano Sonata no. 2 in A major, op. 2, no. 2, *Allegretto*

C.   Mozart, Piano Sonata in C major, K. 330, *Andante cantabile*. This example contains subphrases; consider them as you undertake your phrase analysis.

LISTENING

EXERCISE 20.6 Period Structure and Dictation

Notate missing soprano and/or bass voices (arrows indicate missing pitches) and provide a roman numeral analysis and period diagram.

Mozart, Trio for Piano, Clarinet, and Viola in E♭ major, K. 498, *Allegretto*. The clarinet sounds as written.

PERFORMING

EXERCISE 20.7 Sing and Play: Improvising Period Structures

Below are two antecedent phrases that lack a consequent.

1. Sing and play these phrases. (If you have trouble with the accompaniments as given, you may play block chords in the right hand.)
2. Determine the period type you want. Design a tonal plan and cadence for the second phrase.
3. Improvise/work out a consequent phrase that closes on the tonic to create a period. Improvise both a parallel and a contrasting consequent. Be prepared to perform your periods in class.

A. Beethoven, "Ich liebe dich" ("I Love You"), WoO 132

Ich lie - be dich, so wie, du mich, am A - bend und am Mor - gen,

B. Mendelssohn, "Wenn sich zwei Herzen scheiden" ("When Two Hearts Separate"), op. 99, no. 5

1. Wenn sich zwei Her - zen schei - den, die sich der - einst ge - liebt,

ASSIGNMENT 20.3

LISTENING

DVD 2
CH 20
TRACK 6

EXERCISE 20.8 Period Structures and Dictation

Notate missing soprano and/or bass voices (arrows indicate missing pitches) and provide a roman numeral analysis and period diagram.

A. Beethoven, *Marche funèbre*, Symphony No. 3 in E♭ major ("Eroica") op. 55, *Adagio assai*

B. Mozart, *Romance*, Concerto for Horn in E♭, K. 447

WRITING

EXERCISE 20.9 Completing Figurated Periods

Maintaining the texture and the harmonic rhythm of the given antecedent phrase, write an appropriate consequent phrase on a separate sheet of manuscript paper. Provide a full label for the period.

ASSIGNMENT 20.4

WRITING

EXERCISE 20.10 Figured Bass

The following figured bass is presented in an unmetered context. First, determine roman numerals and possible cadences. Then, on a separate sheet of paper, fit the figured bass into a periodic structure by imposing a meter and providing each note with a duration. Make sure that there is no more than one chord per quarter note in $\frac{3}{4}$ or $\frac{4}{4}$ or one chord per eighth note in $\frac{6}{8}$.

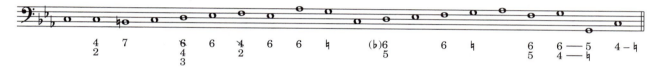

LISTENING

EXERCISE 20.11 Variation and Contrapuntal Expansion of a Harmonic Model

You will hear contrapuntal expansions of a I-V-I harmonic progression. The model bass line below will be fleshed out in variations that maintain the metric placement of the given harmonies implied by the bass notes. Complete the following tasks:

1. Notate the bass and soprano voices of the contrapuntal chords that embellish the given harmonic structure.
2. Provide a two-level harmonic analysis. Your harmonic vocabulary now includes I, I6, IV6, V, V6, V7, V$_5^6$, V$_3^4$, V$_2^4$, vii°6, vii°7, vii°$_5^6$, and vii°$_3^4$, the predominants: ii, ii6, ii7, ii$_5^6$, ii$_3^4$, IV, IV6, IV7, IV$_5^6$, and the new harmonies vi and iii (and VII in minor).

Model (single phrase)

Variation 1

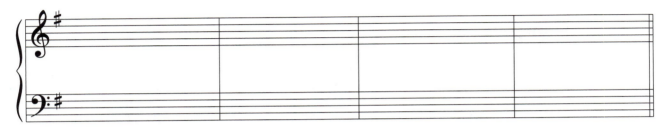

Variation 2

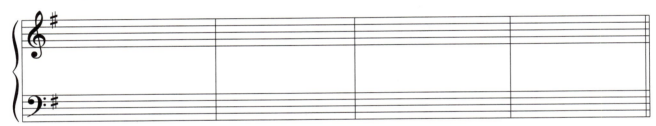

Variation 3

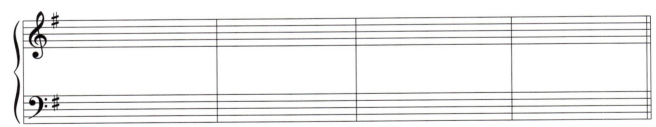

Variation 4

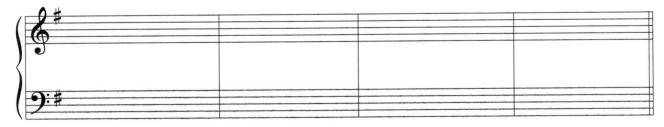

ASSIGNMENT 20.5

WRITING

EXERCISE 20.12 Figured Bass

The following figured bass is presented in an unmetered context. First, determine roman numerals and possible cadences. Then, on a separate sheet of paper, fit the figured bass into a periodic structure by imposing a meter and providing each note with a duration. Make sure that there is no more than one chord per quarter note in $\frac{4}{4}$ or $\frac{4}{4}$ or one chord per eighth note in $\frac{6}{8}$.

LISTENING

EXERCISE 20.13 Variation and Contrapuntal Expansion of a Harmonic Model

DVD 2
CH 20
TRACK 8

You will hear the contrapuntal expansions of a period. The model bass line below will be fleshed out in variations that maintain the metric placement of the given harmonies implied by the bass notes (there are two exceptions). Complete the following tasks.

1. Notate the bass and soprano voices of the contrapuntal chords that embellish the given harmonic structure.
2. Provide a two-level harmonic analysis. Your harmonic vocabulary now includes I, I6, IV6, V, V6, V7, V_5^6, V_3^4, V_2^4, vii°6, vii°7, vii° $_5^6$, and vii°$_3^4$, the predominants ii, ii6, ii7, ii$_5^6$, ii$_3^4$, IV, IV6, IV7, IV$_5^6$, and the new harmonies vi and iii (and VII in minor).

Model period

Beware: Two of the variations do NOT follow the model!

1. Variation 1

2. Variation 2

3. Variation 3

4. Variation 4

5. Variation 5

6. Variation 6

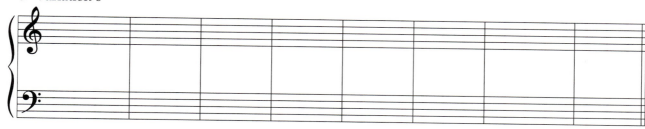

7. Variation 7

Additional Exercises

WRITING

EXERCISE 20.14 Writing Homophonic Periods

Write two different homophonic (SATB) periods. Cast one in major, the other in minor, and use one duple and one triple meter. Each should be eight measures, with each measure containing one but not more than two harmonies. Add tones of figuration to your upper voice. Analyze the period type and the harmonies.

EXERCISE 20.15 Writing Florid Periods

Write two different periods, both of which contain a florid melody that is accompanied by three- or four-voice harmonies. You might approach this exercise in one of two ways. In the first scenario, you would conceive of the work with the harmonic aspect at the forefront of your compositional process. Thus, you would compose for a wind or string trio, voicing individual harmonies for the specific instruments. When the harmonic underpinning was complete, you would add a florid tune above for a solo instrument. In the second scenario, you would first write the soloist's tune and then add the harmonic underpinning in the form of the three-voice accompaniment. If you employ the second technique, you must constantly consider implied harmonies in your soloist's line, perhaps by using roman numerals to remind you of which chords to use when you return to the harmonic underpinning. Your accompaniment may be strictly homophonic, or more figurated, with simple arpeggiations or broken chords derived from offsetting the vertical voices that you have previously written. You could score this for the right hand of the piano, then add a left-hand part that moves more slowly in octaves and carries the harmony.

EXERCISE 20.16 Folk Tunes and Periodic Structure

We now harmonize tunes taken from traditional American songs, Christmas carols, and other familiar sources. All examples contain more than a single phrase, but not every example forms a period; some are simply repeated phrases. Choose two or three tunes from the list below whose first two phrases combine into one of the three period types that we are currently writing (we will postpone writing progressive periods until Chapter 25). Then, write out the tune from memory, making sure that you use a suitable meter. Next, determine the type of period and add the bass line at the cadences and include roman numerals. Then, use an appropriate harmonic rhythm to harmonize the tune; that is, not every note of the tune will be harmonized. You will need to determine the tones of figuration. Add a bass line and inner voices. Use only harmonies that we have studied.

"Shall We Gather at the River"

"Swing Low, Sweet Chariot"

"Amazing Grace"

"Pop Goes the Weasel"

"Beautiful Dreamer"

"The Cowboy's Lament" ("The Streets of Laredo")

"Deck the Halls"

"God Rest Ye Merry, Gentlemen"

"Good King Wenceslas"

"It Came Upon the Midnight Clear"

"Jingle Bells" (refrain)

"Clementine"

"I've Been Workin' on the Railroad"

LISTENING

20.17 Aural Identification of Periods

Listen to each of the following periods from the literature. For each example, provide a formal diagram and a period label. (If the second phrase ends in a new key, mark "x" in the formal diagram.)

A. Haydn, Divertimento in B♭ major, Hob. II. 46; *Lento*, in $\frac{2}{4}$

B. Mozart, Rondo, Concerto for Horn in E♭ major, K. 495, *Allegro vivace*, in $\frac{6}{8}$

C. Haydn, String Quartet in D minor, op. 76, no. 2, Hob. III. 76, *Andante*, in $\frac{6}{8}$

D. Mozart, "Là ci darem la mano" from *Don Giovanni*, K. 527, act 1, scene, *Andante*, in $\frac{2}{4}$

E. Beethoven, *Adagio ma non troppo*, String Quartet in B♭ major, op. 18, no. 6

F. Schubert, *Rondo*, Piano Sonata in A major, op. posth. D. 959

G. Schumann, "Albumblätter" from *Bunte Blätter*, op. 99

H. Haydn, Piano Sonata no. 50 in D major, Hob. XVI: 37, *Allegro con brio*, in $\frac{4}{4}$

I. Schubert, Waltz in F minor, *Eighteen German Dances and Ecossaises*, op. 33, no. 14, D. 783

J. Jacque Christopher Naudot (1690–1762), Gavotte no. 2, Sonata in D, op. 1 no. 3

K. Mozart, Rondo, *Eine kleine Nachtmusik*, K. 525

DVD 2
CH 20
TRACK 10

20.18 Variation and Contrapuntal Expansion of a Harmonic Model

You will hear contrapuntal expansions of a I-V-I harmonic progression. The model bass line below will be fleshed out in variations that maintain the metric placement of the given harmonies implied by the bass notes. Complete the following tasks

1. Notate the bass and soprano voices of the contrapuntal chords that embellish the given harmonic structure.
2. Provide a two-level harmonic analysis. Your harmonic vocabulary now includes I, I6, IV6, V, V6, V7, V$_5^6$, V$_3^4$, V$_2^4$, vii°6, vii°7, vii° $_5^6$, and vii° $_3^4$, the predominants ii, ii6, ii7, ii$_5^6$, ii$_3^4$, IV, IV6, IV7, IV$_5^6$, and the new harmonies vi and iii (and VII in minor).

Model (single phrase)

Model

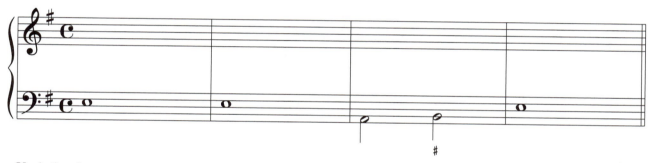

Variation 1

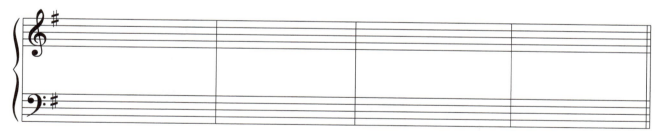

Variation 2

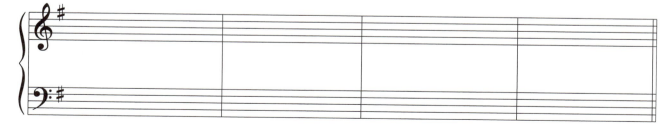

Variation 3

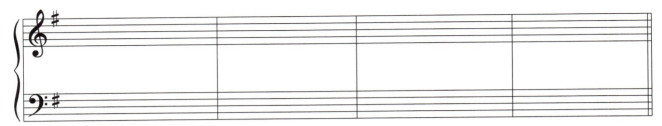

KEYBOARD

EXERCISE 20.19

Accompany your singing of Mozart's tune below by realizing the figured bass.
Mozart, "Ein Mädchen oder Weibchen" ("A Maiden or a Little Wife") from *Die
Zauberflöte*, K. 620, act 2, Scene 6

Other Small Musical Structures: Sentences, Double Periods, and Asymmetrical Periods

ASSIGNMENT 21.1

ANALYSIS/WRITING

EXERCISE 21.1 Melody Harmonization and Period/Sentence Structure

For each example, label the formal type (phrase or period) and whether it is cast in sentence structure. Then, choose one example and determine the harmonic rhythm and harmonize the tune. Provide a harmonic analysis.

A. Mozart, *Rondeau: Tempo di Menuetto*, Bassoon Concerto in B♭ major, K. 191

B. Schubert, "Wiegenlied" ("Cradle Song"), op. 92, no. 2, D. 498

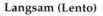

C. Mozart, Horn Concerto in D major, K. 412, *Allegro*

D.   Schubert, "An mein Klavier" ("To My Piano"), D. 342

E.   Mozart, Horn Concerto in D major, K. 412, *Allegro*

KEYBOARD

EXERCISE 21.2 Reduction

Sing the following excerpts from Mozart's *Marriage of Figaro*. Accompany your singing with your reduction. Be able to discuss each excerpt's phrase, period, or sentence structure.

A.   Mozart, "Non so più cosa son', cosa faccio" from *Le Nozze di Figaro* (*The Marriage of Figaro*), K.492, act 1, scene 3

B.   Mozart, "Dove sono" ("Where are they"), from *Le Nozze di Figaro* (*The Marriage of Figaro*), K.492, act 3, scene 8

Do — ve so — no   i bei mo-men — ti,   di   dol-cez — za   e

di — pia — cer, _____   do — ve an-da-ro   i gin-ra men — ti

di   quel lab-bro men-ro-gner, di   quel lab — bro men — ro-gner!

ASSIGNMENT 21.2

WRITING

EXERCISE 21.3 Melody Harmonization: The Sentence

The melodies below are cast in sentence structure. They may take the form of single four-measure phrases or eight-measure periods comprising two four-measure phrases. Determine cadential points and add appropriate bass notes. Then, harmonize the rest of the tune. Remember, the two subphrases that together comprise half the sentence should be related, though they need not have identical harmonizations.

A.

B.

C.

EXERCISE 21.4 Composition

Below is the accompaniment for an antecedent phrase. Write a melody to the accompaniment, and then complete an interrupted period by writing a consequent phrase.

LISTENING

DVD 2
CH 21
TRACK 1

EXERCISE 21.5

You will hear several examples cast as sentence structures or double periods. Notate the bass lines, the grid for which is provided in each case. Begin by identifying cadences, then flesh out the specific harmonic changes. Analyze with two levels.

A.   Haydn, String Quartet, op. 3, no. 5, *Andante cantabile*

B.   Haydn, String Quartet in D minor, op. 42, *Andante ed innocentemente*

C.   Bach, *Menuet I*, Partita no. 1 in B♭ major

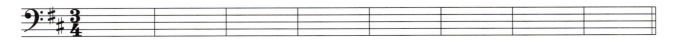

D.   Haydn, *Menuetto* Symphony no. 91 in D major, "The Clock"

E.   Mozart, Symphony no. 40 in G minor, K. 550, *Allegro molto* (in 2)

ASSIGNMENT 21.3

WRITING

EXERCISE 21.6 Writing Sentence Structures

Write an eight-measure period that is cast in sentence structure (2 + 2 + 4 measures). Begin either by improvising on your own instrument, singing, or just exploring ideas at the piano in order to find a suitable melodic and rhythmic motive in a meter, key, and mode of your choice. The first part of your sentence will be a two-measure unit that will be repeated either literally, or with small changes, to comprise four measures. The second part of your sentence will be a single four-measure idea that should borrow at least some elements from the opening two-measure idea. As you write your tunes, consider the underlying harmonic structure and its harmonic rhythm; you may even wish to sketch in a few bass notes and roman numerals. The harmonic structure should approximate the following model.

A (2 mm)	A′ (2mm)	B (4 mm)
I—I or V	I—I or V	I—PAC

KEYBOARD

EXERCISE 21.7 Harmonization

Choose three of the melodies below and determine possible harmonizations and period types. Harmonic changes usually occur once per measure. Accompany yourself with your harmonization.

A.   Foster: "Old Folks at Home"

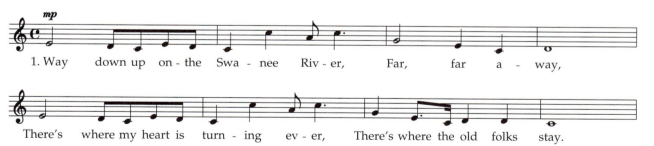

1. Way down up - on - the Swa - nee Riv - er,   Far,   far a - way,

There's where my heart is turn - ing ev - er, There's where the old folks stay.

B. "Auld Lang Syne"

1. Should aul acquain-tance be for-got, And nev - er brought to mind? Should

auld ac-quain - tance be for-got, And __ days of auld lang syne?

C. "Red River Valley"

1. From this val - ley they say you are go - ing; _____ We will miss your bright eyes and sweet

smile, For they say you are tak - ing the sun-shine _ Which has bright-ened our path-way a while.

D. "Home on the Range"

1. Oh, give me a home where the buf - fa-lo roam, Where the deer and the an - te - lope play; _

__ Where sel-dom is heard a dis-cour - ag-ing word, And the skies are not cloud-y all day. __

ASSIGNMENT 21.4

COMPOSITION

EXERCISE 21.8 Harmonic Models and Periods and Sentences

Choose two of the following harmonic models to write periods or double periods. Some examples work well as sentences. Decide on a key, meter, and harmonic rhythm, and add a bass voice. Finally, add a tune for voice or solo instrument and complete the texture by adding the missing chord tones to the implied harmonies above your bass, the result of which will be a homophonic accompaniment to your melody.

Phrase 1	**Phrase 2**
Model 1:	I–extended prolongation of I–either to PD or V V—deceptive progression–cadence: PAC
Model 2:	i–step-descent bass to PD—HC
	i–step-descent bass leading to expanded PD–PAC
Model 3	i–ascending ARP to phrygian cadence i–descending ARP to extended PD–PAC

Additional Exercises

EXERCISE 21.9 Listening

You will hear several examples cast as sentence structures or double periods. Identify the type of formal structure. Begin by identifying cadences, then flesh out the specific roman numerals. Analyze with two levels.

A. Haydn, Finale, String Quartet in E major, op. 54, no. 3

B. Mozart, Piano Trio in E major, K. 542, *Allegro* (iv)

C. Beethoven, Piano Concerto no. 3 in C minor, op. 37, *Allegro con brio*

CHAPTER 22

Harmonic Sequences: Concepts and Patterns

Exercises for Identification and Analysis of Sequences

ASSIGNMENT 22.1

ANALYSIS

DVD 2
CH 22
TRACK 1

EXERCISE 22.1 Analysis of D2 (−5/+4) Sequences

Listen to and study the following sequences. Do not place a roman numeral beneath every chord: The chords within a sequence are members of a linear motion and do not carry individual harmonic weight.

1. Bracket the beginning and end of each sequence.
2. Determine whether root-position chords or alternating first inversions are used. Label each sequence completely.
3. Determine whether each copy maintains the model's voice leading precisely. Label the interval between bass and soprano in the model and in one copy.
4. Mark the location of the single tritone that occurs between IV and vii in major and ii° and V in minor.

A.

B.

C.   Mozart, *Rondeau*, Violin Concerto no 2 in D major, K. 211

EXERCISE 22.2 Analysis of D3 (−4/+2) Sequences

Listen to and study the following sequences. Follow instructions 1–3 from Exercise 22.1.

A.

B.   Bach, Gavotte, French Suite no. 5 in G major, BWV 816

DVD 2
CH 22
TRACK 3

EXERCISE 22.3 Analysis of A2 (+5/−4) Sequences.

Listen to and study the following examples of A2 (+5/−4) sequences. Follow instructions from Exercise 22.1.

A.

B.   Schubert, String Quintet in C major, D. 956, *Adagio*

(continues on next page)

EXERCISE 22.4 Analysis of A2 (−3/+4) Sequences

Listen to and study the following sequence. Follow instructions from Exercise 22.1.
Handel, Trio Sonata in G minor, op. 2, no. 5, HWV 390, *Allegro*

LISTENING

DVD 2
CH 22
TRACK 5

EXERCISE 22.5 Aural Identification of Sequences

This exercise is the same as textbook Exercise 22.5, but now six-three variants are added to the D2 (–5/+4) and D3 (–4/+2), and A2 (D3/A4) sequences. Follow these listening guidelines:

1. Determine whether the sequence ascends or descends. This step reduces sequential possibilities by 50 percent.
2. Listen to the bass to determine which one of the two remaining sequence types is played. Focus on the repetitions of the model. For example, in a descending sequence, does the bass descend by third or second? It is slightly more difficult to distinguish between the two ascending sequences given that both ascend by second. Focus on whether you hear minimal harmonic movement; if so, it is the ascending A2 (D3/A4) sequence. If you hear a hopping bass, then it is the A2 (A5/D4) sequence.

A. _____   B. _____   C. _____
D. _____   E. _____   F. _____

ASSIGNMENT 22.2

KEYBOARD

EXERCISE 22.6

Identify and play each of the sequence models below in major and minor keys up to and including two sharps and two flats. Voicings are given for the model. Be able to sing either outer voice while playing the other three voices.

ANALYSIS

EXERCISE 22.7

The following examples contain a mixture of the four sequence types. Also, all but the A2 (+5/−4) sequence may incorporate first-inversion variants. Bracket the model and copies for each sequence and provide a sequence label.

A.

B.　Mozart Symphony no. 40 in G minor, K. 550, *Andante*

C.　Mozart, Sonata for Violin and Piano in B♭ major, K. 372

(continues on next page)

D.   Corelli, Trio Sonata in D major, op. 4 no. 4

E.   Mozart, Symphony in G minor, "Little G minor," K. 183 *Allegro*

(continues on next page)

LISTENING

EXERCISE 22.8 Sequence Dictation

Label the sequence type and notate the bass and the soprano. Pay close attention to the model, since it determines the repetitions. Make sure that the counterpoint is logical and that pairs of intervals are consistent.

There may be a tonic expansion before the sequence begins.

A.   B.

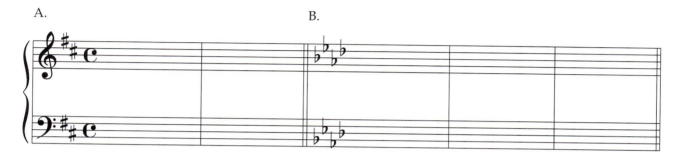

C.

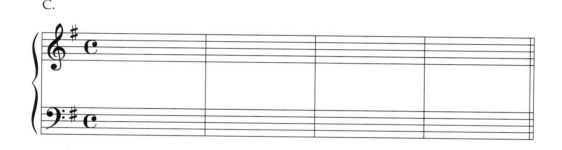

D.   E.

F.

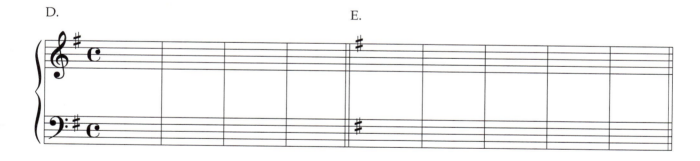

Exercises for Writing Sequences

ASSIGNMENT 22.3

WRITING

EXERCISE 22.9

The following sequences begin on tonic. The model and the outer-voice counterpoint of the first chord of the copy are given.

1. Label sequence type.
2. Continue them and lead each to a pre-dominant.
3. Close with an authentic cadence.
4. Write bass and soprano first, filling in the tenor and alto only after you are sure that the repetitions replicate the model exactly. Use no accidentals within the sequence: these are entirely diatonic sequences.

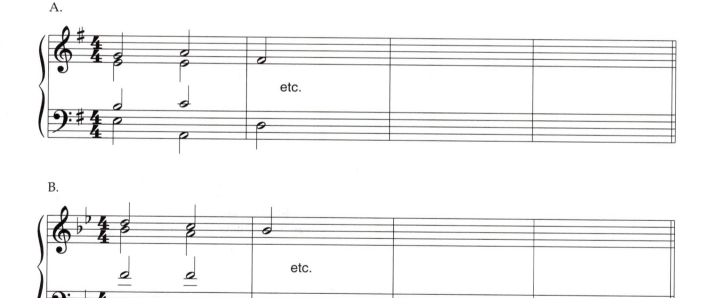

C.

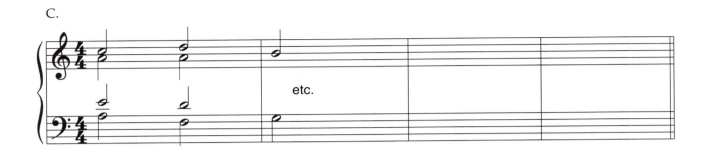

D.

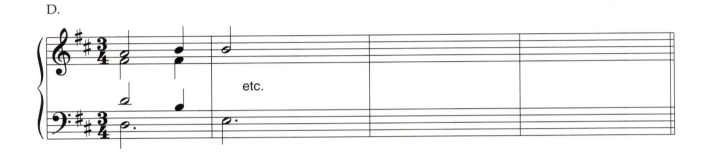

E.

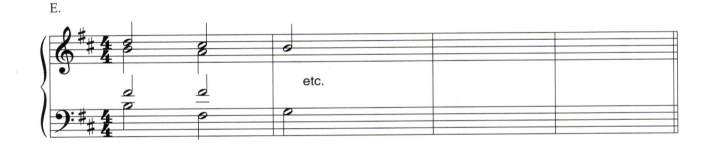

EXERCISE 22.10 Figured Bass and Sequences

Bass, figures, and the soprano are given. Each example includes two or more sequences. Bracket and identify the type of sequence. (Look for the intervallic pattern that repeats every two chords.) Add inner voices and provide a two-level roman numeral analysis. Do not analyze individual chords within a sequence.

A.

ANALYSIS AND REDUCTION

DVD 2
CH 22
TRACK 7

EXERCISE 22.11

The following examples contain a mixture of the four sequence types. Also, all but the A2 (+5/−4) sequence may incorporate first-inversion variants. Bracket the model and copies for each sequence and provide a sequence label. Then, on a separate sheet of manuscript paper, reduce each sequence into its basic four-voice homophonic structure. Be able to play your reductions on the piano or your instrument (you will need to arpeggiate the reductions if you play a melody instrument).

A.   Corelli, Violin Sonata in F major, op. 5, no. 10

B.   C. P. E. Bach, Sonata in A major, *Sechs Sonaten für Kenner und Liebhaber*

ASSIGNMENT 22.4

WRITING

EXERCISE 22.12 Melody Harmonization

Label the sequence implied by the given soprano melody. Then, add a bass voice and inner voices; maintain the model's voicing in each repetition. Be able to sing either outer voice while playing the remaining three voices.

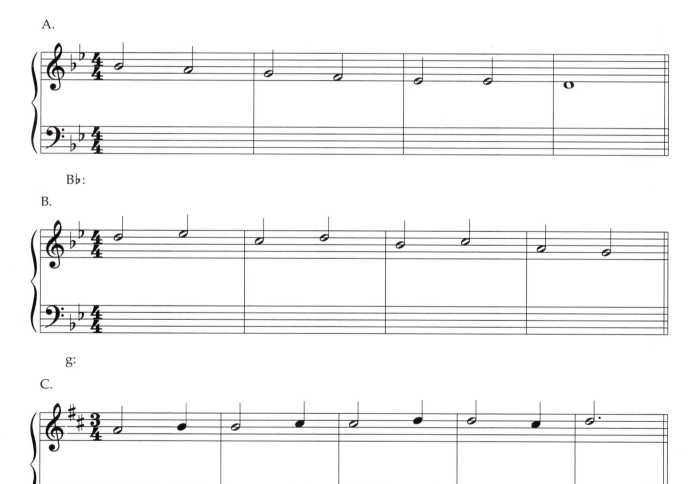

A.

B♭:

B.

g:

C.

D:

(continues on next page)

D.

b:

EXERCISE 22.13 Continuing Sequences

Based on the given models, continue the sequences for two repetitions. Close each example with a cadence. Label each sequence.

A. Bach, Sonata for Flute in E♭ major, BWV 1031, *Allegro*

B. Vivaldi, Sonata for Oboe in B♭ major, RV 34, *Allegro*

B1.

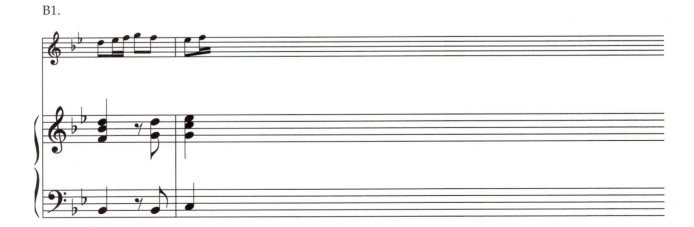

B2.

KEYBOARD

EXERCISE 22.14 Figured Bass

Realize the figured bass below in four voices. Label all sequences. Be able to sing the bass while playing the upper voices. You may write out your soprano.

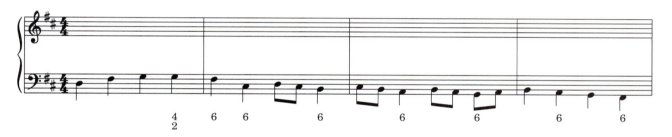

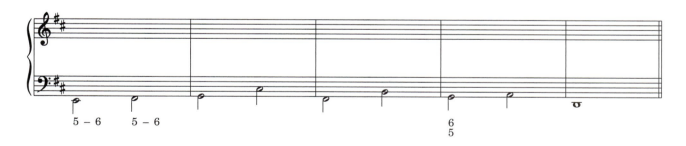

ASSIGNMENT 22.5

WRITING

EXERCISE 22.15 Figured Bass and Sequences

Bass, figures, and soprano are given. Each example includes two or more sequences. Bracket and identify the type of sequence. (Look for the intervallic pattern that repeats every two chords.) Add inner voices and provide a two-level roman numeral analysis. Do not analyze individual chords within a sequence.

DVD 2
CH 22
TRACK 8

EXERCISE 22.16 Analysis and Notation of Sequences

Below are the incomplete scores of excerpts; the bass lines are missing. Identify the sequence type and notate the bass line in each of the excerpts.

A.   Quantz, Trio Sonata in G minor, *Allegro*

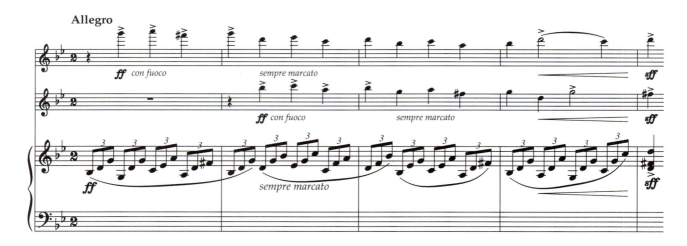

B.   Chopin, Mazurka in F major, op. 68, no. 3, BI 34

C.   Corelli, *Corrente*, Concerto Grosso in C major, op. 6, no. 10.

     Notate only the downbeat bass notes.

ASSIGNMENT 22.6

KEYBOARD

EXERCISE 22.17 Illustrations

Complete the illustrations below.
A. In D minor and a meter of your choice:

1. Establish tonic (*c.* 2 mm.). Include one suspension.
2. Use a descending sequence that leads to a HC (*c.* 2–3 mm.).
3. Begin again on tonic; use any rising sequence to lead to a cadential six-four chord. Close with a PAC. The result will be an interrupted period (whether it is parallel or contrasting is up to you).

B. In E minor and a meter of your choice:

1. Establish tonic; use a voice exchange (*c.* 2 mm.).
2. Use a D3 (−4/+2) sequence to lead to a PD and an IAC.
3. Begin again on tonic; use an A2 (−3/+4) sequence to lead to iv.
4. Close with a PAC; include one suspension. The result will be a sectional period (whether it is parallel or contrasting is up to you).

WRITING

EXERCISE 22.18 Composition

Choose one exercise from the three provided.
A. Given below is the accompaniment of an antecedent phrase. You will add a melody for a solo instrument or voice. Then, realize the figured bass given, which will provide the consequent phrase; use the accompanimental figuration given in the antecedent and compose a suitable melody that is related to the one you wrote for the antecedent phrase.

A.

(continues on next page)

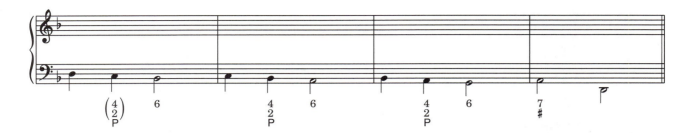

B. Continue the opening of the phrase below and lead to a half cadence; then write a suitable consequent phrase to create a parallel interrupted period.

C. Brahms, "Dort in den Weiden steht ein Haus" ("There in the Willows Stands a House"), *Deutsche Volkslieder*, WoO 33, no. 31 (adapted)

Write an eight-measure continuous consequent phrase that contains a sequence and closes with a PAC. The resulting structure will be a parallel interrupted period cast in sentence structure (4 + 4 + 8).

Additional Exercises

WRITING

EXERCISE 22.19 Elaborating Contrapuntal Models

Below are six 1:1 (first species) outer-voice models of various sequences. Choose a key different from the given key, and a meter. Vary the mode (i.e., use both major and minor modes). Then, using a harmonic rhythm of half notes or even whole notes, embellish each sequence by adding tones of figuration. For example, given the three contrapuntal models below, see how Corelli, Heinichen, and Bach embellished the basic model by adding recurring rhythmic patterns of neighbors, passing tones, and chordal leaps.

A.   Corelli, Trio Sonata in B minor, op. 3, no. 4

B.   Heinichen, Sonata in C minor for Oboe and Bassoon

C.   Bach, Flute Sonata in B♭, BWV 1020

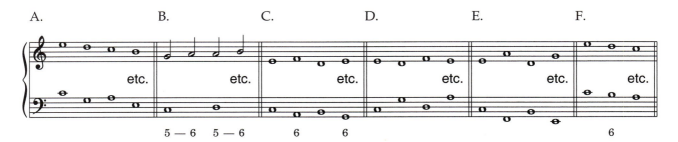

DVD 2
CH 22
TRACK 9

LISTENING

EXERCISE 22.20 Analysis and Notation of Sequences

Below are the incomplete scores of excerpts; the bass lines are missing. Identify the sequence type and notate the bass line in each of the excerpts.

D.   Mozart, *Molto allegro,* Violin Sonata in A major, K. 526

CHAPTER 23

Sequences Within Larger Musical Contexts and Sequences with Seventh Chords

Exercises for Sequences Within the Phrase Model

PERFORMING

The small number of common-sequence types reappear through the common-practice period and continue to this day because composers have found countless ways to mold and embellish them to suit the specific needs of their compositions. In this exercise we both review and embellish sequences. In Example A1, a D2 (−5/+4) sequence with six-three chords is implied by the figured bass, then realized in four voices in Example A2. Example A3 uses compound melody to elaborate the sequence. Example A4 fills the thirds in the outer-voice counterpoint by adding passing tones; this structure is embellished by the added voices in Example A5.

Composers often distribute the pitches between individual instruments, adding embellishments that tie the voices together. The examples from Corelli and Bach show how three- and four-voice homophonic models can be embellished by simple figurations that comprise passing, neighboring, and chordal skipping motions. Study the models, then embellish the homophonic sequence given. Lead each to an authentic cadence.

EXERCISE 23.1 Instrumental Application: Embellishing Sequences

A.

(continues on next page)

B1. A2 (−3/+4)

B2. Corelli Trio Sonata in C major, op. 4 no. 1, *Allegro*

C1. D2 (−5/+4) w/ $\frac{6}{3}$ chords

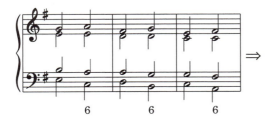

C2. Bach, Prelude in G major, BWV 902

D1. (−5/+4)

etc. ⇒

D2. Corelli Concerto Grosso in F major, op. 6 no. 12, *Giga*

ANALYSIS

EXERCISE 23.2 Comparison of Sequential Passages from the Literature

DVD 2
CH 23
TRACK 1

Below are three examples from Mozart's *Die Zauberflöte* (*The Magic Flute*), K. 620, each of which contains a sequence. Listen to each and then, in a short paragraph, compare and contrast their content. Include in your discussion not only specific types of sequences but also their functions within the larger musical context.

A.   "Drei Knäbchen" ("Three Little Boys"), act I, scene 9

B.   "Holle Rache" ("Hell's Revenge"), act 2, scene 8

mehr, _____

C.   "Wie, wie, wie?" ("What, What, What?"), act 2, scene 5

Allegro

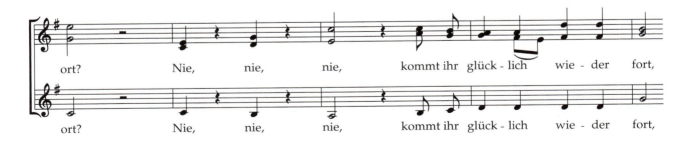

Exercises for Sequences with Seventh Chords, Compound Melody, Parallel $^6_3$ Chords, and Sequences vs. Sequential Progressions

ASSIGNMENT 23.2

ANALYSIS

EXERCISE 23.3

Analyze the examples below that contain D2 (−5/+4) sequences with seventh chords. Circle each chordal seventh and label its preparation and resolution.

A. Mozart, *Allegro,* Symphony in G major, K. 124.
Dissonant suspensions in violin 2 are shown with parentheses.

B.   Telemann, *Adagio*, Sonata in C minor for Flute, Oboe and Basso Continuo, TV 41 no. 2
     One might say that the sevenths of the sequence in the continuo do not resolve correctly. Is this really
     true?

LISTENING

EXERCISE 23.4 Aural Identification of Sequences Within Phrases

Notate the bass of the incomplete scores and provide a roman numeral analysis.
Bracket and label sequences.

A.

B. Write only two bass notes per measure (the other pitches are accompanying arpeggiations).

C.

WRITING

EXERCISE 23.5 Completion of Sequence Patterns

Write at least two repetitions of the sequence models given below. Lead each sequence to an authentic cadence. Analyze. Then, rewrite one completed sequence on a separate sheet of paper by adding at least one tone of figuration (e.g., suspension, passing tone, etc.) to the model and its copies.

A.

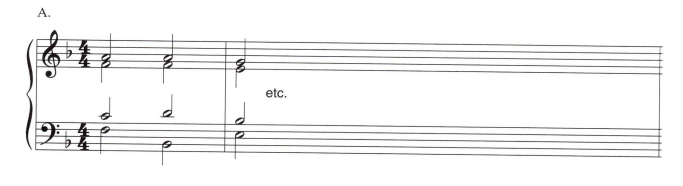

B.

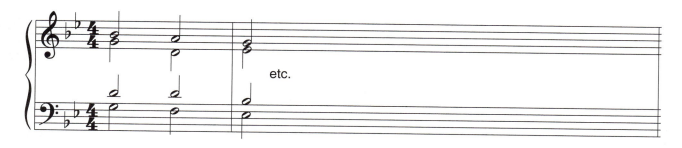

(continues on next page)

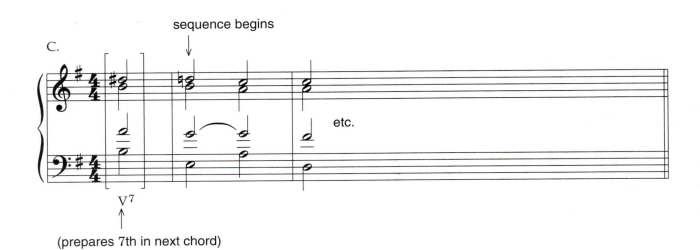

ASSIGNMENT 23.3

LISTENING

DVD 2
CH 23
TRACK 4

EXERCISE 23.6 Analysis and Notation

The following sequences from the literature are missing some notes in A and B and the complete bass line in C. Listen to and study each sequence; then, identify each sequence and notate the bass line.

A. Mozart, Piano Sonata in F major, K. 332, *Allegro*
    Consider this excerpt to be in C minor. What rhythmic device is employed in mm. 64 and 65?

B. Chopin, Etude in G♭ major, op. 25

C.   Haydn, Piano Sonata No. 44 in B♭ major, Hob. XVI:29, *Moderato*

WRITING

EXERCISE 23.7 Figured Bass

Realize the figured bass below, labeling all sequences. Analyze with two levels. Sequence choices are:

1. D2 (–5/+4): five-threes, six-threes, sevenths (alternating or interlocking)
2. A2 (+5/–4)
3. D3 (–4/+2): five-threes or six-threes (the descending 5–6)
4. A2 (–3/+4) (the ascending 5–6)

ASSIGNMENT 23.4

LISTENING

DVD 2
CH 23
TRACK 5

EXERCISE 23.8 Analysis and Notation

The following sequences from the literature are missing bass lines. Listen to and study each sequence; then, identify each sequence and notate the bass line.

A. Geminiani, Violin Sonata in G minor, op. 1, no. 12, *Allegro*
    Notate only the bass pitches that occur on the beat.

B.   Bach, *Allemande*, English Suite no. 3 in G minor, BWV 808

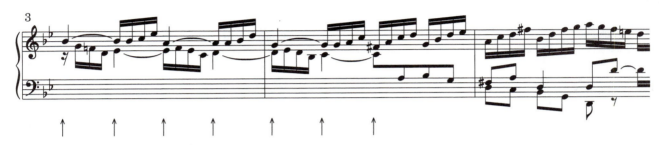

C.   Corelli, Concerto Grosso in F major, op. 6, no. 2, *Allegro*

WRITING

EXERCISE 23.9 Figured Bass

Realize the figured bass below, labeling all sequences. Analyze with two levels. Sequence choices are:

1. D2 (−5/+4): five-threes, six-threes, sevenths (alternating or interlocking)
2. A2 (+5/−4)
3. D3 (−4/+2): five-threes or six-threes (the descending 5–6)
4. A2 (−3/+4) (the ascending 5–6)

ASSIGNMENT 23.5

WRITING

EXERCISE 23.10 Illustrations

Complete the following tasks in four-voice SATB style.

A. In D minor, write a four-measure phrase that includes
1. a D2 (–5/+4) sequence with either alternating or interlocking sevenths leading to a HC
2. at least three suspensions
3. a pedal and cadential six-four chord

B. In B♭ major, write a four-measure phrase that includes

1. a contrapuntal expansion of tonic
2. a D3 (–4/+2) sequence
3. a bass suspension
4. a bass arpeggiation
5. a submediant harmony
6. a deceptive progression

LISTENING

DVD 2
CH 23
TRACK 6

EXERCISE 23.11 Notation of Sequences

You will hear several D2 (–5/+4) sequences with and without sevenths. If the sequence contains sevenths, determine whether it is alternating or interlocking. Notate the bass.

A.

B.

C.

D. Handel, "Pena tiranna io sento" from *Amidigi di Gaula act 1, Largo*

E. Schumann, "Ich will meine Seele tauchen" ("I Want to Delve My Soul"), *Dichterliebe*, op. 48, no. 5
    You will hear the entire song, which is composed of two large phrases. Each phrase may in turn be
    divided into two subphrases. What type of larger musical structure do the two large phrases create?
    Each large phrase begins unusually with a pre-dominant harmony, ii°7, rather than the tonic.

ASSIGNMENT 23.6

KEYBOARD

EXERCISE 23.12 Figured Bass

Realize the figured bass in four voices; a few given soprano pitches will guide your upper line. Sing the bass voice while playing the upper parts. Analyze.

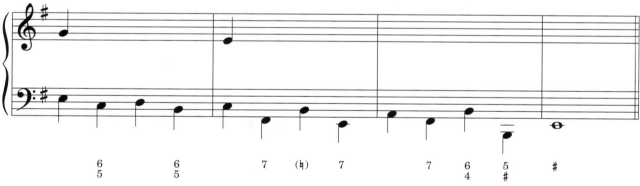

ANALYSIS

DVD 2
CH 23
TRACK 7

EXERCISE 23.13

Analyze the examples below that contain D2 (–5/+4) sequences with inverted seventh chords. Circle each chordal seventh and label its preparation and resolution. Are there any exceptions to the usual practice of preparing and resolving dissonances?

A.   Leclair, Sarabanda, Trio Sonata in D major, op. 2, no. 8

B. Marcello, Trio Sonata in B♭ major, op. 2, no. 2, *Largo*
Focus on the continuo realization.

WRITING

EXERCISE 23.14 Melody Harmonization and Sequences

Based on the contour of the following soprano fragments, determine an appropriate sequence type and then harmonize each in four voices (SATB). Examples A–D require one chord change for each melody note. Examples E–F contain tones of figuration and are incomplete. For these, determine the larger sequential pattern, add the sequential bass and complete the sequence and lead to a cadence. Label each sequence type as shown in the sample solution.

Sample solution

A.

F *and* d

B.

a *and* C

C.

D.

E.

F.

Additional Exercises

EXERCISE 23.15 Figured Bass

Realize the figured bass below; bracket and label sequences. Provide a roman numeral analysis for all harmonies outside of the sequences. Inverted seventh chords must be complete.

EXERCISE 23.16 Conversion

Reduce the excerpts below to homophonic four-voice textures. Then, convert the descending six-three passages into D2 (−5/+4) sequences with seventh chords as shown in the worked solution.

Sample Solution

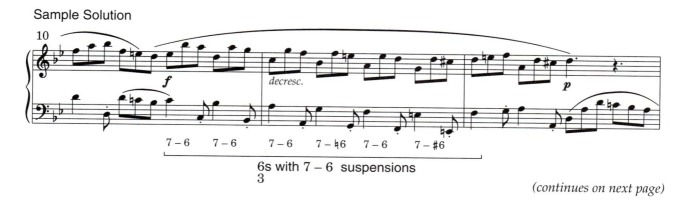

(continues on next page)

DVD 2
CH 23
TRACK 8

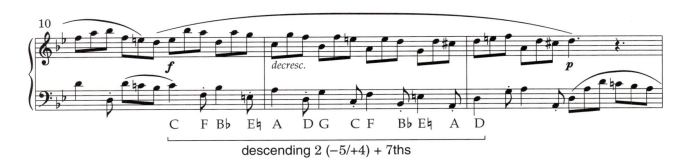

descending 2 (−5/+4) + 7ths

A.   Corelli, *Allemande*, Concerto Grosso in C major, op. 6, no. 10, *Allegro*

B.   Corelli, *Corrente*, Concerto Grosso in C major, op. 6, no. 10

C.   Haydn, Finale, Piano Sonata no. 37 in E major, Hob. XVI:22, *Tempo di Minuet*

ANALYSIS

EXERCISE 23.17 Analysis of Sequences Appearing in Compound Melodies

Determine the sequence type in the compound melodies below and then provide a reductive verticalization of the implied voices (either three or four) as shown in the sample solution.

Sample Solution

(continues on next page)

A. Bach, *Menuet*, French Suite no. 3 in B minor, BWV 814
    Bracket subphrases in this example. What type of formal structure occurs?

B. Schumann, *Kreisleriana*, op. 16, no. 5
    While this is not strictly a compound melody, it is possible to create a five-voice structure.

C. Bach, *Menuet*, French Suite no. 2 in C minor, BWV 813

EXERCISE 23.18 Analysis of Sequential Progressions and Parallel Six-Three Passages

Bracket and label sequences, sequential progressions, and parallel six-three chord streams. Label suspensions and determine whether the six-three chords function transitionally or prolongationally.

A. Handel, Gigue, Suite XVI in G minor, HWV 263
Consider this example to be in D minor. Make a 1:1 contrapuntal reduction of the excerpt. What long-range contrapuntal event takes place between the downbeats of mm. 10 and 12?

d:

B. Handel, "But Who May Abide the Day of His Coming?" *Messiah*, HWV 56

What contrapuntal technique is used at the beginning of this excerpt? Compare this example with the previous one.

C. Schubert, German Dance No. 1, *German Dances and Ecossaises*, D. 643

D. Corelli, *Corrente*, Concerto Grosso in C major, op. 6, no. 10

LISTENING

DVD 2
CH 23
TRACK 11

EXERCISE 23.19 Expansion of Basic Progressions

You will hear two basic chord progressions; each is followed by elaborated versions that include contrapuntal expansions and sequences. Notate the bass and the soprano and include roman numerals. In a sentence or two, describe the way the tonic is expanded.

Model 1

(continues on next page)

Variation 1

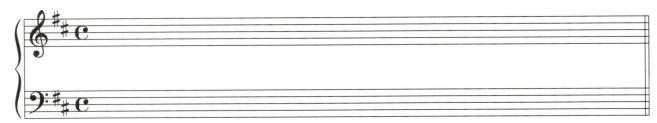

Variation 2

Variation 3

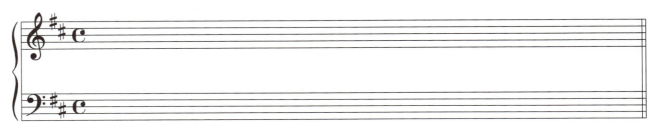

Variation 4

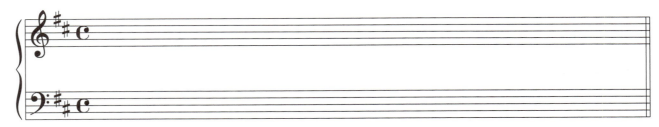

Model 2

DVD 2
CH 23
TRACK 12

(continues on next page)

Variation 1 (3 mm.)   Variation 2 (3 mm.)

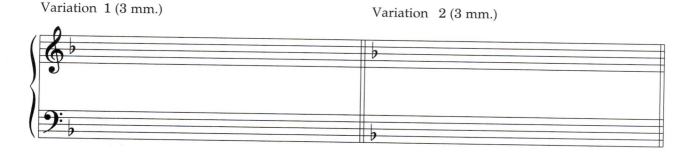

Variation 3 (3 mm.)   Variation 4 (4 mm.)

EXERCISE 23.20 Analysis and Notation

The following sequences from the literature are missing part of their bass lines. Listen to and study each sequence; then, identify each sequence and notate the bass line.

A.   Tchaikovsky, Symphony no. 4, op. 36, *Andantino in modo di canzona*

B.   Corelli, *Gigue*, Concerto Grosso in F major, op. 6, no. 12, *Allegro*